TAKING HUMAN RIGHTS FORWARD

People's Union for Civil Liberties

(PUCL)

Judgments

TAKING HUMAN RIGHTS FORWARD

People's Union for Civil Liberties (PUCL) Judgments

Preface by
Justice Rajindar Sachar
Chief Justice (Retd.), Delhi High Court

Edited by
Sanjay Parikh

VANI PRAKASHAN

VANI PRAKASHAN
4695, 21-A, Daryaganj, New Delhi 110 002
India
Branch
Ashok Rajpath, Patna 800 004
Phone : +91 11 23273167 Fax : +91 11 23275710

www.vaniprakashan.in
vaniprakashan@gmail.com
sales@vaniprakashan.in

TAKING HUMAN RIGHTS FORWARD
PEOPLE'S UNION FOR CIVIL LIBERTIES (PUCL) JUDGMENTS

Preface by Justice Rajindar Sachar
Edited by Sanjay Parikh

ISBN: 978-93-87409-56-9
Law

First Edition 2017

Price : ₹ 695

Printed at City Press, Delhi-110 095 (India)

Vani Prakashan's signature motif is created by Artist Maqbool Fida Husain

Contents

Preface

I must congratulate Mr. Sanjay Parikh for preparing a compilation of various cases on Human Rights, Electoral Reforms and the phone tapping cases etc, filed by the People's Union for Civil liberties (PUCL) and decided by the Supreme Court of India.

Mr. Parikh has collected cases which were argued by PUCL over decades on various aspects of human rights. More important is the fact that I had the pleasure of having his assistance in most of the cases. But let me straightaway admit that the required research culled out in these cases was done by Sanjay Parikh. This collection would show PUCL's incessant fight for the protection of human rights by using constitutional mechanism to change the law for the better.

This fight for human rights was always met with resistance from various sections of the government. But, it was the determination and persistence of PUCL, led by Sanjay Parikh and his colleagues that such fights could continue.

In one of the PUCL cases regarding the Electoral Reforms, the Supreme Court directed that candidates must give information of any criminal case pending against them as well as about their assets in the nomination forms. These directions were given so that the voters can know the antecedents of the candidates so as to enable them to make up their mind before casting their vote to a particular candidate. But, the Parliament was so vain that it passed a unanimous amendment saying that "*notwithstanding the Court directive*", the candidate will not give such information.

Surprisingly, the Parliament consisting of eminent lawyers as MPs from all parties did not realize the implications of this direction as it is well settled that parliament may change the provisions of law but it cannot abrogate to itself the power to pass a contrary direction. Naturally, the Supreme Court struck down the amendment made by the government. It is, however, sad to note that all the political parties had unanimously opposed that there should be a declaration of the antecedents and assets by the MPs/MLAs to make the voter 'better-informed'.

With regard to Right of Privacy, it may be said with pride that this issue was raised by PUCL in the famous phone tapping case. Recently the Constitution Bench has referred to the said judgment of PUCL, while affirming the Right of Privacy.

Right to food has been also accepted in the writ petition filed by PUCL, as a right to life under Article 21 of the Constitution of India.

Similarly, the PUCL was successful in getting NOTA right to the voters. It is a unique contribution by the PUCL. It is again important to point out that the suggestion of Election Commission to introduce 'None of the Above' voting was rejected by all political parties. It is interesting that though political parties pretend to abuse each other but, when it comes to disclosing information and the right of voters to know, they surprisingly show unanimous strength to deny this right to the voters.

Mr. Sanjay Parikh in his introduction has very concisely given the substance of each judgment. This will give readers an immediate idea about the judgments and the questions of law and public importance that have been dealt with.

I urge that this compilation be sent to all our units and especially to the Bar Associations so that they know the contribution of PUCL in the fight for the Human Rights.

–Rajindar Sachar

The PUCL And Its Mission

On June 12, 1975, the Allahabad High Court held Indira Gandhi guilty of corrupt electoral practices and quashed her election to Parliament. She went to the Supreme Court in appeal and prayed to stay the High Court order pending the disposal.. However, on 24th of June, the Apex Court granted her only a conditional stay. The Court allowed her to address the Lok Sabha but barred her from participating in the debates and voting. She was also barred from drawing remuneration as a member of the Lok Sabha. The opposition demanded her resignation while her pending for disposal.. They contended that a person, who could not participate in the debate in Lok Sabha or vote on a motion, should not hold the Prime Minister's august office. A call was given by the opposition for a nationwide *Satyagraha* for her resignation. Desperate to prevent the *Satyagraha* for her resignation, Indira Gandhi obtained the assent of President Fakhruddin Ali Ahmad to promulgate the internal emergency at the mid-night of 25 June 1975. Thus, the emergency was declared without the advice of the Council of Ministers as required under Article 74 of the Constitution. Following the President's assent for the declaration of the emergency, Jaya Prakash Narayan and most of the leaders of the opposition were arrested and detained under MISA (The Maintenance of Internal Security Act, 1971, a law enacted to maintain internal security in the country) in a midnight swoop. Though it was later that the Congress President D.K Barua declared, *"Indira is India and India is Indira*", as Indira had already secured her throne by clamping emergency. The declaration of the emergency was followed by the arrest of most who might had been against her or the emergency. About 35,000 people were detained under MISA alone. The total number of detained people under various other laws went up to approximately 1,10,000. The press was censored. Anyone who was even whispering against the emergency or any Congress leader found himself in jail. There was quiet in the country, but it was the quiet of the grave. Since Article 21 was suspended during the emergency, the government claimed that it could detain, torture or even kill a citizen with impunity. The government also asserted that the court could not come to the rescue of such persons. The Supreme Court also upheld this stand of the government. Such was the terror under which the people had to liveunder a ruthless authoritarian rule unknown to independent India.It was an act of rare courage and determination to think of founding or joining an organisation to raise one's voice for civil liberties and democratic rights. But defying the risk and terror, the People's Union for Civil Liberties and Democratic Rights was founded by Jaya Prakash Narayan on October 17, 1976, with the cooperation and dedication of courageous people committed to democracy. A seminar was held in Delhi, which was inaugurated by J.B. Kripalani, a revered freedom fighter and close associate of Mahatma Gandhi. Earlier, a prominent opposition leader Era Sezhiyan had taken the responsibility of acting as the Convenor of the committee tasked to set up PUCL (People's Union for Civil Liberties) & PUDR (People's Union for Democratic Rights). V.M. Tarkunde (a former judge of Bombay High Court, who had taken voluntary retirement) was elected as President and Krishan Kant, who later was elected as Vice President of India, was elected as the General Secretary. Many courageous persons from all over the country joined the organisation.

Seven months later, Indira Gandhi lifted the emergency on 23 March, 1977 following her own and her party's defeat in the 1977 Parliamentary elections. Her government was succeeded by the Janata Party government headed by Morarji Desai. The PUCL and PUDR became inactive presumably due to a belief that with the fall of Indira Gandhi and the lifting of the emergency, civil liberties and democratic rights of the people had become secure. However, the experience of the Janata Party government gave a lie to this belief. Though it undid many of the distortions in the Constitution introduced by Indira Gandhi, repealed the draconian MISA and removed other extreme measures introduced during the emergency, but in other respects, Janta Party government showed no noticeable difference in its approach to civil liberties and democratic rights. There was unease among those genuinely committed to the cause the PUCL and DR had espoused, and some thinking about the future course of action had begun. Subsequently an event took place which ended all uncertainties in this regard. Indira Gandhi returned to power with an absolute majority at the election of 1980. Her return to power left no one in any doubt that a strong organisation was needed to protect and promote civil liberties and democratic rights.

Hence, a conference was held on November 23, 1980, in Delhi, which was attended by a large number of people including several leaders of the political parties and eminent persons from different walks of life. The conference adopted the constitution of the PUCL (People's Union for Civil Liberties[1]) and elected its National Executive. V.M. Tarkunde and Arun Shourie were elected as President and General Secretary respectively. Some of the eminent persons elected to the National Executive Committee were N.A.Palkhiwala, a famous jurist, Nayantara Sehgal - an author, Girish Kanad - a noted film producer, Cho Ramawsamy - an author and journalist, Siddharaj Dhadda - Sarvodaya leader, Nikhil Chakravarty - Editor, Mainstream, Ram Jethmalani - a well-known advocate , K.G. Kannabiran - a well-known advocate and civil liberty activist, Prof. Raj Krishna - Delhi University, Balraj Puri - journalist and activist from J & K, Madhu Limaye - Socialist leader and a noted Parliamentarian, Asgar Ali Engineer - author and crusader for Islamic reform, Surendra Mohan - a veteran socialist leader, Banka Behari Das - General Secretary AICC, M.M. Thomas - a social worker from Kerala and several other important personalities.

The Constitution framed by the conference was extraordinary in many respects and unique in at least one respect. Departing from the normal practice of forming an organisation with like-minded persons, the first and the most important goal of the PUCL was set up for bringing all those who believed in the protection and promotion of civil liberties in India regardless of their political ideology. The organisation's aims and objects provided that "*The People's Union*

---

1. Many members of the PUCL & PUDR were of the opinion that the door of the organization should not be kept open for all, especially, for the members of the RSS. These members did not join the PUCL. They formed the PUDR, which is actively engaged in fighting for human rights as per its belief.

for Civil Liberties will try to bring together all those who are committed to the defence and promotion of civil liberties in India irrespective of any difference they may have in regard to political and economic institutions suitable for the country". It meant that the new organisation would welcome to its fold a communist, a socialist, a Naxalite, a Sarvodayee, a Gandhian, a Congressman or an RSS member in his personal capacity if they were committed to the aims and objects enshrined in the PUCL Constitution and signed a pledge to this effect. The bulk of its members were the persons who did not belong to any political party. The idea was to make the PUCL a bulwark against the imminent attack on the civil liberties apprehended on Indira Gandhi's return to power and even later. Welcoming, all those who pledged themselves to stand for the civil liberties and democratic rights despite their differences on political and other issues made the organization strong and ensured its impartiality. Its commitment to impartiality was further buttressed by providing that the members of political parties would not be eligible to hold any office. However, time and experience have proved that the idea was not utopian. Wherever, an honest effort had been made to bring in persons with different political persuasions spectacular result had been produced.

The framers of the Constitution were aware that civil liberties and democratic rights could not be protected without the support of a society imbued with democratic consciousness and spirit. The Indian society lacked that consciousness and spirit on account of its history, which denied equality to people on the basis of their caste and other considerations. With that in view, the PUCL constitution does not confine its aims and objects merely to protect democratic rights, but also gives its priority in upholding and promoting 'by peaceful means civil liberties and the democratic way of life' and to protect the institutions indispensable for a democracy. Conscious that democracy cannot survive if the individuals are not accorded equal dignity, securing 'recognition to the principle of the dignity of the individual is set as one of its high priority objectives. But the ultimate aim of the PUCL has been to reach the masses by involving them in the struggle for the rights and liberties which they have been denied till date and make them conscious of their rights and obligations. Way back in 1982, the then President of the organisation V.M. Tarkunde wrote in his article 'The Radicalisation of the PUCL' :

> *"An organisation like the PUCL cannot possibly fulfill its purpose if the appreciation of civil liberties remains confined to a section of the upper classes in the country. So long as civil liberties are not regarded by the masses of the people as their own liberties, laws like the National Security Act and the Maintenance of Essential Services Act will continue to be passed, vital media of mass communication like the radio and the television will continue to be under official control, the daily and the periodical press will continue to be subjected to governmental pressure and the judiciary will gradually cease to be independent. Appreciation of the necessity of civil liberties by the broad masses of the people is the precondition for the survival and continuation of these liberties."*

The observation has proved prophetic.

The PUCL's commitment to the use of peaceful means and the Rule of Law has been total and unwavering. The question of violence and denial of the protection of Constitutional rights to those who did not believe in the Constitution or has taken violence as their means was seriously raised by some very important members at the National Convention of the organisation held in Madras (present Chennai) in March, 1982. After a long debate, the Convention rejected both the use of violence as a means by any organisation and denial of the Constitutional protection to those who did not believe in the Constitution and had taken arms. The Convention adopted the following resolution :

The Question of violence :

(a) *Resolution of the National Convention held on March 7, 1982, at Madras (now Chennai) :*

"The PUCL reaffirms its faith in the democratic way of life. It appeals to all to use to the utmost the agencies and methods available in an open society. Apart from other factors, violence, even for laudable objectives, will legitimize counter violence by the State and other groups. It reaffirms that even those who have taken to violence are entitled to due process of law. We believe that this commitment is the very faith of an open society and also that adhering to this commitment is an effective way of converting all to the democratic and peaceful way of transforming our society."

The PUCL remains wholly committed to this position.

The independence of the judiciary and the freedom of the media are recognized as indispensable for the survival of a real democracy, and the organization has fought many battles in their defence during 1980s. Whenever, the attempts were made to control the press and media by the government either at the centre or the state, the PUCL took up the cudgels for their freedom. Its charter of demands submitted to the political parties before 1989 Parliamentary elections included the demand that 'Radio and Television should be placed under the control of one or more autonomous bodies'. The government control on them was viewed inimical to democracy.

The independence of the judiciary has always been accorded on a very high priority. Indira Gandhi's call for a committed judiciary,(hiatus)she superseded three judges who rejected her government's contention that Parliament had unlimited power to amend the Constitution (Kesavanand Bharati, 1973) and appointed the fourth judge in seniority - Justice A.N. Ray as the Chief Justice of India. Later, she superseded Justice H.R. Khanna and by not appointing him as Chief Justice of India though he was the senior most judge of Supreme Court. This rang the alarm bell for all who stood for the protection of the life, personal liberty and fundamental rights of the people. Justice Khanna was punished for rejecting her government's contention that during the emergency the right to life and personal liberty (Article 21) could not be suspended and a citizen could not be detained, tortured, maimed and killed by the State with impunity (*ADM Jabalpur v. Shivkant Shukla*). During the emergency, several High Court judges were transferred because they had not toed the government's line. Apart, from its faith in independent and impartial judiciary. It was also with this background in the mind that the PUCL was of the firm opinion that the judiciary should be kept independent and free from the pulls and pressures of the executive. In view of the executive seeking to make the judiciary pliant, if not subservient, the PUCL demanded the end of the power of the executive to appoint the judges of the Supreme Court and High Courts and transfer of the judges of the High Court. In its charter of demand presented to the political parties on the eve of 1989 Parliamentary elections, the PUCL demanded :

"The appointment and transfer of judges and Chief Justice of High Courts and the appointment of judges and Chief Justice of the Supreme Court should be made the responsibility of a high powered judicial committee so as to eliminate executive interference in these matters and to maintain the independence and dignity of the judiciary."

Though now the power to appoint the judges of the higher judiciary vests in the collegium of judges, there has been a persistent effort by the executive to have a say in the appointment of the judges of the higher judiciary. There are alleged shortcomings in the present system, but the remedy lies in a better system completely free from the interference or influence of the executive. Allowing the interference of the executive to remove the alleged shortcomings of the existing system would be like jumping from the frying pan into the fire.

The aggrieved citizens individually or collectively have nowhere to go but to the judiciary. The PUCL has also turned to the judiciary on a number of occasions and has succeeded in obtaining relief for the people and the nation which only an independent and impartial judiciary could grant. In the compilation of cases presented in this book, two cases which come to the mind first are pertaining to electoral reform and the right to food. The first has provided the people with the information required for making a choice before casting their votes at the elections, and the second has benefitted millions, including old helpless men, women and school children, in a desperate need of relief from a life of semi-starvation. These could be achieved because of an independent judiciary. In the future also, the role of the judiciary in protecting and promoting human rights is going to be crucial.

The PUCL has a daunting task ahead. The challenge before it is growing more and more difficult because the members of the political parties, who were part of the struggle for civil liberties and democratic rights during the emergency and 1980s when the Congress was in power, have not only deserted the organization but have become friends turned foes. Most of them rose to power in the states or at the centre from the end of the 1980s and have unfortunately turned hostile to the civil liberties and the democratic rights.

But the PUCL continues to move forward towards its mission of promoting a democratic way of life by inculcating democratic consciousness and values in the society, which alone can protect our rights from the onslaughts of a repressive government.

–Prabhakar Sinha

Public Interest Litigation And PUCL's Interventions

Public Interest Litigation (PIL), as it developed in early 80s, marks a significant departure from traditional judicial proceedings. In the earlier years, the Supreme Court interpreted the role of the judiciary as determining the *lis* before it in accordance with the narrow procedural rules. The traditional rules of procedure in the adversarial system of law permit only a person whose rights are rightly affected. Under a common law, a person claiming a writ of mandamus had to show that he was enforcing his own personal rights. In Municipal Council, *Ratlam Vs Shri Vardichand & Ors. (1980 (4) SCC 162)*, the Supreme Court reacted differently to this traditional approach and observed through Justice V.R. Krishna Iyer (sitting with O.Chinnappa Reddy J.) :

> *The truth is that a few profound issues of processual jurisprudence of great strategic significance to our legal system face us and we must zero in on them as they involve problem of access to justice for the people beyond the blinkered rules of* ***'standing'*** *of British–Indian vintage. If the centre of gravity of justice is to shift, as the preamble of our constitution mandates, from the traditional individualism of* ***locus standi*** *to the community orientation of public interest litigation, these issues must be considered.*

On 30.12.81 in the First Judges case, *S.P. Gupta and Ors. Vs Union of India, 1981 Supp (1) SCC 87*, the Supreme Court said :

> *Where a legal wrong or a legal injury is caused to a person or to a determinate class of persons by reason of violation of any constitutional or legal right or any burden is imposed in contravention of any constitutional or legal provision or without authority of law or any such legal wrong or legal injury or legal burden is threatened and such person or determinate class of person is by reasons of poverty, helplessness or disability or socially or economically disadvantaged position, unable to approach the court for any relief, any member of the public can maintain an application for an appropriate direction, order or writ in the High Court under Article 226 and in case of breach of any fundamental right of such persons or class of persons, in this court under Article 32 seeking judicial redress for the legal wrong or injury caused to such person or determinate class of persons .*

Round about the same time in the early 80s, the People's Union for Civil Liberties (PUCL) drafted and adopted its Constitution on 23rd Nov 1980, with its aims and objectives, which included upholding and promoting by peaceful means civil liberties and democratic way of life throughout India and to secure recognition to the principle of dignity of individual and to make legal assistance available for the defence of civil liberties and also to do all acts and things that may be necessary, helpful to its aims and objectives.

As a sequel to these aims and objectives, PUCL filed petitions as public interest litigations involving important issues like electoral reforms, fake encounters, right to privacy, bonded labour, constitutional validity of draconian law (POTA), and right to food etc.

Mr. Sanjay Parikh has prepared this compilation of important judgments on the issues raised by the PUCL. Mr. Sanjay Parikh along with Mr. Rajindar Sachar has appeared in most of these cases. He has, in his introduction, very appropriately elaborated the issues involved in these judgments with an expectation *"that the readers understand that selective interventions were made by the PUCL in important areas where it felt that the constitutional rights and civil liberties were being seriously infringed upon"*.

I hope that this compilation would be useful for the scholars, legal practitioners and human right activists from all over India, besides being a guiding to the PUCL members throughout the country.

–Ravikiran Jain

Introduction

The idea of preparing a compilation of important judgments of the Supreme Court on the issues raised by the People's Union for Civil Liberties (PUCL), was discussed on many occasions in the National Convention as well as in the Executive Committee meetings. However, for one reason or the other, this idea could not materialize. I am happy that ultimately it has taken a concrete shape. Better late than never! I am sure that this book will provide sufficient material and information to our office bearers and members, which they can use at the local level, either in the courts or in creating awareness among the people. This book will also be helpful to the lawyers and human rights activists.

For convenience and continuity, the judgments have been arranged issue-wise instead of following the chronology. A brief summary of the cases has been given in the beginning of the each case. But it is always advisable to read the judgment in its entirety for a better understanding.

The first set of judgments pertain to electoral reforms. All these judgments ultimately aim at empowering the voter, who forms the basis of a healthy democracy. The first judgment (2002) relates to an Article 32 petition filed directly by the PUCL praying that voters have a right to know relevant particulars of the candidates. In that context, the Supreme Court examined whether right to know is derived fromthe concept of *"freedom of speech and expression"* under Article 19(1)(a) of the Constitution. After referring to several judgments, the Court realized that casting of a vote by a misinformed and non-informed voter or a voter having one-sided information only, is bound to affect the democracy seriously.

The Supreme Court held that the citizens who elect MPs or MLAs have a right to know that their representatives do not have tainted records, i.e., criminal antecedents and/or assets beyond the known sources. The following observation in the judgment is extremely important:

"Under our Constitution, Article 19(1)(a) provides for freedom of speech and expression. Voter's speech or expression in case of election would include casting of votes, that is to say, voter speaks out or expresses by casting vote. For this purpose, information about the candidate to be selected is a must. Voter's (little man — citizen's) right to know antecedents including criminal past of his candidate contesting election for MP or MLA is much more fundamental and basic for survival of democracy. The little man may think over before making his choice of electing law-breakers as law-makers."

Finally, the Supreme Court directed the Election Commission to seek information on affidavit from each candidate as a necessary part of the nomination papers, by exercising powers under Article 324 of the Constitution. The information should include, among others, criminal antecedents, if any, assets both movable and immovable as well as the educational qualification.

The second judgment (2003) was a corollary of the first judgment. After the 2002 judgment, all the political parties, without any exception, termed the Supreme Court judgment as *'judicial overreach'* and impressed on passing of an Ordinance. As a result of which, Representation of the People (Amendment) Ordinance, 2002 was promulgated on 24.08.2002 seeking to nullify the directions given in the 2002 judgment. PUCL challenged the said Ordinance by way of a Writ Petition under Article 32 of the Constitution before the Supreme Court. Later, the said Ordinance became an Act.

Therefore, the petition was amended to include challenge to the Act also. By judgment dated 13.03.2003, the Amendment Act i.e. Section 33-B of the Representation of the People Act was struck down as being null and void. Justice M.B. Shah, in his judgment, held that a voter's Fundamental Right to know the antecedents of a candidate is independent of the statutory rights under the Election Law. A voter is first a citizen of this country and apart from statutory rights, he has Fundamental Rights conferred by the Constitution. Therefore, the Right to Vote would be meaningless unless the citizens are well informed about the antecedents of a candidate. Justice P. Venkatarama Reddi wrote a concurring judgment however, he has expressed his views slightly differently. The Learned Judge held that though the initial right i.e. right to cast a vote, cannot be placed on the pedestal of a Fundamental Right. But when the voter goes to the polling booth and casts his vote, his freedom to express arises. The Learned Judge agreed that casting of a vote in favour of one or the other candidate tantamount to freedom of expression of the voter and the exercise of voting right marks the accomplishment of that freedom under Article 19(1)(a) of the Constitution. Though Justice Dharamadhikari agreed with both Justice Shah and Justice Reddi but clarified that the entire election system needs a reformation so that the election process becomes transparent and accountable and the influence of tainted money and physical force of criminals do not make democracy a farce.

The above two judgments gave a new dimension to the democracy by empowering the voter, who, as an informed citizen could freely exercise the choice of his candidate. These judgments converted a voter–*"a little man"*, as said by Sir Winston Churchill into a *"big man"*—big enough to sustain the democracy!

So many things are still required to be done to make the above two judgments of the Supreme Court more meaningful. For example, in spite of the law being laid down by the Supreme Court, in practical reality, the information is not made available to the voters. Some NGOs collect the information about antecedents of the candidates and put them on the internet. But it is not possible for the entire electorate of this country to access this information. What is required is that this information must be made available to voters at each polling booth so that a voter can at least receive the information at that juncture before casting his vote for expressing his right.

Subsequent to the developments pursuant to the aforementioned, two PUCL judgments are required to be mentioned. In *Resurgence India v. Election Commission of India & Anr.* (decided on 13.09.2013), the Supreme Court held that if the information is not fully furnished at the time of filing of affidavit along with the nomination paper, the nomination paper is fit to be rejected. This view was reiterated in *Kisan Shankar Kathore v. Arun Dattatraya Sawant* (decided on 09.05.2014). It was held that if blanks are left in an affidavit, nomination can be rejected then and there. Recently, the Supreme Court in *Krishnamoorthy v. Sivakumar & Ors.* gave a judgment on the question as to what will be the impact of non-disclosure of the offences, as decided by the above mentioned two PUCL judgments. The Supreme Court held that disclosure of criminal antecedents of a candidate, specially pertaining to serious offence(s) relating to corruption or moral turpitude at the time of filing nomination paper as mandated by law is categorical imperative. Non-disclosure creates an impediment in the free exercise of electoral right and the concealment or suppression deprives the voters to make an informed choice as the candidate alone has the special knowledge of pending cases where cognizance has been taken or charges have been framed. The Court has held that non-disclosure would amount to undue influence and, therefore, the election will be declared null and void by the Election Tribunal under Section 100(1)(b) of the 1951 Act. Therefore, the disclosure of information in the nomination paper as held in the above two PUCL judgments has taken larger dimensions towards electoral reforms. In *Mairembam Prithviraj v. Pukhrem Sharatchandra Singh* decided on 28.10.2016, the Supreme Court was considering the case of false declaration with regard to educational qualification and whether that will result in declaration of the election as null and void. The Court, after referring to the PUCL judgments, held that in cases where nomination is declared to have been improperly accepted, there is no requirement to prove that the result of the election of the returned candidate is materially affected. On the ground of improper acceptance only, the election of a candidate can be set aside.

As a sequel to the above, PUCL was faced with many questions. One logical question was that if all the candidates have a tainted record, why should a voter be compelled to cast his/her vote in favour of any one of them? Is abstinence from election, the only way available to a voter or must he have a right to go to the polling booth and say 'no' to all the contesting candidates as a part of his right of expression? This right was recognized in many countries *as "None Of The Above" (NOTA)*. The PUCL took up this issue before the Supreme Court in Article 32 Petition and argued that though the right 'not to vote' is recognized by law and that is also a part of freedom of expression of a voter, therefore if a voter chooses to exercise this right i.e. NOTA, it has to be kept secret. The Supreme Court held that for the survival of democracy, it is essential that the best available man should be chosen as the people's representative and *that* can be attained only if men of high moral and ethical values are elected on a positive vote. The Court held that for a vibrant democracy, the voter must be given an opportunity to choose NOTA button, which will indeed compel the political parties to nominate a sound candidate. The following observations of the Supreme Court, in this context, are important :

"Giving right to a voter not to vote for any candidate while protecting his right of secrecy is extremely important in a democracy. Such an option gives the voter the right to express his disapproval with the kind of candidates that are being put up by the political parties. When the political parties will realise that a large number of people are expressing their disapproval with the candidates being put up by them, gradually there will be a systemic change and the political parties will be forced to accept the will of the people and field candidates who are known for their integrity."

After NOTA, yet another logical query arose. What should happen in a constituency if out of total votes 50% or more than 50% votes are cast in favour of NOTA? Whether a candidate who gets less than 50% of the votes cast has any moral/legal right to act as a representative of the people? The logic is quite sound and the time is not very far when need for a legal provision giving solution to this problem will arise? In the elections conducted subsequent to the NOTA judgment, it is found that in many constituencies the percentage of NOTA votes are quite high. The message from the people should be taken up seriously by all the political parties in nominating their candidates,otherwise either the Legislature or the Courts will be compelled to step in to remedy the situation.

The second series of judgments are on the topic of police encounters. The first case was in 1997, wherein, the Supreme Court had awarded compensation for a fake police encounter, in spite of reservation by India in ratifying Article 9(5) of the International Covenant on Civil and Political Rights (ICCPR) 1966, which provides enforceable right to compensation in cases of unlawful arrest or detention. In the said judgment, there was an interesting discussion as to how the important principles of International Law can be read into Municipal Law. However, it was clearly stated that *"the provisions of the covenant, which elucidate and go to effectuate the fundamental rights guaranteed by our Constitution, can certainly be relied upon by courts as facets of those fundamental rights and hence, enforceable as such."*

This principle of incorporation of covenants in the Constitution laid down in above PUCL Judgment has been relied upon in several subsequent judgments by the Supreme Court. In the second judgment (2014), the Supreme Court laid down several guidelines to ensure a standard procedure for thorough, effective and independent investigation in cases of police encounters resulting in death or grievous injury. The Supreme Court further directed that the guidelines laid by it must be strictly observed in all cases of death and grievous injury in police encounters by treating them as law declared under Article 141 of the Constitution.

Yet another important case (1997) which has been included in the compilation relates to telephone tapping, which results in serious invasion of right to privacy of an individual. The Supreme Court said that the right to privacy being part of right to life under Article 21, it cannot be curtailed except according to the procedure established by law. The Supreme Court found that no rules were framed under the Indian Telegraph Act, 1885 laying down the precautions to be taken for preventing the improper interception or disclosure of messages. Therefore, in order to rule out the arbitrariness and till the Central Government lay down such rules, the Supreme Court laid down guidelines providing for necessary procedural safeguards for exercising the power of telephone tapping. This judgment is also recognized as landmark in protecting Constitutional rights and civil liberties of the citizens. This judgment has also been followed and referred to in umpteen number of cases decided subsequently. In recent Constitution Judgment by 11 Judges, recognizing Right to Privacy as part of fundamental rights, PUCL Judgment has been referred to and relied upon.

The compilation also includes judgments relating to bonded labour, sewage workers, appointment of member of NHRC disregarding the Paris Principles and challenge to Prevention of Terrorism Act ("POTA"). With regard to the Right to Food petition, I may add that the PUCL along with Indian Council for Legal Aid and Advice had taken up the issue of starvation deaths in Koraput, Balangir and Kalahandi ("KBK") districts of Odisha which also involved the question of Right to Food. On a reference from the Supreme Court, the NHRC had given various directions and monitored the situation for nearly a decade to enforce the Right to Food in the context of starvation deaths in the KBK region. The PUCL had thereafter taken up the issue of Right to Food in the Supreme Court with regard to all the States/Union Territories in which a number of orders were passed, particularly in relation to the Public Distribution System ("PDS"). The series of directions have resulted in strengthening of the PDS system throughout the country.

PUCL had challenged the constitutional validity of section 66A of the IT Act by filing an independent Writ Petition. This Writ Petition has been decided along with other Writ Petitions carrying the title of the lead case, *Shreya Singhal v. Union of India. (NO.167 OF 2012).* In this compilation, we have given the submissions made by PUCL and a gist of findings arrived at by the Supreme Court. As the judgment is quite lengthy and due to size constraint of the book, the citation where the said judgment can be accessed has been given.

I would like to refer to another important fact. This compilation contains judgments of the Supreme Court only. Our branch offices in different states across the county have also taken up many important causes and significant judgments have been given by different High Courts. We have requested the State units to send important judgments so that another compilation of PUCL judgments given by different High Courts can be published.

A brief introduction to the important judgments compiled in this book has been made so that the readers understand that selective interventions were made by the PUCL in important areas where it felt that the constitutional rights and civil liberties were being seriously infringed upon. PUCL has also made interventions in the areas which fall under social, cultural and economic rights, as that area was considered important to give dignity to the constitutionally guaranteed Right to Life. Above all, without the strong and vibrant democracy, the Constitutional rights and pledges become illusory and therefore, PUCL decided to take up the issue of electoral reforms as a mission.

Compilation of these cases also signify the importance of my association with Justice Rajindar Sachar for more than two decades. I consider myself fortunate and blessed that this association not only enriched my knowledge of law but also developed in me a strong commitment to fight for social causes.

Shri Prabhakar Sinha has given a brief background of PUCL touching upon important miles stones, association of eminent people and the ideology which PUCL has followed. Shri Ravi Kiran Jain, while describing origin of PIL, has narrated how PUCL has in public interest, used the liberal locus standi principle in the Courts to strengthen human rights and democracy.

I am thankful to Ms. Ninni Susan Thomas and Ms. Karishma Maria for their help in preparing this compilation. I hope that this book will be useful to not only the office bearers and members of PUCL but also to other organizations, lawyers and human rights activists which deal with the similar problems and issues of human rights violations in the country.

—Sanjay Parikh

In the Supreme Court of India

Civil Appeal No. 7178 of 2001
Union of India v. Association for Democratic Reforms & Anr.[2]

Writ Petition (Civil) No. 294 of 2001
People's Union for Civil Liberties (PUCL) & Anr. v. Union of India & Anr.

Date of Judgement : 02.05.2002

Bench : M.B. Shah, Bisheshwar Prasad Singh and H.K. Sema, JJ.

[This judgment relates to the question whether, before casting their vote, voters have a right to know relevant particulars of their candidates. The Delhi High Court in a Writ Petition filed by the Association for Democratic Reforms had held that for making the right choice, it is essential for a voter to know the past of a candidate. Keeping information about the candidate in the dark would not be in the interest of democracy as well as the well-being of the country. The Delhi High Court, therefore, gave appropriate directions to the Election Commission. This judgment was challenged by the Union of India before the Supreme Court in a Special Leave Petition. PUCL had filed a Writ Petition under Article 32 of the Constitution seeking directions that there should be declaration of assets by candidates and that such declaration should be made every year during the tenure as an elected representative. PUCL also prayed that guidelines be framed under Article 141 of the Constitution by the Supreme Court. In the judgment, the Supreme Court has decided that the voters have a right to know the antecedents of the candidates as it is a right flowing from Article 19(1)(a) of the Constitution. The Court directed the Election Commission that every MP/MLA, as a necessary part of his nomination paper, should furnish his antecedents pertaining to criminal offences, declaration of his assets (movable, immovable, bank balance, etc.) and educational qualifications.]

2. (2002) 5 SCC 294

Judgment

M.B. Shah, J.

1. Short but important question involved in these matters is — in a nation wedded to republican and democratic form of government, where election as a Member of Parliament or as a Member of Legislative Assembly is of utmost importance for governance of the country, whether, before casting votes, voters have a right to know relevant particulars of their candidates? Further connected question is — whether the High Court had jurisdiction to issue directions, as stated below, in a writ petition filed under Article 226 of the Constitution of India?

2. Before dealing with the aforesaid questions, we would refer to the brief facts as alleged by the petitioner Association for Democratic Reforms in Writ Petition No. 7257 of 1999 filed before the High Court of Delhi for direction to implement the recommendations made by the Law Commission in its 170th Report and to make necessary changes under Rule 4 of the Conduct of Elections Rules, 1961. It has been pointed out that the Law Commission of India had, at the request of the Government of India, undertaken comprehensive study of the measures required to expedite hearing of election petitions and to have a thorough review of the Representation of the People Act, 1951 (hereinafter referred to as "the Act") so as to make the electoral process more fair, transparent and equitable and to reduce the distortions and evils that have crept into the Indian electoral system and to identify the areas where the legal provisions required strengthening and improvement. It is pointed out that the Law Commission has made recommendation for debarring a candidate from contesting an election if charges have been framed against him by a court in respect of certain offences and necessity for a candidate seeking to contest election to furnish details regarding criminal cases, if any, pending against him. It has also suggested that true and correct statement of assets owned by the candidate, his/her spouse and dependent relations should also be disclosed. The petitioner has also referred para 6.2 of the report of the Vohra Committee of the Government of India, Ministry of Home Affairs, which reads as follows :

> *"6.2. Like the Director CBI, DIB has also stated that there has been a rapid spread and growth of criminal gangs, armed senas, drug mafias, smuggling gangs, drug peddlers and economic lobbies in the country which have, over the years, developed an extensive network of contacts with the bureaucrats/government functionaries at the local levels, politicians, media persons and strategically located individuals in the non-State sector. Some of these syndicates also have international linkages, including the foreign intelligence agencies. In this context DIB has given the following examples:*
>
> *I. In certain States like Bihar, Haryana and U.P., these gangs enjoy the patronage of local-level politicians, cutting across party lines and the protection of governmental functionaries. Some political leaders become the leaders of these gangs, armed senas and over the years get themselves elected to local bodies, State Assemblies and the national Parliament. Resultantly, such elements have acquired considerable*

political clout seriously jeopardising the smooth functioning of the administration and the safety of life and property of the common man causing a sense of despair and alienation among the people.

II. The big smuggling syndicates having international linkages have spread into and infected the various economic and financial activities, including hawala transactions, circulation of black money and operations of a vicious parallel economy causing serious damage to the economic fibre of the country. These syndicates have acquired substantial financial and muscle power and social respectability and have successfully corrupted the government machinery at all levels and yield enough influence to make the task of investigating and prosecuting agencies extremely difficult; even the members of the judicial system have not escaped the embrace of the mafia.

III. Certain elements of the mafia have shifted to narcotics, drugs and weapon-smuggling and established narco-terrorism networks specially in the States of J&K, Punjab, Gujarat and Maharashtra. The cost of contesting elections has thrown the politician into the lap of these elements and led to a grave compromise by officials of the preventive/detective systems. The virus has spread to almost all the centres in the country, the coastal and the border States have been particularly affected.

IV. The Bombay bomb blast case and the communal riots in Surat and Ahmedabad have demonstrated how the Indian underworld has been exploited by the Pak ISI and the latter's network in UAE to cause sabotage, subversion and communal tension in various parts of the country. The investigations into the Bombay bomb blast cases have revealed extensive linkages of the underworld in the various governmental agencies, political circles, business sector and the film world."

3. It is also contended that despite the reports of the Law Commission and the Vohra Committee, successive Governments have failed to take any action and, therefore, petition was filed for implementation of the said reports and for a direction to the Election Commission to make mandatory for every candidate to provide information by amending Forms 2-A to 2-E prescribed under the Conduct of Elections Rules, 1961. After hearing the parties, the High Court by judgment and order dated 02.11.2000, held that it is the function of Parliament to make necessary amendments in the Representation of the People Act, 1951 or the Elections Rules and, therefore, the Court cannot pass any order, as prayed, for amending the Act or the Rules.

4. However, the Court considered whether or not an elector, a citizen of the country has a fundamental right to receive information regarding the criminal activities of a candidate to the Lok Sabha or the Legislative Assembly for making an estimate for himself — as to whether the person who is contesting the election has a background making him worthy of his vote, by peeping into the past of the candidate. After considering the relevant submissions and the reports as well as the say of the Election Commission, the High Court held that for making a right choice, it is essential that the past of the candidate should not be kept in the dark as it is not in the interest of the democracy and well being of the country. The Court directed the Election Commission to secure to voters the following information pertaining to each of the candidates contesting election to Parliament and to the State Legislatures and the parties they represent :

1. Whether the candidate is accused of any offence(s) punishable with imprisonment. If so, the details thereof.
2. Assets possessed by a candidate, his or her spouse and dependent relations.
3. Facts giving insight into the candidate's competence, capacity and suitability for acting as a parliamentarian or a legislator including details of his/her educational qualifications.
4. Information which the Election Commission considers necessary for judging the capacity and capability of the political party fielding the candidate for election to Parliament or the State Legislature.

That order is challenged by the Union of India by filing the present appeal.

5. On behalf of Indian National Congress I.A. No. 2 of 2001 is also filed for impleadment/intervention in the appeal filed by the Union of India by *inter alia* contending that the High Court ought to have directed the writ petitioners to approach Parliament for appropriate amendments to the Act instead of directing the Election Commission of India to implement the same. I.A. for intervention is granted.

6. Further, People's Union for Civil Liberties (PUCL) has filed Writ Petition No. 294 of 2001 under Article 32 of the Constitution praying that writ, order or direction be issued to the respondents (a) to bring in such measures which provide for declaration of assets by the candidate for the elections and for such mandatory declaration every year during the tenure as an elected representative as MP/MLA; (b) to bring in such measures which provide for declaration by the candidate contesting election, whether any charge in respect of any offence has been framed against him/her; and (c) to frame such guidelines under Article 141 of the Constitution by taking into consideration the 170th Report of the Law Commission of India.

Submissions

7. We have heard the learned counsel for the parties at length. Mr. Harish N. Salve, learned Solicitor-General appearing for the Union of India submitted that till suitable amendments are made in the Act and the Rules thereunder, the High Court should not have given any direction to the Election Commission. He referred to various sections of the Act and submitted that Section 8 provides for disqualification on conviction for certain offences and Section 8-A provides for disqualification on the ground of corrupt practices. Section 32 provides nomination of candidate for election if he is qualified to be chosen to fill that seat under the provisions of the Constitution and the Act or under the provisions of the Government of Union Territories Act, 1963. Thereafter, elaborate procedure is prescribed for presentation of nomination paper and requirements for a valid nomination. Finally, Section 36 provides for scrutiny of nominations and empowers the returning officer to reject any nomination on the following grounds :

> *"(a) that on the date fixed for the scrutiny of nominations the candidate either is not qualified or is disqualified for being chosen to fill the seat under any of the following provisions that may be applicable, namely—*
>
> *Articles 84, 102, 173 and 191,*
>
> *Part II of this Act and Sections 4 and 14 of the Government of Union Territories Act, 1963 (20 of 1963); or*
>
> *(b) that there has been a failure to comply with any of the provisions of Section 33 or Section 34; or*
>
> *(c) that the signature of the candidate or the proposer on the nomination paper is not genuine."*

8. It is his submission that it is for the political parties to decide whether such amendments should be brought and carried out in the Act and the Rules. He further submitted that as the Act or the Rules nowhere disqualify a candidate for non-disclosure of the assets or pending charge in a criminal case, therefore, directions given by the High Court would be of no consequence and such directions ought not to have been issued.

9. Supplementing the aforesaid submission, Mr. Ashwani Kumar, learned Senior Counsel appearing on behalf of intervenor Indian National Congress submitted that the Constituent Assembly had discussed and negatived requirement of educational qualification and possession of assets to contest election. For that purpose, he referred to the debates in the Constituent Assembly. He submitted that 3/4th of the population is illiterate and providing education as a qualification for contesting election was not accepted by the Constituent Assembly. Similarly, prescribing of property qualification for the candidates to contest election was also negatived by the Constituent Assembly. He, therefore, submitted that furnishing of information regarding assets and educational qualification of a candidate is not at all relevant for contesting election and even for casting votes. Voters are not influenced by the educational qualification or by possession of wealth by a contesting candidate. It is his say that the party whom he represents is interested in purity of election and wants to stop entry of criminals in politics or its criminalisation but it is for Parliament to decide the said question. It is submitted that a delicate balance is required to be maintained with regard to the jurisdiction of Parliament and that of courts and once Parliament has not amended the Act or the Rules despite the recommendation made by the Law Commission or the report submitted by the Vohra Committee, there was no question of giving any direction by the High Court to the Election Commission.

10. Mr. K.K. Venugopal, learned Senior Counsel appearing on behalf of the Election Commission exhaustively referred to the counter-affidavit filed on behalf of the Election Commission. At this stage, we would refer to some part from the said affidavit. It is stated that the issue of 'persons with criminal background' contesting election has been engaging the attention of the Election Commission of India for quite some time; even Parliament in the debates on

50 years of independence and the resolution passed in its special session in August 1997 had shown great concern about the increasing criminalisation of politics; it is widely believed that there is criminal nexus between the political parties and anti-social elements which is leading to criminalisation of politics; the criminals themselves are now joining the election fray and often even getting elected in the process. Some of them have even adorned ministerial berths and, thus, law-breakers have become law-makers. The Commission has suggested that a candidate should be required to furnish information in respect of—

> *(a) all cases in which he has been convicted of any offence and punished with any kind of imprisonment or amount of fine, and whether any appeal or application for review is pending in respect of any such cases of conviction; and*
> *(b) all pending cases in which he is involved before any court of law in any offence, punishable with imprisonment for two years or more, and where the appropriate court has on prima facie satisfaction framed the charges against him for proceeding with the trial.*

11. For declaration of assets, it has been suggested by the Election Commission that the candidate should be asked to disclose his assets, all immovable and movable properties which would include cash, bank balances, fixed deposits and other savings such as shares, stocks, debentures etc. The candidate also should be directed to disclose for voters' information, not only his assets but his liabilities like overdues to public financial institutions and government dues and charges on his/her properties.

12. For other directions issued by the High Court, it has been pointed out that it is for the political parties to project the capacity and capability of a candidate and that directions issued by the High Court are required to be set aside. Finally, the Election Commission has suggested as under :

> *"I. Each candidate for election to Parliament or a State Legislature should submit, along with his nomination paper, a duly sworn affidavit, for the truth of which he is liable, as a necessary part of his nomination paper, furnishing therein, information on the following aspects in relation to his candidature:*
>
> *I. whether the candidate is convicted of any offence in any case in the past, and punished with imprisonment or fine; if so, the details thereof, together with the details of any pending appeals or applications for revision in any such cases of conviction;*
>
> *II. whether the candidate is accused in any pending case, of any offence punishable with imprisonment for two years or more, and in which charges have been framed against him by the competent court of law; if so, the details thereof, together with the details of any pending appeals or applications for revision in respect of the charges framed in any such cases;*

III. whether the candidate is an income tax and/or wealth tax assessee and has been paying his tax(es) and filing his returns regularly, wherever he is liable, and if so, the financial year for which the last income tax/wealth tax returns have been filed;

IV. the liabilities of the candidate, his/her spouse and minor children; that is to say, overdues to any public financial institutions, any government dues, and charges on his/her properties;

V. the educational qualifications of the candidate.

II. The information by each candidate in respect of all the foregoing aspects shall be furnished by the candidate in a format to be prescribed by the Election Commission and shall be supported by a duly sworn affidavit, making him responsible for the correctness of the information so furnished and liable for any false statement.

III. The information so furnished by each candidate in the prescribed format and supported by a duly sworn affidavit shall be disseminated by the Election Commission, through the respective Returning Officers, by displaying the same on the notice board of the Returning Officer and making the copies thereof available freely and liberally to all other contesting candidates and the representatives of the print and electronic media.

If any rival candidate furnishes information to the contrary, by means of a duly sworn affidavit, then such affidavit of the rival candidate may also be disseminated along with the affidavit of the candidate concerned.

The Court may lay down that it would be mandatory for each candidate for election to Parliament or State Legislature, to file along with his nomination paper, the aforesaid duly sworn affidavit, furnishing therein the information on the aspects detailed above and that the nomination paper of such a candidate who fails or refuses to file the required affidavit or files an incomplete affidavit shall be deemed to be an incomplete nomination paper within the meaning of Section 33(1) of the Representation of the People Act, 1951 and shall suffer consequences according to law."

13. The aforesaid suggestions made by the Election Commission would certainly mean that except certain modifications, the Election Commission virtually supports the directions issued by the High Court and that candidates must be directed to furnish necessary information with regard to pending criminal cases as well as assets and educational qualification.

14. Mr. Rajindar Sachar, learned Senior Counsel appearing on behalf of the petitioners relied upon the decision rendered by this Court in *Vineet Narain v. Union of India* [(1998) 1 SCC 226] and submitted that considering the widespread illiteracy of the voters, and at the same time their overall culture and character, if they are well informed about the candidates contesting election as MP or MLA, they would be in a position to decide independently to cast their votes in favour of a candidate who, according to them, is much more efficient to discharge his functions as MP or MLA. He, therefore, submitted that presuming that the High Court has no jurisdiction to pass orders to fill in the gaps, this Court can do so by exercising its powers under Article 142 which have the effect of law.

15. In *Vineet Narain case* [(1998) 1 SCC 226] this Court dealt with the writ petitions under Article 32 of the Constitution of India brought in public interest wherein allegation was against the Central Bureau of Investigation (CBI) of inertia in matters where accusation made was against high dignitaries. Primary question considered was — whether it was within the domain of judicial review and it could be an effective instrument for activating the investigating process which is under the control of the executive? While discussing the powers of this Court, it was observed :

> *"The powers conferred on this Court by the Constitution are ample to remedy this defect and to ensure enforcement of the concept of equality.*
>
> *There are ample powers conferred by Article 32 read with Article 142 to make orders which have the effect of law by virtue of Article 141 and there is mandate to all authorities to act in aid of the orders of this Court as provided in Article 144 of the Constitution. In a catena of decisions of this Court, this power has been recognised and exercised, if need be, by issuing necessary directions to fill the vacuum till such time the legislature steps in to cover the gap or the executive discharges its role." (emphasis supplied)*

16. In paragraph 51, the Court pointed out previous precedents for exercise of such power :

> *"51. In exercise of the powers of this Court under Article 32 read with Article 142, guidelines and directions have been issued in a large number of cases and a brief reference to a few of them is sufficient. In Erach Sam Kanga v. Union of India [WP No. 2632 of 1978, decided on 20.03.1979] the Constitution Bench laid down certain guidelines relating to the Emigration Act. In Lakshmi Kant Pandey v. Union of India [(1984) 2 SCC 244] (In re, Foreign Adoption), guidelines for adoption of minor children by foreigners were laid down. Similarly in State of W.B. v. Sampat Lal [(1985) 1 SCC 317] , K. Veeraswami v. Union of India [(1991) 3 SCC 655] , Union Carbide Corpn. v. Union of India [(1991) 4 SCC 584] , Delhi Judicial Service Association v. State of Gujarat (Nadiad case) [(1991) 4 SCC 406], Delhi Development Authority v. Skipper Construction Co. P. Ltd. [(1996) 4 SCC 622] and Dinesh Trivedi, M.P. v. Union of India [(1997) 4 SCC 306] guidelines were laid down having the effect of law, requiring rigid compliance. In Supreme Court Advocates-on-Record Association v. Union of India (IInd Judges case) [(1993) 4 SCC 441] a nine-Judge Bench laid down guidelines and norms for the appointment and transfer of Judges which are being rigidly followed in the matter of appointments of High Court and Supreme Court Judges and transfer of High Court Judges. More recently in Vishaka v. State of Rajasthan [(1997) 6 SCC 241] elaborate*

guidelines have been laid down for observance in workplaces relating to sexual harassment of working women. In Vishaka [(1997) 6 SCC 241] it was said (SCC pp. 249-50, para 11)

'11. The obligation of this Court under Article 32 of the Constitution for the enforcement of these fundamental rights in the absence of legislation must be viewed along with the role of judiciary envisaged in the Beijing Statement of Principles of the Independence of Judiciary in the LAWASIA region. These principles were accepted by the Chief Justices of Asia and the Pacific at Beijing in 1995 (As amended at Manila, 28th August, 1997) as those representing the minimum standards necessary to be observed in order to maintain the independence and effective functioning of the judiciary. The objectives of the judiciary mentioned in the Beijing Statement are:

"Objectives of the Judiciary :

10. The objectives and functions of the judiciary include the following: (a) to ensure that all persons are able to live securely under the rule of law;

(b) to promote, within the proper limits of the judicial function, the observance and the attainment of human rights; and

(c) to administer the law impartially among persons and between persons and the State."

Thus, an exercise of this kind by the court is now a well-settled practice which has taken firm roots in our constitutional jurisprudence. This exercise is essential to fill the void in the absence of suitable legislation to cover the field.' "

17. Ms. Kamini Jaiswal, learned counsel appearing on behalf of the respondents in support of the decision rendered by the High Court referred to the decision in *Kihoto Hollohan v. Zachillhu* [1992 Supp (2) SCC 651] wherein while considering the validity of the Tenth Schedule of the Constitution, the Court observed :

"179. Democracy is a part of the basic structure of our Constitution; and rule of law, and free and fair elections are basic features of democracy. One of the postulates of free and fair elections is provision for resolution of election disputes as also adjudication of disputes relating to subsequent disqualifications by an independent authority."

She, therefore, contended that for free and fair elections and for survival of democracy, entire history, background and the antecedents of the candidate are required to be disclosed to the voters so that they can judiciously decide in whose favour they should vote; otherwise, there would not be true reflection of electoral mandate. For interpreting Article 324, she submitted that this provision outlines broad and general principles giving power to the Election Commission and it should be interpreted in a broad perspective as held by this Court in various decisions.

18. In these matters, questions requiring consideration are :

1. Whether the Election Commission is empowered to issue directions as ordered by the High Court?

2. Whether a voter — a citizen of this country — has right to get relevant information, such as assets, qualification and involvement in offence for being educated and informed for judging the suitability of a candidate contesting election as MP or MLA?

For deciding the aforesaid questions, we would proceed on the following accepted legal position.

19. At the outset, we would say that it is not possible for this Court to give any directions for amending the Act or the statutory Rules. It is for Parliament to amend the Act and the Rules. It is also established law that no direction can be given, which would be contrary to the Act and the Rules.

20. However, it is equally settled that in case when the Act or Rules are silent on a particular subject and the authority implementing the same has constitutional or statutory power to implement it, the Court can necessarily issue directions or orders on the said subject to fill the vacuum or void till the suitable law is enacted.

21. Further, it is to be stated that (a) one of the basic structures of our Constitution is "republican and democratic form of government"; (b) the election to the House of People and the Legislative Assembly is on the basis of adult suffrage, that is to say, every person who is a citizen of India and who is not less than 18 years of age on such date as may be fixed in that behalf by or under any law made by the appropriate legislature and is not otherwise disqualified under the Constitution or any law on the ground of non-residence, unsoundness of mind, crime or corrupt or illegal practice, shall be entitled to be registered as a voter at any such election (Article 326); (c) holding of any asset (immovable or movable) or any educational qualification is not the eligibility criteria to contest election; and (d) under Article 324, the superintendence, direction and control of the "conduct of all elections" to Parliament and to the legislature of every State vests in the Election Commission. The phrase "conduct of elections" is held to be of wide amplitude which would include power to make all necessary provisions for conducting free and fair elections.

Question-1. Whether the Election Commission is empowered to issue directions as ordered by the High Court

22. For health of democracy and fair election, whether the disclosure of assets by a candidate, his/her qualification and particulars regarding involvement in criminal cases are necessary for informing voters, maybe illiterate, so that they can decide intelligently, whom to vote for. In our opinion, the decision of even an illiterate voter, if properly educated and informed about the contesting candidate, would be based on his own relevant criteria of selecting a candidate. In democracy, periodical elections are conducted for having efficient governance for the country and for the benefit of citizens — voters. In a democratic form of government, voters are of utmost importance. They have right to elect or re-elect on the basis of the antecedents and past performance of the candidate. The voter has the choice of deciding whether holding of educational qualification or holding of property is relevant for electing or re-electing a person to be his representative. Voter has to decide whether he should cast vote in favour of a candidate who is involved in a criminal case. For maintaining purity of elections and a healthy democracy, voters are required to be educated and well informed about the contesting candidates. Such information would include assets held by the candidate, his qualification including educational qualification and antecedents of his life including whether he was involved in a criminal case and if the case is decided — its result, if pending — whether charge is framed or cognizance is taken by the court. There is no necessity of suppressing the relevant facts from the voters.

23. The Constitution Bench of this Court in *Mohinder Singh Gill v. Chief Election Commr.* [(1978) 1 SCC 405] while dealing with a contention that the Election Commission has no power to cancel the election and direct re-poll, referred to the pervasive philosophy of democratic elections which Sir Winston Churchill vivified in matchless words:

> " *'At the bottom of all tributes paid to democracy is the little man, walking into a little booth, with a little pencil, making a little cross on a little bit of paper — no amount of rhetoric or voluminous discussion can possibly diminish the overwhelming importance of the point.'*
>
> *If we may add, the little, large Indian shall not be hijacked from the course of free and fair elections by mob muscle methods, or subtle perversion of discretion by men 'dressed in little, brief authority'. For 'be you ever so high, the law is above you'.*

The moral may be stated with telling terseness in the words of William Pitt: 'Where laws end, tyranny begins.' Embracing both these mandates and emphasizing their combined effect is the elemental law and politics of power best expressed by Benjamin Disraeli (Vivian Grey, Bk VI Ch 7) :

> *'I repeat … that all power is a trust — that we are accountable for its exercise — that, from the people and for the people, all springs, and all must exist.'* "
>
> (emphasis supplied)

Further, the Court (in para 23) observed thus :

> *"23. Democracy is government by the people. It is a continual participative operation, not a cataclysmic, periodic exercise. The little man, in his multitude, marking his vote at the poll does a social audit of his Parliament plus political choice of this proxy. Although the full flower of participative government rarely blossoms, the minimum credential of popular government is appeal to the people after every term for a renewal of confidence. So we have adult franchise and general elections as constitutional compulsions. 'The right of election is the very essence of the Constitution' (Junius). It needs little argument to hold that the heart*

of the parliamentary system is free and fair elections periodically held, based on adult franchise, although social and economic democracy may demand much more."

(emphasis supplied)

Thereafter, the Court dealt with the scope of Article 324 and observed (in para 39) thus :

"Article 324, in our view, operates in areas left unoccupied by legislation and the words 'superintendence, direction and control', as well as 'conduct of all elections', are the broadest terms."

The Court further held:

"41. Our conclusion on this limb of the contention is that Article 324 is wide enough to supplement the powers under the Act, as here, but subject to the several conditions on its exercise we have set out."

The Court also held (in para 77) thus:

"77. We have been told that wherever Parliament has intended a hearing it has said so in the Act and the rules and inferentially where it has not specificated it is otiose. There is no such sequitur. The silence of a statute has no exclusionary effect except where it flows from necessary implication. Article 324 vests a wide power and where some direct consequence on candidates emanates from its exercise we must read this functional obligation."

(emphasis supplied)

In the concluding portion of paragraph 92, the Court *inter alia* observed thus :

"(1)(b) Election, in this context, has a very wide connotation commencing from the Presidential notification calling upon the electorate to elect and culminating in the final declaration of the returned candidate.

(2)(a) The Constitution contemplates a free and fair election and vests comprehensive responsibilities of superintendence, direction and control of the conduct of elections in the Election Commission. This responsibility may cover powers, duties and functions of many sorts, administrative or other, depending on the circumstances.

(b) Two limitations at least are laid on its plenary character in the exercise thereof. Firstly, when Parliament or any State Legislature has made valid law relating to or in connection with elections, the Commission, shall act in conformity with, not in violation of, such provisions but where such law is silent Article 324 is a reservoir of power to act for the avowed purpose of, not divorced from, pushing forward a free and fair election with expedition."

In concurring judgment, Goswami, J. with regard to Article 324 observed (in para 113) thus :

"Since the conduct of all elections to the various legislative bodies and to the offices of the President and the Vice-President is vested under Article 324(1) in the Election Commission, the framers of the Constitution took care to leaving scope for exercise of residuary power by the Commission, in its own right, as a creature of the Constitution, in the infinite variety of situations that may emerge from time to time in such a large democracy as ours. Every contingency could not be foreseen, or anticipated with precision. That is why there is no hedging in Article 324. The Commission may be required to cope with some situation which may not be provided for in the enacted laws and the rules."

(emphasis supplied)

24. The aforesaid decision of the Constitution Bench unreservedly lays down that in democracy the little man voter has overwhelming importance on the point and the little-large Indian (voter) should not be hijacked from the course of free and fair elections by subtle perversion of discretion of casting votes. In a continual participative operation of periodical election, the voter does a social audit of his candidate and for such audit he must be well informed about the past of his candidate. Further, Article 324 operates in areas left unoccupied by legislation and the words "superintendence, direction and control" as well as "conduct of all elections" are the broadest terms. The silence of statute has no exclusionary effect except where it flows from necessary implication. Therefore, in our view, it would be difficult to accept the contention raised by Mr. Salve, learned Solicitor-General and Mr. Ashwani Kumar, learned Senior Counsel appearing on behalf of the intervenor that if there is no provision in the Act or the Rules, the High Court ought not to have issued such directions to the Election Commission. It is settled that the power of the Commission is plenary in character in exercise thereof. In statutory provisions or rules, it is known that every contingency could not be foreseen or anticipated with precision, therefore, the Commission can cope with a situation where the field is unoccupied by issuing necessary orders.

25. Further, this Court in *Kanhiya Lal Omar v. R.K. Trivedi* [(1985) 4 SCC 628] dealt with the constitutional validity of the Election Symbols (Reservation and Allotment) Order, 1968 which was issued by the Election Commission in its plenary exercise of power under Article 324 of the Constitution read with Rules 5 and 10 of the Conduct of Elections Rules, 1961. The challenge was on the ground that the Symbols Order which is legislative in character could not be issued by the Commission because the Commission is not entrusted by law the power to issue such an Order regarding the specification, reservation and allotment of symbols that may be chosen by the candidates at elections in parliamentary and assembly constituencies. It was urged that Article 324 of the Constitution which vests the power of superintendence, direction and control of all elections to Parliament and to the legislature of a State in the Commission cannot be construed as conferring the power on the Commission to issue the symbols. The Court negatived the said contention and pertinently observed that :

"The word 'elections' in Article 324 is used in a wide sense so as to include the entire process of election which consists of several stages and

it embraces many steps, some of which may have an important bearing on the result of the process. India is a country which consists of millions of voters. Although they are quite conscious of their duties politically, unfortunately, a large percentage of them are still illiterate."

The Court in paragraph 16 held :

"16. Even if for any reason, it is held that any of the provisions contained in the Symbols Order are not traceable to the Act or the Rules, the power of the Commission under Article 324(1) of the Constitution which is plenary in character can encompass all such provisions. Article 324 of the Constitution operates in areas left unoccupied by legislation and the words 'superintendence', 'direction' and 'control' as well as 'conduct of all elections' are the broadest terms which would include the power to make all such provisions. (See Mohinder Singh Gill v. Chief Election Commr. [(1978) 1 SCC 405] and A.C. Jose v. Sivan Pillai [(1984) 2 SCC 656])."

The Court further observed :

"While construing the expression 'superintendence, direction and control' in Article 324(1), one has to remember that every norm which lays down a rule of conduct cannot possibly be elevated to the position of legislation or delegated legislation. There are some authorities or persons in certain grey areas who may be sources of rules of conduct and who at the same time cannot be equated to authorities or persons who can make law, in the strict sense in which it is understood in jurisprudence. A direction may mean an order issued to a particular individual or a precept which many may have to follow. It may be a specific or a general order. One has also to remember that the source of power in this case is the Constitution, the highest law of the land, which is the repository and source of all legal powers and any power granted by the Constitution for a specific purpose should be construed liberally so that the object for which the power is granted is effectively achieved. Viewed from this angle it cannot be said that any of the provisions of the Symbols Order suffers from want of authority on the part of the Commission, which has issued it."

26. Thereafter, this Court in *Common Cause (A Registered Society) v. Union of India* [(1996) 2 SCC 752] dealt with election expenses incurred by political parties and submission of return and the scope of Article 324 of the Constitution, where it was contended that cumulative effect of the three statutory provisions, namely, Section 293-A of the Companies Act, 1956, Section 13-A of the Income Tax Act, 1961 and Section 77 of the Representation of the People Act, 1951, is to bring transparency in the election funding and the people of India must know the source of expenditure incurred by the political parties and by the candidates in the process of election. It was contended that elections in the country are fought with the help of money power which is gathered from black sources and once elected to power, it becomes easy to collect tons of black money, which is used for retaining power and for re-election and that this vicious circle has totally polluted the basic democracy in the country. The Court held that purity of election is fundamental to democracy and the Commission can ask the candidates about the expenditure incurred by the candidates and by a political party for this purpose. The Court also held :

> *"The political parties in their quest for power spend more than one thousand crore of rupees on the General Election (Parliament alone), yet nobody accounts for the bulk of the money so spent and there is no accountability anywhere. Nobody discloses the source of the money. There are no proper accounts and no audit. From where does the money come nobody knows. In a democracy where rule of law prevails this type of naked display of black money, by violating the mandatory provisions of law, cannot be permitted."*

Thereafter, the Court observed that under Article 324, the Commission can issue suitable directions to maintain the purity of election and in particular to bring transparency in the process of election. The Court also held (paragraph 26) thus :

> *"26. Superintendence and control over the conduct of elections by the Election Commission include the scrutiny of all expenses incurred by a political party, a candidate or any other association or body of persons or by any individual in the course of the election. The expression 'Conduct of election' is wide enough to include in its sweep, the power to issue directions — in the process of the conduct of an election — to the effect that the political parties shall submit to the Election Commission, for its scrutiny, the details of the expenditure incurred or authorised by the parties in connection with the election of their respective candidates."*

27. The Court further observed that the Constitution has made comprehensive provision under Article 324 to take care of surprise situations and it operates in areas left unoccupied by legislation.

Question-2. Right to know about the candidates contesting elections

28. Now we would refer to various decisions of this Court dealing with citizens' right to know, which is derived from the concept of "freedom of speech and expression". The people of the country have a right to know every public act, everything that is done in a public way by the public functionaries. MPs or MLAs are undoubtedly public functionaries. Public education is essential for functioning of the process of popular government and to assist the discovery of truth and strengthening the capacity of an individual in participating in the decision-making process. The decision-making process of a voter would include his right to know about public functionaries who are required to be elected by him.

29. In *State of Uttar Pradesh v. Raj Narain & Ors.* [(1975) 4 SCC 428] the Constitution Bench considered a question — whether privilege can be claimed by the Government of Uttar Pradesh under Section 123 of the Evidence Act in respect of what has been described for the sake of brevity to be the Blue Book summoned from the Government of Uttar Pradesh and certain documents summoned from the Superintendent of Police, Rae Bareli, Uttar Pradesh? The Court observed that :

> *"The right to know, which is derived from the concept of freedom of speech, though not absolute, is a factor which should make one wary, when secrecy is claimed for transactions which can, at any rate, have no repercussion on public security."*

The Court pertinently observed as under :

> *"74. In a Government of responsibility like ours, where all the agents of the public must be responsible for their conduct, there can be but few secrets. The people of this country have a right to know every public act, everything that is done in a public way, by their public functionaries. They are entitled to know the particulars of every public transaction in all its bearing."*

30. In *Indian Express Newspapers (Bombay) (P) Ltd. v. Union of India* [(1985) 1 SCC 641] this Court dealt with the validity of customs duty on the newsprint in context of Article 19(1)(a). The Court observed (in para 32) thus :

> *"The purpose of the press is to advance the public interest by publishing facts and opinions without which a democratic electorate cannot make responsible judgments."*

31. The Court further referred (in para 35) the following observations made by this Court in *Romesh Thappar v. State of Madras* [1950 SCR 594] :

> *"(The freedom) lay at the foundation of all democratic organisations, for without free political discussion no public education, so essential for the proper functioning of the processes of popular government, is possible. A freedom of such amplitude might involve risks of abuse. But ... 'it is better to leave a few of its noxious branches to their luxuriant growth, than, by pruning them away, to injure the vigour of those yielding the proper fruits'."*

Again in paragraph 68, the Court observed :

> *" 'The public interest in freedom of discussion (of which the freedom of the press is one aspect) stems from the requirement that members of a democratic society should be sufficiently informed that they may influence intelligently the decisions which may affect themselves.' (Per Lord Simon of Glaisdale in Attorney-General v. Times Newspapers Ltd. [(1973) 3 All ER 54]). Freedom of expression, as learned writers have observed, has four broad social purposes to serve: (i) it helps an individual to attain self-fulfilment, (ii) it assists in the discovery of truth, (iii) it strengthens the capacity of an individual in participating in decision-making and (iv) it provides a mechanism by which it would be possible to establish a reasonable balance between stability and social change. All members of*

society should be able to form their own beliefs and communicate them freely to others. In sum, the fundamental principle involved here is the people's right to know. Freedom of speech and expression should, therefore, receive a generous support from all those who believe in the participation of people in the administration."

32. From the afore-quoted paragraph, it can be deduced that the members of a democratic society should be sufficiently informed so that they may influence intelligently the decisions which may affect themselves and this would include their decision of casting votes in favour of a particular candidate. If there is a disclosure by a candidate as sought for then it would strengthen the voters in taking appropriate decision of casting their votes.

33. In *Secy., Ministry of Information and Broadcasting, Govt. of India v. Cricket Association of Bengal* [(1995) 2 SCC 161] this Court considered the question of right to telecast sports event and after considering various decisions, the Court referred to Article 10 of the European Convention on Human Rights which inter alia states as follows (para 36) :

"10.1. Everyone has the right to freedom of expression. This right shall include freedom to hold opinions and to receive and impart information and ideas without interference by public authority and regardless of frontiers."

Thereafter, the Court summarised the law on the freedom of speech and expression under Article 19(1)(a) as restricted by Article 19(2) thus :

"The freedom of speech and expression includes right to acquire information and to disseminate it. Freedom of speech and expression is necessary, for self-fulfilment. It enables people to contribute to debates on social and moral issues. It is the best way to find a truest model of anything, since it is only through it that the widest possible range of ideas can circulate. It is the only vehicle of political discourse so essential to democracy. Equally important is the role it plays in facilitating artistic and scholarly endeavours of all sorts."

The Court dealt with the right of telecast and (in paragraph 75) held thus :

"In a team event such as cricket, football, hockey etc., there is both individual and collective expression. It may be true that what is protected by Article 19(1)(a) is an expression of thought and feeling and not of the physical or intellectual prowess or skill. It is also true that a person desiring to telecast sports events when he is not himself a participant in the game, does not seek to exercise his right of self-expression. However, the right to freedom of speech and expression also includes the right to educate, to inform and to entertain and also the right to be educated, informed and entertained. The former is the right of the telecaster and the latter that of the viewers. The right to telecast sporting event will therefore also include the right to educate and inform the present and the prospective sportsmen

interested in the particular game and also to inform and entertain the lovers of the game. Hence, when a telecaster desires to telecast a sporting event, it is incorrect to say that the free-speech element is absent from his right."

The Court thereafter (in paragraph 82) held :

"True democracy cannot exist unless all citizens have a right to participate in the affairs of the polity of the country. The right to participate in the affairs of the country is meaningless unless the citizens are well informed on all sides of the issues, in respect of which they are called upon to express their views. One-sided information, disinformation, misinformation and non-information all equally create an uninformed citizenry which makes democracy a farce when medium of information is monopolised either by a partisan central authority or by private individuals or oligarchic organisations. This is particularly so in a country like ours where about 65 per cent of the population is illiterate and hardly 1½ per cent of the population has an access to the print media which is not subject to pre-censorship."

The Court also observed :

"A successful democracy posits an 'aware' citizenry".

34. If right to telecast and right to view sport games and the right to impart such information is considered to be part and parcel of Article 19(1)(a), we fail to understand why the right of a citizen/voter — a little man — to know about the antecedents of his candidate cannot be held to be a fundamental right under Article 19(1)(a). In our view, democracy cannot survive without free and fair election, without free and fairly informed voters. Votes cast by uninformed voters in favour of *X* or *Y* candidate would be meaningless. As stated in the aforesaid passage, one-sided information, disinformation, misinformation and non-information, all equally create an uninformed citizenry which makes democracy a farce. Therefore, casting of a vote by a misinformed and non-informed voter or a voter having one-sided information only is bound to affect the democracy seriously. Freedom of speech and expression includes right to impart and receive information which includes freedom to hold opinions. Entertainment is implied in freedom of "speech and expression" and there is no reason to hold that freedom of speech and expression would not cover right to get material information with regard to a candidate who is contesting election for a post which is of utmost importance in the democracy.

35. In *Dinesh Trivedi, M.P. v. Union of India* [(1997) 4 SCC 306] the Court dealt with a petition for disclosure of a report submitted by a Committee established by the Union of India on 09.07.1993 which was chaired by the erstwhile Home Secretary Shri N.N. Vohra which subsequently came to be popularly known as the Vohra Committee. During July 1995, a known political activist Naina Sahni was murdered and one of the persons arrested happened to be an active politician who had held important political posts and a newspaper report published a series of articles on the criminalisation of politics within the country and the growing links between political leaders and mafia members. The attention of the masses was drawn towards the existence of the Vohra Committee Report. It was suspected that the contents of the report were such that the Union Government was reluctant to make it public.

36. In the said case, the Court dealt with citizens' right to freedom of information and observed :

> *"16. In modern constitutional democracies, it is axiomatic that citizens have a right to know about the affairs of the Government which, having been elected by them, seeks to formulate sound policies of governance aimed at their welfare."*

The Court also observed :

> *"Democracy … expects openness and openness is a concomitant of a free society. Sunlight is the best disinfectant."*

37. Mr. Ashwani Kumar, learned Senior Counsel appearing on behalf of the intervenor submitted that the aforesaid observations are with regard to citizens' right to know about the affairs of the Government, but this would not mean that citizens have a right to know the personal affairs of MPs or MLAs. In our view, this submission is totally misconceived. There is no question of knowing the personal affairs of MPs or MLAs. The limited information is — whether the person who is contesting election is involved in any criminal case and if involved, what is the result? Further, there are widespread allegations of corruption against the persons holding post and power. In such a situation, question is not of knowing personal affairs but to have openness in democracy for attempting to cure cancerous growth of corruption by few rays of light. Hence, citizens who elect MPs or MLAs are entitled to know that their representative has not misconducted himself in collecting wealth after being elected. This information could be easily gathered only if prior to election, the assets of such person are disclosed. For this purpose, learned counsel Mr. Muralidhar referred to the practice followed in the United States and the form which is required to be filled in by a candidate for the Senate, which provides that such candidate is required to disclose all his assets and that of his spouse and dependants. The form is required to be refilled every year. Penalties are also prescribed which include removal from ballot.

38. Learned counsel Mrs. Kamini Jaiswal referred to the All India Service (Conduct) Rules, 1968 and pointed out that a member of all-India service is required to disclose his/her assets including that of spouse and dependent children. She referred to Rule 16 of the said Rules, which provides for declaration of movable, immovable and valuable property by a person who becomes a member of the service. Relevant part of Rule 16 is as under :

> *"16. (1) Every person shall, where such person is a member of the service at the commencement of these Rules, before such date after such commencement as may be specified by the Government in this behalf, or, where such person becomes a member of the service after such commencement, on his first appointment to the service, submit a return of his assets and liabilities in such form as may be prescribed by the*

Government giving the full particulars regarding—

(a) the immovable property owned by him, or inherited or acquired by him or held by him on lease or mortgage, either in his own name or in the name of any member of his family or in the name of any other person;

(b) shares, debentures, postal cumulative time deposits and cash including bank deposits inherited by him or similarly owned, acquired or held by him;

(c) other movable property inherited by him or similarly owned, acquired or held by him; and

(d) debts and other liabilities incurred by him directly or indirectly."

39. Such officer is also required to submit an annual return giving full particulars regarding the immovable and movable property inherited by him or owned or acquired or held by him on lease or mortgage either in his own name or in the name of any member of his family or in the name of any other person.

40. It is also submitted that even the gazetted officers in all government services are required to disclose their assets and thereafter to furnish details of any acquisition of property annually. In our view, it is rightly submitted that in a democratic form of government, MP or MLA is having higher status and duty to the public. In *P.V. Narasimha Rao v. State (CBI/SPE)* [(1998) 4 SCC 626], the Court inter alia considered whether Member of Parliament is a public servant. The Court (in para 162) held thus :

> *"162. A public servant is 'any person who holds an office by virtue of which he is authorised or required to perform any public duty'. Not only, therefore, must the person hold an office but he must be authorised or required by virtue of that office to perform a public duty. Public duty is defined by Section 2(b) of the said Act to mean 'a duty in the discharge of which the State, the public or that community at large has an interest'. In a democratic form of government it is the Member of Parliament or a State Legislature who represents the people of his constituency in the highest law-making bodies at the Centre and the State respectively. Not only is he the representative of the people in the process of making the laws that will regulate their society, he is their representative in deciding how the funds of the Centre and the States shall be spent and in exercising control over the executive. It is difficult to conceive of a duty more public than this or of a duty in which the State, the public and the community at large would have greater interest."*

The aforesaid underlined portion highlights the important status of an MP or an MLA.

41. Finally, in our view this Court would have ample power to direct the Commission to fill the void, in the absence of suitable legislation covering the field and the voters are required to be well informed and educated about contesting candidates so that they can elect a proper candidate by their own assessment. It is the duty of the executive to fill the vacuum by executive orders because its field is coterminous with that of the legislature, and where there is inaction by the executive, for whatever reason, the judiciary must step in, in exercise of its constitutional obligations to provide a solution till such time the legislature acts to perform its role by enacting proper legislation to cover the field. The adverse impact of lack of probity in public life leading to a high degree of corruption is manifold. Therefore, if the candidate is directed to declare his/her spouse's and dependants' assets—immovable, movable and valuable articles—it would have its own effect. This Court in *Vishaka v. State of Rajasthan* [(1997) 6 SCC 241] dealt with the incident of sexual harassment of a woman at work place which resulted in violation of fundamental right of gender equality and the right to life and liberty and laid down that in the absence of legislation, it must be viewed along with the role of the judiciary envisaged in the Beijing Statement of Principles of Independence of Judiciary in the LAWASIA region. The decision has laid down the guidelines and prescribed the norms to be strictly observed in all work places until suitable legislation is enacted to occupy the field. In the present case also, there is no legislation or rules providing for giving necessary information to the voters. As stated earlier, this case was relied upon in *Vineet Narain case* [(1998) 1 SCC 226] where the Court has issued necessary guidelines to CBI and the Central Vigilance Commission (CVC) as there was no legislation covering the said field to ensure proper implementation of the rule of law.

42. To sum up the legal and constitutional position which emerges from the aforesaid discussion, it can be stated tha :

1. The jurisdiction of the Election Commission is wide enough to include all powers necessary for smooth conduct of elections and the word "elections" is used in a wide sense to include the entire process of election which consists of several stages and embraces many steps.

2. The limitation on plenary character of power is when Parliament or State Legislature has made a valid law relating to or in connection with elections, the Commission is required to act in conformity with the said provisions. In case where law is silent, Article 324 is a reservoir of power to act for the avowed purpose of having free and fair election. The Constitution has taken care of leaving scope for exercise of residuary power by the Commission in its own right as a creature of the Constitution in the infinite variety of situations that may emerge from time to time in a large democracy, as every contingency could not be foreseen or anticipated by the enacted laws or the rules. By issuing necessary directions, the Commission can fill the vacuum till there is legislation on the subject. In *Kanhiya Lal Omar case* [(1985) 4 SCC 628] the Court construed the expression "superintendence, direction and control" in Article 324(1) and held that a direction may mean an order issued to a particular individual or a precept which many may have

to follow and it may be a specific or a general order and such phrase should be construed liberally empowering the Election Commission to issue such orders.

3. The word "elections" includes the entire process of election which consists of several stages and it embraces many steps, some of which may have an important bearing on the process of choosing a candidate. Fair election contemplates disclosure by the candidate of his past including the assets held by him so as to give a proper choice to the candidate according to his thinking and opinion. As stated earlier, in *Common Cause case* [(1996) 2 SCC 752] the Court dealt with a contention that elections in the country are fought with the help of money power which is gathered from black sources and once elected to power, it becomes easy to collect tons of black money, which is used for retaining power and for re-election. If on an affidavit a candidate is required to disclose the assets held by him at the time of election, the voter can decide whether he could be re-elected even in case where he has collected tons of money.

   Presuming, as contended by the learned Senior Counsel Mr. Ashwani Kumar, that this condition may not be much effective for breaking a vicious circle which has polluted the basic democracy in the country as the amount would be unaccounted. Maybe true, still this would have its own effect as a step-in-aid and voters may not elect law-breakers as law-makers and some flowers of democracy may blossom.

4. To maintain the purity of elections and in particular to bring transparency in the process of election, the Commission can ask the candidates about the expenditure incurred by the political parties and this transparency in the process of election would include transparency of a candidate who seeks election or re-election. In a democracy, the electoral process has a strategic role. The little man of this country would have basic elementary right to know full particulars of a candidate who is to represent him in Parliament where laws to bind his liberty and property may be enacted.

5. The right to get information in democracy is recognised all throughout and it is a natural right flowing from the concept of democracy. At this stage, we would refer to Article 19(1) and (2) of the International Covenant on Civil and Political Rights, which is as under :

   "(1) Everyone shall have the right to hold opinions without interference.

   (2) Everyone shall have the right to freedom of expression; this right shall include freedom to seek, receive and impart

information and ideas of all kinds, regardless of frontiers, either orally, in writing or in print, in the form of art, or through any other media of his choice."

6. On cumulative reading of a plethora of decisions of this Court as referred to, it is clear that if the field meant for legislature and executive is left unoccupied detrimental to the public interest, this Court would have ample jurisdiction under Article 32 read with Articles 141 and 142 of the Constitution to issue necessary directions to the executive to subserve public interest.

7. Under our Constitution, Article 19(1)(a) provides for freedom of speech and expression. Voter's speech or expression in case of election would include casting of votes, that is to say, voter speaks out or expresses by casting vote. For this purpose, information about the candidate to be selected is a must. Voter's (little man — citizen's) right to know antecedents including criminal past of his candidate contesting election for MP or MLA is much more fundamental and basic for survival of democracy. The little man may think over before making his choice of electing law-breakers as law-makers.

43. In this view of the matter, it cannot be said that the directions issued by the High Court are unjustified or beyond its jurisdiction. However, considering the submissions made by the learned counsel for the parties at the time of hearing of this matter, the said directions are modified as stated below.

44. The Election Commission is directed to call for information on affidavit by issuing necessary order in exercise of its power under Article 324 of the Constitution of India from each candidate seeking election to Parliament or a State Legislature as a necessary part of his nomination paper, furnishing therein, information on the following aspects in relation to his/her candidature :

(1) Whether the candidate is convicted/acquitted/discharged of any criminal offence in the past — if any, whether he is punished with imprisonment or fine.

(2) Prior to six months of filing of nomination, whether the candidate is accused in any pending case, of any offence punishable with imprisonment for two years or more, and in which charge is framed or cognizance is taken by the court of law. If so, the details thereof.

(3) The assets (immovable, movable, bank balance, etc.) of a candidate and of his/her spouse and that of dependants.

(4) Liabilities, if any, particularly whether there are any overdues of any public financial institution or government dues.

(5) The educational qualifications of the candidate.

45. It is to be stated that the Election Commission has from time to time issued instructions/orders to meet with the situation where the field is unoccupied by the legislation. Hence, the norms and modalities to carry out and give effect to the aforesaid directions should be drawn up properly by the Election Commission as early as possible and in any case within two months.

46. In the result, Civil Appeal No. 7178 of 2001 is partly allowed and the directions issued by the High Court are modified as stated above. Appeal stands disposed of accordingly.

47. Writ Petition (C) No. 294 of 2001 is allowed to the aforesaid extent.

48. There shall be no order as to costs.

In the Supreme Court of India

Writ Petition (Civil) No. 490 of 2002
People's Union for Civil Liberties (PUCL) & Anr. v. Union of India & Anr.[3]

Writ Petition (Civil) No. 509 of 2002
Lok Satta & Ors. v. Union of India

Writ Petition (Civil) No. 515 of 2002
Association for Democratic Reforms v. Union of India & Anr.

Date of Judgement : 13.03.2003
Bench : M.B. Shah, P. Venkatarama Reddi and D.M. Dharamadhikari, JJ.

[This case was a sequel of the earlier PUCL case. All the political parties had unanimously opposed the judgment which led to promulgation of an Ordinance, which later became an Act. PUCL had challenged the Ordinance/ Act by filing a Writ Petition directly before the Supreme Court under Article 32 of the Constitution. The Court held that the earlier judgment (dated 02.05.2002) had attained finality and therefore could not be reopened. Section 33-B of the Representation of People Act was struck down as illegal, null and void. The judgment reaffirmed the voter's right to know the antecedents of candidates under Article 19(1)(a) of the Constitution. All three Hon'ble judges had given separate judgments.]

Judgment

M.B. Shah, J.

1. These writ petitions under Article 32 of the Constitution of India have been filed challenging the validity of the Representation of the People (Amendment) Ordinance, 2002 (4 of 2002) ("the Ordinance" for short) promulgated by the President of India on 24.08.2002.

2. There was an era when a powerful or a rich or a strong or a dacoit aged more than 60 years married a beautiful young girl despite her resistance. Except to weep, she had no choice of selecting her mate. To a large extent, such situation does not prevail today. Now, young

3. (2003) 4 SCC 399

persons are selecting mates of their choice after verifying full details thereof. Should we not have such a situation in selecting a candidate contesting elections? In a vibrant democracy — is it not required that a little voter should know the biodata of his/her would-be rulers, law-makers or destiny-makers of the nation?

3. Is there any necessity of keeping in the dark the voters that their candidate was involved in criminal cases of murder, dacoity or rape or has acquired the wealth by unjustified means? Maybe, that he is acquitted because the investigating officer failed to unearth the truth or because the witnesses turned hostile. In some cases, apprehending danger to their life, witnesses fail to reveal what was seen by them. Is there any necessity of permitting candidates or their supporters to use unaccounted money during elections? If assets are declared, would it not amount to having some control on unaccounted election expenditure?

4. It is equally true that right step in that direction is taken by amending the Representation of the People Act, 1951 (hereinafter referred to as "the Act") on the basis of judgment rendered by this Court in *Union of India v. Association for Democratic Reforms* [(2002) 5 SCC 294]. Still however, question to be decided is — whether it is in accordance with what has been declared in the said judgment.

5. After concluding hearing of the arguments on 23.10.2002, the matter was reserved for pronouncement of judgment. Before the judgment could be pronounced, the Ordinance was repealed and on 28.12.2002, the Representation of the People (Third Amendment) Act, 2002 ("the Amended Act" for short) was notified to come into force with retrospective effect. Thereafter, an amendment application was moved before us challenging the validity of Section 33-B of the Amendment Act which was granted because there is no change in the cause of action nor in the wording of Section 33-B of the Amended Act, validity of which is under challenge. At the request of learned counsel for the respondent Union of India, time to file additional counter was granted and the matter was further heard on 31.01.2003.

6. It is apparent that there is no change in the wording (even fullstop or comma) of Sections 33-A and 33-B of the Ordinance and Sections 33-A and 33-B of the Amended Act. The said sections read as under :

> *"33-A. Right to information.—(1) A candidate shall, apart from any information which he is required to furnish, under this Act or the rules made thereunder, in his nomination paper delivered under sub-section (1) of Section 33, also furnish the information as to whether—*
>
> > *(i) he is accused of any offence punishable with imprisonment for two years or more in a pending case in which a charge has been framed by the court of competent jurisdiction;*
> >
> > *(ii) he has been convicted of an offence other than any offence referred to in sub-section (1) or sub-section (2), or covered in sub-section (3), of Section 8 and sentenced to imprisonment for one year or more.*
>
> *(2) The candidate or his proposer, as the case may be, shall, at the time of*

delivering to the Returning Officer the nomination paper under sub-section (1) of Section 33, also deliver to him an affidavit sworn by the candidate in a prescribed form verifying the information specified in sub-section (1).

(3) The Returning Officer shall, as soon as may be after the furnishing of information to him under sub-section (1), display the aforesaid information by affixing a copy of the affidavit, delivered under sub-section (2), at a conspicuous place at his office for the information of the electors relating to a constituency for which the nomination paper is delivered.

33-B. Candidate to furnish information only under the Act and the rules.— Notwithstanding anything contained in any judgment, decree or order of any court or any direction, order or any other instruction issued by the Election Commission, no candidate shall be liable to disclose or furnish any such information, in respect of his election, which is not required to be disclosed or furnished under this Act or the rules made thereunder."

7. For the directions, which were issued in *Association for Democratic Reforms* [(2002) 5 SCC 294] it is contended that some of them are incorporated by the statutory provisions but with regard to the remaining directions it has been provided therein that no candidate shall be liable to disclose or furnish any such information in respect of his election which is not required to be disclosed or furnished under the Act or the rules made thereunder, despite the directions issued by this Court. Therefore, the aforesaid Section 33-B is under challenge.

8. At the outset, we would state that such exercise of power by the legislature giving similar directions was undertaken in the past and this Court in unequivocal words declared that the legislature in this country has no power to ask the instrumentalities of the State to disobey or disregard the decisions given by the courts. For this, we would quote some observations on the settled legal position having direct bearing on the question involved in these matters:

(A) Dealing with the validity of the Bombay Provincial Municipal Corporation (Gujarat Amendment and Validating Provisions) Ordinance, 1969, this Court in *Municipal Corporation of the City of Ahmedabad v. New Shrock Spg. and Wvg. Co. Ltd.* [(1970) 2 SCC 280] observed thus :

"7. This is a strange provision. Prima facie that provision appears to command the Corporation to refuse to refund the amount illegally collected despite the orders of this Court and the High Court. The State of Gujarat was not well advised in introducing this provision. That provision attempts to make a direct inroad into the judicial powers of the State. The Legislatures under our Constitution have within the prescribed limits, powers to make laws prospectively as well as retrospectively. By exercise of those powers, the Legislature can remove the basis of a decision rendered by a competent court thereby rendering that decision ineffective. But no Legislature in this country has power to ask the instrumentalities of the State to disobey or disregard the decisions given by courts."

(emphasis supplied)

Further, Khanna, J. in *Indira Nehru Gandhi v. Raj Narain* [1975 Supp SCC 1] succinctly and without any ambiguity observed thus :

> *"190. A declaration that an order made by a court of law is void is normally part of the judicial function and is not a legislative function. Although there is in the Constitution of India no rigid separation of powers, by and large the spheres of judicial function and legislative function have been demarcated and it is not permissible for the Legislature to encroach upon the judicial sphere. It has accordingly been held that a Legislature while it is entitled to change with retrospective effect the law which formed the basis of the judicial decision, it is not permissible to the Legislature to declare the judgment of the court to be void or not binding…."*

(emphasis supplied)

It is also settled law that the legislature may remove the defect which is the cause for invalidating the law by the Court by appropriate legislation if it has power over the subject-matter and competence to do so under the Constitution.

(B) Secondly, we would reiterate that the primary duty of the judiciary is to uphold the Constitution and the laws without fear or favour, without being biased by political ideology or economic theory. Interpretation should be in consonance with the constitutional provisions, which envisage a republic democracy. Survival of democracy depends upon free and fair election. It is true that the elections are fought by political parties, yet election would be a farce if the voters are unaware of the antecedents of candidates contesting elections. Their decision to vote either in favour of A or B candidate would be without any basis. Such election would be neither free nor fair.

For this purpose, we would refer to the observations made by Khanna, J. in *Kesavananda Bharati v. State of Kerala* [(1973) 4 SCC 225] which read thus :

> *"That all constitutional interpretations have political consequences should not obliterate the fact that the decision has to be arrived at in the calm and dispassionate atmosphere of the courtroom, that Judges in order to give legitimacy to their decision have to keep aloof from the din and controversy of politics and that the fluctuating fortunes of rival political parties can have for them only academic interest. Their primary duty is to uphold the Constitution and the laws without fear or favour and in doing so, they cannot allow any political ideology or economic theory, which may have caught their fancy, to colour the decision."*

(emphasis supplied)

(C) It is also equally settled law that the court should not shirk its duty of performing its function merely because it has political thicket.

Following observations (of Bhagwati, J., as he then was) made in *State of Rajasthan v. Union of India* [(1977) 3 SCC 592] (at SCC pages 660-661 para 149) were referred to and relied upon by this Court in *B.R. Kapur v. State of T.N.* [(2001) 7 SCC 231] :

"53. … 'But merely because the question has a political complexion, that by itself is no ground why the court should shrink from performing its duty under the Constitution if it raises an issue of constitutional determination. Every constitutional question concerns the allocation and exercise of governmental power and no constitutional question can, therefore, fail to be political. … So long as a question arises whether an authority under the Constitution has acted within the limits of its power or exceeded it, it can certainly be decided by the court. Indeed it would be its constitutional obligation to do so. It is necessary to assert in the clearest possible terms, particularly in the context of recent history, that the Constitution is suprema lex, the paramount law of the land, and there is no department or branch of Government above or beyond it.' "

(emphasis supplied)

Submissions

9. It is contended by learned Senior Counsel Mr. Rajindar Sachar and Mr. P.P. Rao for the petitioners that Section 33-B is, on the face of it, arbitrary and unjustifiable. It is their contention that the aforesaid section is on the face of it void as a law cannot be passed which violates/abridges the fundamental rights of the citizens/voters, declared and recognised by this Court. It is submitted that without exercise of the right to know the relevant antecedents of the candidate, it will not be possible to have free and fair elections. Therefore, the impugned section violates the very basic features of the Constitution, namely, republic democracy. For having free and fair elections, anywhere in the territory of this country, it is necessary to give effect to the voters' fundamental right as declared by this Court in the above judgment.

10. It has been contended that, in our country, at present about 700 legislators and twenty-five to thirty Members of Parliament are having criminal record. It is also contended that almost all political parties declare that persons having criminal record should not be given tickets, yet for one or the other reason, political parties under some compulsion give tickets to some persons having criminal records and some persons having no criminal records get support from criminals. It is contended by learned Senior Counsel Mr. Sachar that by issuing the Ordinance, the Government has arrogated to itself the power to decide unilaterally for nullifying the decision rendered by this Court without considering whether it can pass legislation which abridges fundamental right guaranteed under Article 19(1)(a). It is his submission that the Ordinance is issued and thereafter the Act is amended because it appears that the Government is interested in having uninformed ignorant voters.

11. Contra, learned Solicitor-General Mr. Kirit N. Raval and learned Senior Counsel Mr. Arun Jaitley appearing on behalf of the intervener, with vehemence, submitted that the aforesaid Ordinance/Amended Act is in consonance with the judgment rendered by this Court and the vacuum pointed out by the said judgment is filled in by the enactment. It is also contended by learned Senior Counsel Mr. Jaitley that voters' right to know the antecedents of the candidate is not part of the fundamental rights, but it is a derivative fundamental right on the basis of interpretation of Article 19(1)(a) given by this Court. It is submitted that the Ordinance/Amended Act is in public interest and, therefore, it cannot be held to be illegal or void. In support of their contentions, learned counsel for the parties have referred to various decisions rendered by this Court.

Whether Ordinance/Amended Act covers the directions issued by this Court :

12. Before dealing with the rival submissions, we would refer to the following directions given by this Court in *Association for Democratic Reforms case* [(2002) 5 SCC 294] :

> *"48. The Election Commission is directed to call for information on affidavit by issuing necessary order in exercise of its power under Article 324 of the Constitution of India from each candidate seeking election to Parliament or a State Legislature as a necessary part of his nomination paper, furnishing therein, information on the following aspects in relation to his/her candidature :*
>
> *(1) Whether the candidate is convicted/acquitted/discharged of any criminal offence in the past — if any, whether he is punished with imprisonment or fine.*
>
> *(2) Prior to six months of filing of nomination, whether the candidate is accused in any pending case, of any offence punishable with imprisonment for two years or more, and in which charge is framed or cognizance is taken by the court of law. If so, the details thereof.*
>
> *(3) The assets (immovable, movable, bank balance etc.) of a candidate and of his/her spouse and that of dependants.*
>
> *(4) Liabilities, if any, particularly whether there are any overdues of any public financial institution or government dues.*
>
> *(5) The educational qualifications of the candidate."*

13. The learned counsel for the respondent submitted that the directions issued by this Court are, to a large extent, implemented by the aforesaid Amended Act. It is true that some part of the directions issued by this Court are implemented. Comparative chart on the basis of judgment and Ordinance would make the position clear :

Subject	Discussion in judgment dated 2-5-2002	Provisions under the impugned Ordinance/Amended Act
Past criminal record	Para 48(1) All past convictions/acquittals/ discharges, whether punished with imprisonment or fine.	Section 33-A(1)(ii) Conviction of any offence (except Section 8 offence) and sentenced to imprisonment of one year or more.No such declaration in case of acquittals or discharge.(Section 8 offences to be disclosed in nomination paper itself)
Pending criminal cases	Para 48(2) Prior to six months of filing of nomination, whether the candidate has been accused of any criminal offence punishable with imprisonment of two years or more, and charge framed or cognizance taken.	Section 33-A(1)(i) Any case in which the candidate has been accused of any criminal offence punishable with imprisonment of two years or more, and charge framed.
Assets and liabilities	Para 48(3) Assets of candidate (contesting the elections), spouse and dependants. Para 48(4) Liabilities, particularly to Government and public financial institutions.	Section 75-A No such declaration by a candidate who is contesting election. After elected election, candidate is required to furnish information relating to him as well as his spouse and dependent children's assets to the Speaker of the House of the People. No provision is made for the candidate contesting election. However, after election, Sections 75-A(1)(ii) and (iii) provide for elected candidate.
Educational qualifications Breach of provisions	Para 48(5) To be declaredNo direction regarding consequences of non-compliance.	No provision. Section 125-A Creates an offence punishable by imprisonment for six months or fine for failure to furnish affidavit in accordance with Section 33-A, as well as for falsity or concealment in affidavit or nomination paper. Section 75-A(5)Wilful contravention of rules regarding asset disclosure may be treated as breach of privilege

of the House.

14. From the aforesaid chart, it is clear that a candidate is not required to disclose (a) the cases in which he is acquitted or discharged of criminal offence(s); (b) his assets and liabilities; and (c) his educational qualification. With regard to assets, it is sought to be contended that under the Act the candidate would be required to disclose the same to the Speaker after being elected. It is also contended that once the person is acquitted or discharged of any criminal offence, there is no necessity of disclosing the same to the voters.

Finality of the judgment

15. Firstly, it is to be made clear that the judgment rendered by this Court in *Association for Democratic Reforms* [(2002) 5 SCC 294] has attained finality. The voters' right to know the antecedents of the candidates is based on interpretation of Article 19(1)(a) which provides that all citizens of this country would have fundamental right to "freedom of speech and expression" and this phrase is construed to include fundamental right to know relevant antecedents of the candidate contesting the elections.

16. Further, even though we are not required to justify the directions issued in the aforesaid judgment, to make it abundantly clear that it is not ipse dixit and is based on sound foundation, it can be stated thus:

- Democratic republic is part of the basic structure of the Constitution.
- For this, free and fair periodical elections based on adult franchise are a must.
- For having unpolluted healthy democracy, citizens-voters should be well informed.

17. So, the foundation of a healthy democracy is to have well-informed citizens-voters. The reason to have right of information with regard to the antecedents of the candidate is that voter can judge and decide in whose favour he should cast his vote. It is the voter's discretion whether to vote in favour of an illiterate or literate candidate. It is his choice whether to elect a candidate against whom criminal cases for serious or non-serious charges were filed but is acquitted or discharged. He is to consider whether his candidate may or may not have sufficient assets so that he may not be tempted to indulge in unjustified means for accumulating wealth. For assets or liability, the voter may exercise his discretion in favour of a candidate whose liability is minimum and/or there are no overdues of public financial institution or government dues. From this information, it would be, to some extent, easy to verify whether unaccounted money is utilized for contesting election and whether a candidate is contesting election for getting rich or after being elected to what extent he became richer. Exposure to public scrutiny is one of the known means for getting clean and less polluted persons to govern the country. A little man — a citizen — a voter is the master of his vote. He must have necessary information so that he can intelligently decide in favour of a candidate who satisfies his criterion of being elected as an MP or MLA. On occasions, it is stated that we are not having such intelligent voters. This is no excuse. This would be belittling a little citizen/voter. He himself may be illiterate but still he would have the guts to decide in whose favour he should cast his vote. In any case, for having free and fair election and not to convert democracy into a mobocracy and mockery or a farce, information to voters is a necessity.

18. Further, in context of Section 8 of the Act, the Law Commission in its Report submitted in 1999 observed as under :

"5.1. The Law Commission had proposed that in respect of offences provided in sub-section (1) [except the offence mentioned in clause (b) of sub-section (1)], a mere framing of charge should serve as a disqualification. This provision was sought to be made in addition to existing provision which provides for disqualification arising on account of conviction. The reason for this proposal was that most of the offences mentioned in sub-section (1) are either election offences or serious offences affecting the society and that the persons committing these offences are mostly persons having political clout and influence. Very often these elements are supported by unsocial persons or group of persons, with the result that no independent witness is prepared to come forward to depose against such persons. In such a situation, it is proving extremely difficult to obtain conviction of these persons. It was suggested that inasmuch as charges were framed by a court on the basis of the material placed before it by the prosecution including the material disclosed by the charge-sheet, providing for disqualification on the ground of framing of the charge-sheet would be neither unjust nor unreasonable or arbitrary."

The Law Commission also observed :

"6.3.1. There has been mounting corruption in all walks of public life. People are generally lured to enter politics or contest elections for getting rich overnight. Before allowing people to enter public life the public has a right to know the antecedents of such persons. The existing conditions in which people can freely enter the political arena without demur, especially without the electorate knowing about any details of the assets possessed by the candidate are far from satisfactory. It is essential by law to provide that a candidate seeking election shall furnish the details of all his assets (movable/immovable) possessed by him/her, wife/husband, dependent relations, duly supported by an affidavit.

6.3.2. Further, in view of recommendations of the Law Commission for debarring a candidate from contesting an election if charges have been framed against him by a court in respect of offences mentioned in the proposed Section 8-B of the Act, it is also necessary for a candidate seeking to contest election to furnish details regarding criminal case, if any, pending against him, including a copy of the FIR/complaint and any order made by the court concerned.

6.3.3. In order to achieve the aforesaid objectives, it is essential to insert a new Section 4-A after the existing Section 4 of the Representation of the People Act, 1951, as follows :

'4-A. Qualification for membership of the House of the People, the Council of States, Legislature Assembly of a State or Legislative Council.—A person shall not be qualified to file his nomination for contesting any election for a seat in the House of the People, the Council of States, Legislature Assembly or Legislative Council of a State unless he or she files—

(a) a declaration of all his assets (movable/immovable) possessed by him/her, his/her spouse and dependent relations, duly supported by an affidavit, and

(b) a declaration as to whether any charge in respect of any offence referred to in Section 8-B has been framed against him by any criminal court.' "

19. It is to be stated that similar views are expressed in the Report submitted in March 2002 by the National Commission to Review the Working of the Constitution appointed by the Union Government for reviewing the working of the Constitution. Relevant recommendations are as under:

"Successes and failures

4.4. During the last half-a-century, there have been thirteen general elections to the Lok Sabha and a much large number to various State Legislative Assemblies. We can take legitimate pride in that these have been successful and generally acknowledged to be free and fair. But, the experience has also brought to the fore many distortions, some very serious, generating a deep concern in many quarters. There are constant references to the unhealthy role of money power, muscle power and mafia power and to criminalisation, corruption, communalism and casteism.

4.12. Criminalisation

4.12.2. The Commission recommends that the Representation of the People Act be amended to provide that any person charged with any offence punishable with imprisonment for a maximum term of five years or more, should be disqualified for being chosen as, or for being, a Member of Parliament or Legislature of a State on the expiry of a period of one year from the date the charges were framed against him by the court in that offence and unless cleared during that one year period, he shall continue to remain so disqualified till the conclusion of the trial for that offence. In case a person is convicted of any offence by a court of law and sentenced to imprisonment for six months or more the bar should apply during the period under which the convicted person is undergoing the sentence and for a further period of six years after the completion of the period of the sentence. If any candidate violates this provision, he should be disqualified.

Also, if a party puts up such a candidate with knowledge of his antecedents, it should be derecognised and deregistered.

4.12.3. Any person convicted for any heinous crime like murder, rape, smuggling, dacoity etc. should be permanently debarred from contesting for any political office.

4.12.8. The Commission feels that the proposed provision laying down that a person charged with an offence punishable with imprisonment which may extend to five years or more should be disqualified from contesting elections after the expiry of a period of one year from the date the charges were framed in a court of law should equally be applicable to sitting Members of Parliament and State Legislatures as to any other such person.

4.14. High cost of elections and abuse of money power

4.14.1. One of the most critical problems in the matter of electoral reforms is the hard reality that for contesting an election one needs large amounts of money. The limits of expenditure prescribed are meaningless and almost never adhered to. As a result, it becomes difficult for the good and the honest to enter legislatures. It also creates a high degree of compulsion for corruption in the political arena. This has progressively polluted the entire system. Corruption, because it erodes performance, becomes one of the leading reasons for non-performance and compromised governance in the country. The sources of some of the election funds are believed to be unaccounted criminal money in return for protection, unaccounted funds from business groups who expect a high return on this investment, kickbacks or commissions on contracts etc. No matter how we look at it, citizens are directly affected because apart from compromised governance, the huge money spent on elections pushes up the cost of everything in the country. It also leads to unbridled corruption and the consequences of widespread corruption are even more serious than many imagine. Electoral compulsions for funds become the foundation of the whole superstructure of corruption.

4.14.3. Transparency in the context of election means both the sources of finance as well as their utilization as are listed out in an audited statement. If the candidates are required to list the sources of their income, this can be checked back by the Income Tax Authorities. The Commission recommends that the political parties as well as individual candidates be made subject to a proper statutory audit of the amounts they spend. These accounts should be monitored through a system of checking and cross-checking through the income tax returns filed by the candidates, parties and their well-wishers. At the end of the election each candidate should submit an audited statement of expenses under specific heads. EC should devise specific formats for filing such statements so that fudging of accounts becomes difficult. Also, the audit should not only be mandatory but it should be enforced by the Election Commission.

Any violation or misreporting should be dealt with strongly.

4.14.4. The Commission recommends that every candidate at the time of election must declare his assets and liabilities along with those of his close relatives. Every holder of a political position must declare his assets and liabilities along with those of his close relations annually. Law should define the term 'close relatives'.

4.14.6. All candidates should be required under law to declare their assets and liabilities by an affidavit and the details so given by them should be made public. Further, as a follow-up action, the particulars of the assets and liabilities so given should be audited by a special authority created specifically under law for the purpose. Again, the legislators should be required under law to submit their returns about their liabilities every year and a final statement in this regard at the end of their term of office.

Candidates owing government dues

4.23. It is recommended that all candidates should be required to clear government dues before their candidatures are accepted. This pertains to payment of taxes and bills and unauthorised occupation of accommodation and availing of telephones and other government facilities to which they are no longer entitled. The fact that matters regarding government dues in respect of the candidate are pending before a court of law should be no excuse."

20. *Mr. P.P. Rao, learned Senior Counsel has drawn our attention to the "Ethics Manual for Members, Officers and Employees of the U.S. House of Representatives", which inter alia provides as under:*

"Financial interests and investments of Members and employees, as well as those of candidates for the House of Representatives, may present conflicts of interest with official duties. Members and employees need not, however, divest themselves of assets upon assuming their positions, nor must Members disqualify themselves from voting on issues that generally affect their personal financial interests. Instead, public financial disclosure provides a means of monitoring and deterring conflicts.

All Members, officers, and employees are prohibited from improperly using their official positions for personal gain. Members, officers, candidates, and certain employees must file annual financial disclosure statements, summarizing financial information concerning themselves, their spouses, and dependent children. Such statements must indicate outside compensation, holdings and business transactions, generally for the calendar year preceding the filing date.

Who must file

The following individuals must file financial disclosure statements:

— Members of the House of Representatives;

— candidates for the House of Representatives;

When to file

Candidates who raise or spend more than $ 5000 for their campaigns must file within 30 days of doing so, or by May 15, whichever is later, but in any event at least 30 days prior to the elections in which they run.

Termination reports must be filed within 30 days of leaving government employment by Members, officers, and employees who file financial disclosure statements.

Policies Underlying Disclosure

Members, officers, and certain employees must annually disclose personal financial interests, including investments, income, and liabilities. Financial disclosure provisions were enacted to monitor and to deter possible conflicts of interest due to outside financial holdings. Proposals for divestiture of potentially conflicting assets and mandatory disqualification of Members from voting rejected as impractical or unreasonable. Such disqualification could result in the disenfranchisement of a Member's entire constituency on particular issues. A Member may often have a community of interests with his constituency, may arguably have been elected because of and to serve these common interests, and thus would be ineffective in representing the real interests of his constituents if he were disqualified from voting on issues touching those matters of mutual concern. In rare instances, the House rule on abstaining from voting may apply where a direct personal interest in a matter exists.

At the other extreme, a conflict of interest becomes corruption when an official uses his position of influence to enhance his personal financial interests. Between these extremes are those ambiguous circumstances which may create a real or potential conflict of interest. The problem is identifying those instances in which an official allows his personal economic interests to impair his independence of judgment in the conduct of his public duties.

The House has required public financial disclosure by rule since 1968 and by statute since 1978.

Specific Disclosure Requirements

The Ethics in Government Act of 1978 mandated annual financial disclosure by all senior Federal personnel, including all Members and some employees of the House. The Ethics Reform Act of 1989 totally revamped these provisions and condensed what had been different requirements for each branch into one uniform title covering the entire Federal Government. Financial disclosure statements must indicate outside compensation, holdings, and business transactions, generally for the calendar year preceding the filing date. In all instances, filers may disclose additional information or explanation at their discretion."

21. At this stage, it would be worthwhile to note some observations made by the Committee on State Funding of Elections headed by Shri Indrajit Gupta as Chairman and others, which submitted its Report in 1998. In the concluding portion, it has mentioned as under:

"Conclusion

1. Before concluding, the Committee cannot help expressing its considered view that its recommendations being limited in nature and confined to only one of the aspects of the electoral reforms may bring about only some cosmetic changes in the electoral sphere. What is needed, however, is an immediate overhauling of the electoral process whereby elections are freed from evil influence of all vitiating factors, particularly, criminalisation of politics. It goes without saying that money power and muscle power go together to vitiate the electoral process and it is their combined effect which is sullying the purity of electoral contests and affecting free and fair elections. Meaningful electoral reforms in other spheres of electoral activity are also urgently needed if the present recommendations of the Committee are to serve the intended useful purpose."

22. From the aforesaid Reports of the Law Commission, National Commission to Review the Working of the Constitution, conclusion drawn in the Report of Shri Indrajit Gupta and the Ethics Manual applicable in an advance democratic country, it is apparent that for saving the democracy from the evil influence of criminalisation of politics, for saving the election from muscle and money power, for having true democracy and for controlling corruption in politics, the candidate contesting the election should be asked to disclose his antecedents including assets and liabilities. Thereafter, it is for the voters to decide in whose favour he should cast his vote.

23. Further, we would state that this Court has construed "freedom of speech and expression" in various decisions and on the basis of tests laid therein, directions were issued. In short, this aspect is discussed in paras 31, 32 and 33 of our earlier judgment which read as under:

"31. In State of U.P. v. Raj Narain [(1975) 4 SCC 428] the Constitution Bench considered a question — whether privilege can be claimed by the Government of Uttar Pradesh under Section 123 of the Evidence Act in respect of what has been described for the sake of brevity to be the Blue Book summoned from the Government of Uttar Pradesh and certain documents summoned from the Superintendent of Police, Rae Bareli, Uttar Pradesh? The Court observed that :

> *'The right to know, which is derived from the concept of freedom of speech, though not absolute, is a factor which should make one wary, when secrecy is claimed for transactions which can, at any rate, have no repercussion on public security.'*

The Court pertinently observed as under :

> *'74. In a Government of responsibility like ours, where all the agents of the public must be responsible for their conduct, there can be but few secrets. The people of this country have a right to know every public act, everything that is done in a public way, by their public functionaries. They are entitled to know the particulars of every public transaction in all its bearing.'*

32. In Indian Express Newspapers (Bombay) (P) Ltd. v. Union of India [(1985) 1 SCC 641] this Court dealt with the validity of customs duty on the newsprint in context of Article 19(1)(a). The Court observed (in para 32) thus :

> *'The purpose of the press is to advance the public interest by publishing facts and opinions without which a democratic electorate cannot make responsible judgments.'*

33. The Court further referred the following observations made by this Court in Romesh Thappar v. State of Madras [1950 SCR 594] :

> *'(The freedom) lay at the foundation of all democratic organisations, for without free political discussion no public education, so essential for the proper functioning of the processes of popular government, is possible. A freedom of such amplitude might involve risks of abuse. But … "it is better to leave a few of its noxious branches to their luxuriant growth, than, by pruning them away, to injure the vigour of those yielding the proper fruits".'*

Again in SCC pages 685-686 para 68, the Court observed :

'"The public interest in freedom of discussion (of which the freedom of the press is one aspect) stems from the requirement that members of a democratic society should be sufficiently informed that they may influence intelligently the decisions which may affect themselves." (Per Lord Simon of Glaisdale in Attorney General v. Times Newspapers Ltd. [(1973) 3 All ER 54] Freedom of expression, as learned writers have observed, has four broad social purposes to serve: (i) it helps an individual to attain self-fulfilment, (ii) it assists in the discovery of truth, (iii) it strengthens the capacity of an individual in participating in decision-making and (iv) it provides a mechanism by which it would be possible to establish a reasonable balance between stability and social change. All members of society should be able to form their own beliefs and communicate them freely to others. In sum, the fundamental principle involved here is the people's right to know. Freedom of speech and expression should, therefore, receive a generous support from all those who believe in the participation of people in the administration.' "

(emphasis supplied)

24. Even with regard to telecasting of events such as cricket, football and hockey etc. this Court in *Secretary, Ministry of Information and Broadcasting, Govt. of India* v. *Cricket Association of Bengal* [(1995) 2 SCC 161] held (at SCC page 224 para 75) that "the right to freedom of speech and expression also includes the right to educate, to inform and to entertain and also the right to be educated, informed and entertained". The Court further held as under:

"82. ... True democracy cannot exist unless all citizens have a right to participate in the affairs of the polity of the country. The right to participate in the affairs of the country is meaningless unless the citizens are well informed on all sides of the issues, in respect of which they are called upon to express their views. One-sided information, disinformation, misinformation and non-information all equally create an uninformed citizenry which makes democracy a farce when medium of information is monopolised either by a partisan central authority or by private individuals or oligarchic organisations. This is particularly so in a country like ours where about 65 per cent of the population is illiterate and hardly 1 ½ per cent of the population has an access to the print media which is not subject to pre-censorship."

(emphasis supplied)

25. The aforesaid passage leaves no doubt that right to participate by casting vote at the time of election would be meaningless unless the voters are well informed about all sides of the issues, in respect of which they are called upon to express their views by casting their votes. Disinformation, misinformation, non-information, all equally create an uninformed citizenry which would finally make democracy a mobocracy and farce. On this aspect, no further discussion is required. However, we would narrate some observations made by Bhagwati, J. (as he then was) in *S.P. Gupta v. Union of India* [1981 Supp SCC 87] while dealing with the contention of right to secrecy that: (SCC page 274 para 66) "There can be little doubt that exposure to public gaze and scrutiny is one of the surest means of achieving a clean and healthy administration." (Emphasis supplied)

Further, it has been explicitly and lucidly held thus :

> *"64. Now it is obvious from the Constitution that we have adopted a democratic form of government. Where a society has chosen to accept democracy as its credal faith, it is elementary that the citizens ought to know what their Government is doing. The citizens have a right to decide by whom and by what rules they shall be governed and they are entitled to call on those who govern on their behalf to account for their conduct. No democratic Government can survive without accountability and the basic postulate of accountability is that the people should have information about the functioning of the Government. It is only if people know how Government is functioning that they can fulfil the role which democracy assigns to them and make democracy a really effective participatory democracy. 'Knowledge' said James Madison, 'will forever govern ignorance and a people who mean to be their own governors must arm themselves with the power knowledge gives. A popular Government without popular information or the means of obtaining it, is but a prolague to a farce or tragedy or perhaps both'. The citizens' right to know the facts, the true facts, about the administration of the country is thus one of the pillars of a democratic State. And that is why the demand for openness in the Government is increasingly growing in different parts of the world.*
>
> *65. The demand for openness in the Government is based principally on two reasons. It is now widely accepted that democracy does not consist merely in people exercising their franchise once in five years to choose their rules and, once the vote is cast, then retiring in passivity and not taking any interest in the Government. Today it is common ground that democracy has a more positive content and its orchestration has to be continuous and pervasive. This means inter alia that people should not only cast intelligent and rational votes but should also exercise sound judgment on the conduct of the Government and the merits of public policies, so that democracy does not remain merely a sporadic exercise in voting but becomes a continuous process of Government — an attitude and habit of mind. But this important role people can fulfil in a democracy only if it is an open Government where there is full access to information in regard to the functioning of the Government."*
>
> (emphasis supplied)

It was further observed :

"67. … *The concept of an open Government is the direct emanation from the right to know which seems to be implicit in the right of free speech and expression guaranteed under Article 19(1)(a).* … *The approach of the court must be to attenuate the area of secrecy as much as possible consistently with the requirement of public interest, bearing in mind all the time that disclosure also serves an important aspect of public interest. It is in the context of this background that we must proceed to interpret Section 123 of the Indian Evidence Act.*"

26. From the aforesaid discussion it can be held that it is expected by all concerned and as has been laid down by various decisions of this Court that for survival of true democracy, the voter must be aware of the antecedents of his candidate. Voter has to cast intelligent and rational vote according to his own criteria. A well-informed voter is the foundation of democratic structure. That information to a voter, who is the citizen of this country, is one facet of the fundamental right under Article 19(1)(a).

Article 145(3) of the Constitution of India

27. Mr. Arun Jaitley, learned Senior Counsel and Mr. Kirit N. Raval, learned Solicitor-General submitted that the question involved in these petitions is a substantial question of law as to the interpretation of the Constitution and, therefore, the matter may be referred to a Bench consisting of five Judges.

28. In our view, this contention is totally misconceived. Article 19(1)(a) is interpreted in numerous judgments rendered by this Court. After considering various decisions and following tests laid therein, this Court in *Association for Democratic* [(2002) 5 SCC 294] arrived at the conclusion that for survival of the democracy, right of the voter to know antecedents of a candidate would be part and parcel of his fundamental right. It would be the basis for free and fair election which is a basic structure of the Constitution. Therefore, the question relating to interpretation of Article 19(1)(a) is concluded and there is no other question which requires interpretation of the Constitution. Dealing with a similar contention, a five-Judge Bench of this Court in *State of J&K v. Thakur Ganga Singh* [AIR 1960 SC 356] succinctly held thus :

"7. *What does interpretation of a provision mean? Interpretation is the method by which the true sense or the meaning of the word is understood. The question of interpretation can arise only if two or more possible constructions are sought to be placed on a provision — one party suggesting one construction and the other a different one. But where the parties agree on the true interpretation of a provision or do not raise any question in respect thereof, it is not possible to hold that the case involves any question of law as to the interpretation of the Constitution. On an interpretation of Article 14, a series of decisions of this Court evolved the doctrine of classification. As we have pointed out, at no stage of the proceedings either the correctness of the interpretation of Article 14 or the principles governing the doctrine of classification have been questioned by either of the parties. Indeed accepting the said doctrine, the appellants contended that there was a valid classification under the rule while the respondents argued contra. The learned Additional Solicitor-General contended, for the first time, before us that the appeal raised a new facet of the doctrine of equality, namely, whether an artificial person and a natural person have equal attributes within the meaning of the equality clause, and, therefore, the case involves a question of interpretation of the Constitution. This argument, if we may say so, involves the same contention in a different garb. If analysed, the argument only comes to this: as an artificial person and a natural person have different attributes, the classification made between them is valid. This argument does not suggest a new interpretation of Article 14 of the Constitution, but only attempts to bring the rule within the doctrine of classification. We, therefore, hold that the question raised in this case does not involve any question of law as to the interpretation of the Constitution."*

(emphasis supplied)

29. The aforesaid judgment is referred to and relied upon in *Sardar Sardul Singh Caveeshar v. State of Maharashtra* [AIR 1965 SC 682].

30. From the judgment rendered by this Court in *Association for Democratic Reforms* [(2002) 5 SCC 294] it is apparent that no such contention was raised by the learned Solicitor-General, who appeared in appeal filed on behalf of the Union of India that question involved in that matter was required to be decided by a five-Judge Bench, as provided under Article 145(3) of the Constitution. The question raised before us has been finally decided and no other substantial question of law regarding the interpretation of the Constitution survives. Hence, the matter is not required to be referred to a five-Judge Bench.

Whether impugned Section 33-B can be considered as validating provision

31. The learned counsel for the respondent submitted that by the impugned legislation, most of the directions issued by the Court are complied with and vacuum pointed out is filled in by the legislation. It is their contention that the legislature did not think it fit that the remaining information as directed by this Court is required to be given by a contesting candidate.

32. This submission is, on the face of it, against well-settled legal position. In a number of decisions rendered by this Court, similar submission is negatived. The legislature has no power to review the decision and set it at naught except by removing the defect which is the cause pointed out by the decision rendered by the Court. If this is permitted it would sound the death knell of the rule of law as observed by this Court in various decisions. In *P. Sambamurthy v. State of A.P.* [(1987) 1 SCC 362] this Court observed :

"4. ... It is a basic principle of the rule of law that the exercise of power by the executive or any other authority must not only be conditioned by the Constitution but must also be in accordance with law and the power of

judicial review is conferred by the Constitution with a view to ensuring that the law is observed and there is compliance with the requirement of law on the part of the executive and other authorities. It is through the power of judicial review conferred on an independent institutional authority such as the High Court that the rule of law is maintained and every organ of the State is kept within the limits of the law. Now if the exercise of the power of judicial review can be set at naught by the State Government by overriding the decision given against it, it would sound the death knell of the rule of law. The rule of law would cease to have any meaning, because then it would be open to the State Government to defy the law and yet to get away with it. The proviso to clause (5) of Article 371-D is therefore clearly violative of the basic structure doctrine."

(emphasis supplied)

33. In *Cauvery Water Disputes Tribunal, In re* [1993 Supp (1) SCC 96 (II)] the Court referred to and relied upon the decision in *P. Sambamurthy* [(1995) 2 SCC 161]. In that case, the Court dealt with the validity of the Karnataka Cauvery Basin Irrigation Protection Ordinance, 1991 issued by the Government of Karnataka giving overriding effect that notwithstanding anything contained in any order, report or decision of any court or tribunal except the final decision under the provisions of sub-section (2) of Section 5 read with Section 6 of the Inter-State Water Disputes Act, 1956 shall have any effect and held that the Ordinance in question which seeks directly to nullify the order of the Tribunal impinges on the judicial power of the State and is, therefore, ultra vires. After referring to the earlier decisions, the Court observed thus :

"74. ... it would be unfair to adopt legislative procedure to undo a settlement which had become the basis of a decision of the High Court. Even if legislation can remove the basis of a decision, it has to do it by alteration of general rights of a class but not by simply excluding the specific settlement which had been held to be valid and enforceable by a High Court. The object of the Act was in effect to take away the force of the judgment of the High Court. The rights under the judgment would be said to arise independently of Article 19 of the Constitution.

***

76. The principle which emerges from these authorities is that the legislature can change the basis on which a decision is given by the Court and thus change the law in general, which will affect a class of persons and events at large. It cannot, however, set aside an individual decision inter partes and affect their rights and liabilities alone. Such an act on the part of the legislature amounts to exercising the judicial power of the State and to functioning as an appellate court or tribunal."

(emphasis supplied)

34. Further, in *Municipal Corporation of the City of Ahmedabad v. New Shrock Spg. and*

Wvg. Co. Ltd. [(1970) 2 SCC 280] this Court (in SCC pages 285-286 para 7) held thus :

> *"But no Legislature in this country has power to ask the instrumentalities of the State to disobey or disregard the decisions given by courts. The limits of the power of Legislatures to interfere with the directions issued by courts were considered by several decisions of this Court. In Shri Prithvi Cotton Mills Ltd. v. Broach Borough Municipality [(1969) 2 SCC 283] our present Chief Justice speaking for the Constitution Bench of the Court observed :*
>
> > *'Before we examine Section 3 to find out whether it is effective in its purpose or not we may say a few words about validating statutes in general. When a Legislature sets out to validate a tax declared by a court to be illegally collected under an ineffective or an invalid law, the cause for ineffectiveness or invalidity must be removed before validation can be said to take place effectively. The most important condition of course, is that the Legislature must possess the power to impose the tax, for, if it does not, the action must ever remain ineffective and illegal. Granted legislative competence, it is not sufficient to declare merely that the decision of the court shall not bind for that is tantamount to reversing the decision in exercise of judicial power which the Legislature does not possess or exercise. A court's decision must always bind unless the conditions on which it is based are so fundamentally altered that the decision could not have been given in the altered circumstances. Ordinarily, a court holds a tax to be invalidly imposed because the power to tax is wanting or the statute or the rules or both are invalid or do not sufficiently create the jurisdiction. Validation of a tax so declared illegal may be done only if the grounds of illegality or invalidity are capable of being removed and are in fact removed and the tax thus made legal. Sometimes this is done by providing for jurisdiction where jurisdiction had not been properly invested before. Sometimes this is done by re-enacting retrospectively a valid and legal taxing provision and then by fiction making the tax already collected to stand under the re-enacted law.'*
> >
> > (emphasis supplied)

In Mahal Chand Sethia v. State of West Bengal [1969 UJ (SC) 616] Mitter, J., speaking for the Court stated the legal position in these words :

> *"The argument of counsel for the appellant was that although it was open to the State Legislature by an Act and the Governor by an ordinance to amend the West Bengal Criminal Law Amendment (Special Courts) Act, 1949, it was incompetent for either of them to validate an order of transfer*

which had already been quashed by the issue of a writ of certiorari by the High Court and the order of transfer being virtually dead, could not be resuscitated by the Governor or the Legislature and the validating measures could not touch any adjudication by the Court.

... A court of law can pronounce upon the validity of any law and declare the same to be null and void if it was beyond the legislative competence of the Legislature or if it infringed the rights enshrined in Part III of the Constitution. Needless to add it can strike down or declare invalid any Act or direction of a State Government which is not authorised by law. The position of a Legislature is however different. It cannot declare any decision of a court of law to be void or of no effect.' "

(Emphasis supplied)

35. For the purpose of deciding these petitions, the principles emerging from various decisions rendered by this Court from time to time can inter alia be summarised thus :

> The Legislature can change the basis on which a decision is rendered by this Court and change the law in general. However, this power can be exercised subject to constitutional provision, particularly, legislative competence and if it is violative of fundamental rights enshrined in Part III of the Constitution, such law would be void as provided under Article 13 of the Constitution. The legislature also cannot declare any decision of a court of law to be void or of no effect.

36. As stated above, this Court has held that Article 19(1)(a) which provides for freedom of speech and expression would cover in its fold right of the voter to know specified antecedents of a candidate, who is contesting election. Once it is held that a voter has a fundamental right to know the antecedents of his candidate, that fundamental right under Article 19(1)(a) could be abridged by passing such legislation only as provided under Article 19(2) which provides as under :

*"19. Protection of certain rights regarding freedom of speech, etc.—(1) ****

(2) Nothing in sub-clause (a) of clause (1) shall affect the operation of any existing law, or prevent the State from making any law, insofar as such law imposes reasonable restrictions on the exercise of the right conferred by the said sub-clause in the interests of the sovereignty and integrity of India, the security of the State, friendly relations with foreign States, public order, decency or morality or in relation to contempt of court, defamation or incitement to an offence."

37. So legislative competence to interfere with a fundamental right enshrined in Article 19(1)(a) is limited as provided under Article 19(2).

38. Learned counsel for the respondents have not pointed out how the impugned legislation could be justified or saved under Article 19(2).

Derivative fundamental right

39. Learned Senior Counsel Mr. Jaitley developed an ingenious submission that as there is no specific fundamental right of the voter to know the antecedents of a candidate, the declaration by this Court of such fundamental right can be held to be derivative, therefore, it is open to the legislature to nullify it by appropriate legislation.

40. In our view, this submission requires to be rejected as there is no such concept of derivative fundamental rights. Firstly, it should be properly understood that the fundamental rights enshrined in the Constitution such as, right to equality and freedoms have no fixed contents. From time to time, this Court has filled in the skeleton with soul and blood and made it vibrant. Since the last more than 50 years, this Court has interpreted Articles 14, 19 and 21 and given meaning and colour so that the nation can have a truly republic democratic society. This cannot be undone by such an Ordinance/Amended Act. For this, we would refer to the discussion by Mohan, J. in *Unni Krishnan, J.P. v. State of A.P.* [(1993) 1 SCC 645] while considering the ambit of Article 21, he succinctly placed it thus :

> *"25. In Kesavananda Bharati v. State of Kerala [(2002) 5 SCC 294] Mathew, J. stated therein that the fundamental rights themselves have no fixed content, most of them are empty vessels into which each generation must pour its content in the light of its experience. It is relevant in this context to remember that in building up a just social order it is sometimes imperative that the fundamental rights should be subordinated to directive principles.*
>
> *26. In Pathumma v. State of Kerala [(1978) 2 SCC 1] it has been stated :*
>
> > *'The attempt of the court should be to expand the reach and ambit of the fundamental rights rather than accentuate their meaning and content by process of judicial construction.... Personal liberty in Article 21 is of the widest amplitude.'*
>
> *27. In this connection, it is worthwhile to recall what was said of the American Constitution in Missouri v. Holland [252 US 416, 433] :*
>
> > *"[W]hen we are dealing with words that also are constituent act, like the Constitution of the United States, we must realize that they have called into life a being the development of which could not have been foreseen completely by the most gifted of its begetters.' "*
>
> *(Emphasis supplied)*

41. Thereafter, the Court pointed out that several unenumerated rights fall within the ambit of Article 21 since personal liberty is of the widest amplitude and categorized them (in SCC pages 669-670 para 30) thus :

> *"(1) The right to go abroad. Satwant Singh Sawhney v. D. Ramarathnam, A.P.O. [AIR 1967 SC 1836]*

(2) The right to privacy. Gobind v. State of M.P. [(1975) 2 SCC 148] In this case reliance was placed on the American decision in Griswold v. Connecticut [381 US 479] (US at p. 510).

(3) The right against solitary confinement. Sunil Batra v. Delhi Administration [(1978) 4 SCC 494] (SCC at page 545).

(4) The right against bar fetters. Charles Sobraj v. Supdt., Central Jail [(1978) 4 SCC 104].

(5) The right to legal aid. Madhav Hayawadanrao Hoskot v. State of Maharashtra [(1978) 3 SCC 544].

(6) The right to speedy trial. Hussainara Khatoon (I) v. Home Secretary, State of Bihar [(1980) 1 SCC 81].

(7) The right against handcuffing. Prem Shankar Shukla v. Delhi Administration [(1980) 3 SCC 526]

(8) The right against delayed execution. T.V. Vatheeswaran v. State of T.N. [(1983) 2 SCC 68]

(9) The right against custodial violence. Sheela Barse v. State of Maharashtra [(1983) 2 SCC 96].

(10) The right against public hanging. Attorney General of India v. Lachma Devi [1989 Supp (1) SCC 264].

(11) Doctor's assistance. Parmanand Katara v. Union of India [(1989) 4 SCC 286].

(12) Shelter. Shantistar Builders v. Narayan Khimalal Totame [(1990) 1 SCC 520]."

42. Further, learned Senior Counsel Mr. Sachar referred to the following decisions of this Court giving meaning to the phrase "freedom of speech and expression" :

(1) Romesh Thappar v. State of Madras [(1977) 3 SCC 592]

Freedom of speech and expression includes freedom of propagation of ideas which is ensured by freedom of circulation. [AIR Headnote (ii)]

(2) Brij Bhushan v. State of Delhi [AIR 1950 SC 129]

Pre-censorship of a journal is restriction on the liberty of press. (AIR para 9)

(3) Hamdard Dawakhana v. Union of India [AIR 1960 SC 554]

Advertisements meant for propagation of ideas or furtherance

of literature or human thought is a part of freedom of speech and expression.
(AIR page 563 para 17)

(4) Sakal Papers (P) Ltd. v. Union of India [AIR 1962 SC 305]

Freedom of speech and expression carries with it the right to publish and circulate one's ideas, opinions and views.
(AIR page 311 para 29)

(5) Bennett Coleman and Co. v. Union of India [(1972) 2 SCC 788]

Freedom of press means right of citizens to speak, publish and express their viewsas well as right of people to read.
(SCC page 813 para 45)

(6) Indian Express Newspapers (Bombay) (P) Ltd. v. Union of India [(1973) 4 SCC 225]

"Freedom of expression, as learned writers have observed, has four broad social purposes to serve: (i) it helps an individual to attain self-fulfilment, (ii) it assists in the discovery of truth, (iii) it strengthens the capacity of an individual in participating in decision-making and (iv) it provides a mechanism by which it would be possible to establish a reasonable balance between stability and social change."
(SCC page 686 para 68)

(7) Odyssey Communications (P) Ltd. v. Lokvidayan Sanghatana [(1988) 3 SCC 410]

Freedom of speech and expression includes right of citizens to exhibit films on Doordarshan.(SCC page 414 para 5)

(8) S. Rangarajan v. P. Jagjivan Ram [(1989) 2 SCC 574]

Freedom of speech and expression means the right to express one's opinion by words of mouth, writing, printing, picture or in any other manner. It would thus include the freedom of communication and the right to propagate or publish opinion.
(SCC page 582 para 8)

(9) LIC of India v. Manubhai D. Shah [(1992) 3 SCC 637]

Freedom of speech and expression is a natural right which a human being acquires by birth. It is, therefore, a basic human right (Article 19 of Universal Declaration of Human Rights relied on.) Every citizen, therefore, has a right to air his or her views through the printing and/or electronic media or through any communication method.(SCC page 648 & 650 para 5 and 8)

(10) Secretary, Ministry of Information and Broadcasting, Govt. of India v. Cricket Association of Bengal [(1975) 4 SCC 428]

"3. (b) The right of free speech and expression includes the right to receive and impart information. For ensuring the free speech right of the citizens of this country, it is necessary that the citizens have the benefit of plurality of views and a range of opinions on all public issues. A successful democracy posits an 'aware' citizenry. Diversity of opinions, views, ideas and ideologies is essential to enable the citizens to arrive at informed judgment on all issues touching them."(Emphasis supplied)(SCC page 300 para 201)

(11) *S.P. Gupta v. Union of India [(1985) 1 SCC 641]*
Right to know is implicit in the right of free speech and expression. Disclosure of information regarding functioning of the Government must be the rule(SCC page 275 para 67)

(12) *State of U.P. v. Raj Narain [1975 Supp SCC 1]*
Freedom of speech and expression includes the right to know every public act, everything that is done in a public way, by their public functionaries.(SCC page 453 para 74)

(13) *Dinesh Trivedi, MP v. Union of India [(1997) 4 SCC 306]*
Freedom of speech and expression includes right of the citizens to know about the affairs of the Government. (SCC page 313 para 16)

43. There are many other judgments which are not required to be reiterated in this judgment. All these developments of law giving meaning to freedom of speech and expression or personal liberty are not required to be reconsidered nor could there be legislation so as to nullify such interpretation except as provided under the exceptions to fundamental rights.

44. Learned counsel for the respondents relied upon *R. Rajagopal v. State of T.N.* [(1994) 6 SCC 632] and submitted that in the said case the Court observed that right to privacy is not enumerated as a fundamental right in our Constitution but has been inferred from Article 21. In that case, reliance was placed on *Kharak Singh v. State of U.P.* [AIR 1963 SC 1295], *Gobind v. State of M.P.* [1969 UJ (SC) 616] and other decisions of English and American courts and thereafter, the Court held that the petitioners have a right to publish what they alleged to be a life story/autobiography of Auto Shankar insofar as it appears from the public records, even without his consent or authorisation. But if they go beyond that and publish his life story, they may be invading his right to privacy for the consequences in accordance with law. For this purpose, the Court held that a citizen has a right to safeguard the privacy of his own, his family, marriage, procreation, motherhood, child-bearing and education among other matters. None can publish anything concerning the above matters without his consent — whether truthful or otherwise and whether laudatory or critical. Position may, however, be different, if a person voluntarily thrusts himself into controversy or voluntarily invites or raises a controversy. The Court also pointed out an exception namely :

"This is for the reason that once a matter becomes a matter of public record, the right to privacy no longer subsists and it becomes a legitimate subject for comment by press and media among others. We are, however, of the opinion that in the interests of decency [Article 19(2)] an exception must be carved out to this rule, viz., a female who is the victim of a sexual assault, kidnap, abduction or a like offence should not further be subjected to the indignity of her name and the incident being publicised in press/media."

45. From the aforesaid observations learned Solicitor-General Mr. Raval and learned Senior Counsel Mr. Jaitley contended that rights which are derivatives would be subject to reasonable restriction. Secondly, it was sought to be contended that by insisting for declaration of assets of a candidate, right to privacy is affected. In our view, the aforesaid decision nowhere supports the said contention. This Court only considered — to what extent a citizen would have right to privacy under Article 21. The Court itself has carved out the exceptions and restrictions on absolute right of privacy. Further, by declaration of a fact, which is a matter of public record that a candidate was involved in various criminal cases, there is no question of infringement of any right of privacy. Similarly, with regard to the declaration of assets also, a person having assets or income is normally required to disclose the same under the Income Tax Act or such similar fiscal legislation. Not only this, but once a person becomes a candidate to acquire public office, such declaration would not affect his right of privacy. This is the necessity of the day because of statutory provisions of controlling widespread corrupt practices as repeatedly pointed out by all concerned including various reports of the Law Commission and other committees as stated above.

46. Even the Prime Minister of India in one of his speeches has observed to the same effect. This has been reproduced in *B.R. Kapur case* [(2001) 7 SCC 231] by Pattanaik, J. (as he then was) (in SCC page 314 para 74) as under:

"Mr. Divan in course of his arguments, had raised some submissions on the subject — 'Criminalisation of Politics' and participation of criminals in the electoral process as candidates and in that connection, he had brought to our notice the order of the Election Commission of India dated 28.08.1997. ... — 'Whither Accountability', published in The Pioneer, Shri Atal Behari Vajpayee had called for a national debate on all the possible alternatives for systematic changes to cleanse our democratic governing system of its present mess. He has expressed his dissatisfaction that neither Parliament nor the State Vidhan Sabhas are doing, with any degree of competence or commitment, what they are primarily meant to do: legislative function. According to him, barring exceptions, those who get elected to these democratic institutions are neither trained, formally or informally, in law-making nor do they seem to have an inclination to develop the necessary knowledge and competence in their profession. He has further indicated that those individuals in society who are generally interested in serving the electorate and performing legislative functions are finding it increasingly

difficult to succeed in today's electoral system and the electoral system has been almost totally subverted by money power, muscle power, and vote bank considerations of castes and communities. Shri Vajpayee also had indicated that the corruption in the governing structures has, therefore, corroded the very core of elective democracy. According to him, the certainty of scope of corruption in the governing structure has heightened opportunism and unscrupulousness among political parties, causing them to marry and divorce one another at will, seek opportunistic alliances and coalitions often without the popular mandate. Yet they capture and survive in power due to inherent systematic flows. He further stated that casteism, corruption and politicisation have eroded the integrity and efficacy of our civil service structure also. The manifestos, policies, programmes of the political parties have lost meaning in the present system of governance due to lack of accountability."

(emphasis supplied)

47. Further, this Court while dealing with the election expenses observed in *Common Cause v. Union of India* [(1996) 2 SCC 752] thus :

"18. ... Flags go up, walls are painted, and hundreds of thousands of loudspeakers play out the loud exhortations and extravagant promises. VIPs and VVIPs come and go, some of them in helicopters and air taxis. The political parties in their quest for power spend more than one thousand crore of rupees on the General Election (Parliament alone), yet nobody accounts for the bulk of the money so spent and there is no accountability anywhere. Nobody discloses the source of the money. There are no proper accounts and no audit. From where does the money come nobody knows. In a democracy where rule of law prevails this type of naked display of black money, by violating the mandatory provisions of law, cannot be permitted."

(Emphasis supplied)

48. To combat this naked display of unaccounted/black money by the candidate, declaration of assets is likely to have a check on violation of the provisions of the Act and other relevant Acts including the Income Tax Act.

49. Further, the doctrine of parliamentary sovereignty as it obtains in England does not prevail here except to the extent and in the fields provided by the Constitution. The entire scheme of the Constitution is such that it ensures the sovereignty and integrity of the country as a republic and the democratic way of life by parliamentary institutions based on free and fair elections. In *P.V. Narasimha Rao v. State (CBI/SPE)* [(1998) 4 SCC 626] this Court observed thus :

"47. ... Parliamentary democracy is a part of the basic structure of the Constitution. ... It is settled law that in interpreting the constitutional provisions the court should adopt a construction which strengthens the foundational features and the basic structure of the Constitution. (See: Sub-

Committee on Judicial Accountability v. Union of India [(1991) 4 SCC 699], SCC at page 719.)"

50. In *C. Narayanaswamy v. C.K. Jaffer Sharief* [1994 Supp (3) SCC 170] the Court observed (in SCC page 186 para 22) thus :

> *"If the call for 'purity of elections' is not to be reduced to a lip service or a slogan, then the persons investing funds, in furtherance of the prospect of the election of a candidate must be identified and located. The candidate should not be allowed to plead ignorance about the persons who have made contributions and investments for the success of the candidate concerned at the election. But this has to be taken care of by Parliament."*

51. In *T.N. Seshan, CEC of India v. Union of India* [(1995) 4 SCC 611] this Court observed thus :

> *"10. The preamble of our Constitution proclaims that we are a Democratic Republic Democracy being the basic feature of our constitutional set-up, there can be no two opinions that free and fair elections to our legislative bodies alone would guarantee the growth of a healthy democracy in the country."*

52. As observed in *Kesavananda Bharati case* [(2002) 5 SCC 294] the fundamental rights themselves have no fixed content and it is also to be stated that the attempt of the Court should be to expand the reach and ambit of the fundamental rights. The Constitution is required to be kept young, energetic and alive. In this view of the matter, the contention raised by the learned counsel for the respondents, that as the phrase "freedom of speech and expression" is given the meaning to include citizens' right to know the antecedents of the candidates contesting election of MP or MLA, such rights could be set at naught by the legislature, requires to be rejected.

Right to vote is a statutory right

53. Learned counsel for the respondents vehemently submitted that right to elect or to be elected is a pure and simple statutory right and in the absence of statutory provision neither has the citizen a right to elect nor has he a right to be elected because such right is neither a fundamental right nor a common law right. It is, therefore, submitted that it cannot be held that a voter has any fundamental right of knowing the antecedents/assets of a candidate contesting the election. Learned Solicitor-General Mr. Raval also submitted that on the basis of the decision rendered by this Court, the Act is amended by the impugned Ordinance/ Amendment Act. However, for the directions which are left out, the presumption would be — it is deliberate omission on the part of the legislature and, therefore, there is no question of it being violative of Article 19(1)(a). He submitted that law pertaining to election depends upon statutory provisions. Right to vote, elect or to be elected depends upon statutory rights. For this purpose, he referred to the decision in *N.P. Ponnuswami v. Returning Officer* [AIR 1952 SC 64], *G. Narayanaswami v. G. Pannerselvam* [(1972) 3 SCC 717] and *C. Narayanaswamy v. C.K. Jaffer Sharief* [(1994) 6 SCC 632].

54. There cannot be any dispute that the right to vote or stand as a candidate for election and decision with regard to violation of election law is not a civil right but is a creature of statute or special law and would be subject to the limitations envisaged therein. It is for the legislature to examine and provide provisions relating to validity of election and the jurisdiction of the Court would be limited in accordance with such law which creates such Election Tribunal.

55. In the case of *N.P. Ponnuswami* [(1996) 2 SCC 752] a person whose nomination paper was rejected, filed a writ of certiorari, which was dismissed on the ground that it had no jurisdiction to interfere with the order of the Returning Officer by reason of Article 329(b) of the Constitution.

56. In the case of *G. Narayanaswami* [(1998) 4 SCC 626] this Court was dealing with an election petition wherein the issue which was required to be decided was whether the respondent was not qualified to stand for election to the graduates' constituency on all or any of the grounds set out by the petitioner in paras 7 to 9 of the election petition. The Court referred to Article 171 and thereafter observed that the term "electorate" used in Articles 171(3)(a), (b) and (c) has neither been defined by the Constitution nor in any enactment by Parliament. The Court thereafter referred to the definition of "elector" given in Section 2(1)(a) of the RP Act and held that considering the language as well as the legislative history of Articles 171 and 173 of the Constitution and Section 6 of the RP Act, there could be a presumption of deliberate omission of the qualification that the representative of the graduates should also be a graduate.

57. Similarly, in *C. Narayanaswamy case* [(1994) 6 SCC 632] the Court was dealing with the validity of an election of a candidate on the ground of alleged corrupt practice as provided under Section 123(1)(A) of the Act and in that context the Court held that right of a person to question the validity of an election is dependent on conditions prescribed in the different sections of the Act and the rules framed thereunder. The Court thereafter held that as the Act does not provide that any expenditure incurred by a political party or by any other association or body of persons or any individual other than the candidate or his election agent, it shall not be deemed to be expenditure in connection with the election or authorised by a candidate or his election agent for the purpose of sub-section (1) of Section 77 read with Rule 90.

58. Learned counsel further referred to the decision in *Jyoti Basu v. Debi Ghosal* [(1982) 1 SCC 691] wherein similar observations are made by this Court while deciding election petition :

> *"8. A right to elect, fundamental though it is to democracy, is, anomalously enough, neither a fundamental right nor a common law right. It is pure and simple, a statutory right. So is the right to be elected. So is the right to dispute an election. Outside of statute, there is no right to elect, no right to be elected and no right to dispute an election. Statutory creations they are, and therefore, subject to statutory limitation. ...Concepts familiar to common law and equity must remain strangers to election law unless statutorily embodied. A court has no right to resort to them on considerations of alleged policy because policy in such matters as those, relating to the trial of election disputes, is what the statute lays down. ... We have already referred to the scheme of the Act. We have noticed the necessity to rid ourselves of notions based on common law or equity. We*

see that we must seek an answer to the question within the four corners of the statute. What does the Act say?"

59. It has to be stated that in an election petition challenging the validity of election, rights of the parties are governed by the statutory provisions for setting aside the election but this would not mean that a citizen who has right to be a voter and elect his representative in the Lok Sabha or Legislative Assembly has no fundamental right. Such a voter who is otherwise eligible to cast vote to elect his representative has statutory right under the Act to be a voter and has also a fundamental right as enshrined in Chapter III. Merely because a citizen is a voter or has a right to elect his representative as per the Act, his fundamental rights could not be abridged, controlled or restricted by statutory provisions except as permissible under the Constitution. If any statutory provision abridges fundamental right, that statutory provision would be void. It also requires to be well understood that democracy based on adult franchise is part of the basic structure of the Constitution. The right of an adult to take part in election process either as a voter or a candidate could be restricted by a valid law which does not offend constitutional provisions. Hence, the aforesaid judgments have no bearing on the question whether a citizen who is a voter has fundamental right to know the antecedents of his candidate. It cannot be held that as there is deliberate omission in law, the right of the voter to know the antecedents of the candidates, which is his fundamental right under Article 19(1)(a), is taken away.

60. Mr. Raval, learned Solicitor-General submitted that an enactment cannot be struck down on the ground that the Court thinks it unjustified. Members of Parliament or the Legislature are representatives of the people and are supposed to know and be aware of what is good and bad for the people. The Court cannot sit in judgment over their wisdom. He relied upon the decision rendered by this Court in *P. Nalla Thampy Terah (Dr.) v. Union of India* [1985 Supp SCC 189] wherein the Court considered the validity of Section 77(1) of the Act and referred to Report of the Santhanam Committee on Prevention of Corruption, which says :

> *"The public belief in the prevalence of corruption at high political levels has been strengthened by the manner in which funds are collected by political parties, especially at the time of elections. Such suspicions attach not only to the ruling party but to all parties, as often the opposition can also support private vested interests as well as members of the government party. It is, therefore, essential that the conduct of political parties should be regulated in this matter by strict principles in relation to collection of funds and electioneering. It has to be frankly recognised that political parties cannot be run and elections cannot be fought without large funds. But these funds should come openly from the supporters or sympathisers of the parties concerned."*

The Court also referred to various decisions and thereafter held thus :

> *"13. We have referred to this large data in order to show that the influence of big money on the election process is regarded universally as an evil of great magnitude. But then, the question which we, as Judges, have to consider is whether the provision contained in Explanation 1 suffers from*

any constitutional infirmity and, particularly, whether it violates Article 14. On that question we find it difficult, reluctantly though, to accept the contention that Explanation 1 offends against the right to equality. Under that provision, (i) a political party or (ii) any other association or body of persons or (iii) any individual, other than the candidate or his election agent, can incur expenses, without any limitation whatsoever, in connection with the election of a candidate. Such expenses are not deemed to be expenditure in connection with the election, incurred or authorised by the candidate or by his election agent for the purposes of Section 77(1)."

(emphasis supplied)

61. Learned Solicitor-General heavily relied upon para 19, wherein the Court observed thus :

"19. The petitioner is not unjustified in criticising the provision contained in Explanation 1 as diluting the principle of free and fair elections, which is the cornerstone of any democratic polity. But, it is not for us to lay down policies in matters pertaining to elections. If the provisions of the law violate the Constitution, they have to be struck down. We cannot, however, negate a law on the ground that we do not approve of the policy which underlies it."

(Emphasis supplied)

62. From the aforesaid discussion it is apparent that the Court in that case was dealing with the validity of Explanation 1 and was deciding whether it suffered from any constitutional infirmity, particularly, whether it was violative of Article 14. The question of Article 19(1)(a) was not required to be considered and the Court had not even touched it. At the same time, there cannot be any dispute that if the provisions of the law violate the constitutional provisions, they have to be struck down and that is what is required to be done in the present case. It is made clear that no provision is nullified on the ground that the Court does not approve the underlying policy of the enactment.

63. As against this, Mr. Sachar, learned Senior Counsel rightly referred to a decision rendered by this Court in *Bennett Coleman & Co. v. Union of India* [(1989) 4 SCC 286] where similar contentions were raised and negatived while imposing restrictions by the Newspaper Control Order. The Court's relevant discussion is as under :

"31. Article 19(1)(a) provides that all citizens shall have the right to freedom of speech and expression, Article 19(2) states that nothing in sub-clause (a) of clause (1) shall affect the operation of any existing law, or prevent the State from making any law, insofar as such law imposes reasonable restrictions on the exercise of the right conferred by the said sub-clause in the interests of the security of the State, friendly relations with foreign States, public order, decency or morality, or in relation to contempt of court, defamation or incitement to an offence. Although Article 19(1)(a) does not mention the freedom of the press, it is the settled view of this Court that freedom of speech and expression includes freedom of the press and circulation.

32. In the Express Newspapers case [(1973) 4 SCC 225] it is said that there can be no doubt that liberty of the press is an essential part of the freedom of speech and expression guaranteed by Article 19(1)(a). The press has the right of free propagation and free circulation without any previous restraint on publication. If a law were to single out the press for laying down prohibitive burdens on it that would restrict the circulation, penalise its freedom of choice as to personnel, prevent newspapers from being started and compel the press to government aid. This would violate Article 19(1)(a) and would fall outside the protection afforded by Article 19(2).

33. In Sakal Papers case [1989 Supp (1) SCC 264] it is said that the freedom of speech and expression guaranteed by Article 19(1) gives a citizen the right to propagate and publish his ideas to disseminate them, to circulate them either by words of mouth or by writing. This right extends not merely to the matter it is entitled to circulate but also to the volume of circulation. In Sakal Papers case [1989 Supp (1) SCC 264] the Newspaper (Price and Page) Act, 1956 empowered the Government to regulate the prices of newspapers in relation to their pages and sizes and to regulate the allocation of space for advertisement matter. The Government fixed the maximum number of pages that might be published by a newspaper according to the price charged. The Government prescribed the number of supplements that would be issued. This Court held that the Act and the Order placed restraints on the freedom of the press to circulate. This Court also held that the freedom of speech could not be restricted for the purpose of regulating the commercial aspects of activities of the newspapers."

(emphasis supplied)

64. The Court also dealt with the contention that newsprint policy does not directly deal with the fundamental right mentioned in Article 19(1)(a). It was also contended that regulatory statutes which do not control the content of speech but incidentally limit the ventured exercise are not regarded as a type of law. Any incidental limitation or incidental restriction on freedom of speech is permissible as the same is essential to the furtherance of important governmental interest in regulating speech and freedom. The Court negatived the said contention and in para 39 held thus :

"39. Mr. Palkhivala said that the tests of pith and substance of the subject-matter and of direct and of incidental effect of the legislation are relevant to questions of legislative competence but they are irrelevant to the question of infringement of fundamental rights. In our view this is a sound and correct approach to interpretation of legislative measures and State action in relation to fundamental rights. The true test is whether the effect of the impugned action is to take away or abridge fundamental rights. If it be assumed that the direct object of the law or action has to be direct abridgement of the right of free speech by the impugned law or

action it is to be related to the directness of effect and not to the directness of the subject-matter of the impeached law or action. The action may have a direct effect on a fundamental right although its direct subject-matter may be different."

(emphasis supplied)

The Court observed in SCC para 80 at p. 823 :

"The faith in the popular Government rests on the old dictum, 'let the people have the truth and the freedom to discuss it and all will go well'. The liberty of the press remains an 'Art of the Covenant' in every democracy."

65. Further, the freedom of speech and expression, as has been held repeatedly, is basic to and indivisible from a democratic polity. It includes right to impart and receive information. (*Secretary, Min. of Information & Broadcasting* [(1975) 4 SCC 428].) Restriction to the said right could be only as provided in Article 19(2). This aspect is also discussed in SCC para 151 (page 270) thus :

"151. Article 19(1)(a) declares that all citizens shall have the right of freedom of speech and expression. Clause (2) of Article 19, at the same time, provides that nothing in sub-clause (i) of clause (1) shall affect the operation of any existing law or prevent the State from making any law, insofar as such law imposes reasonable restrictions on the exercise of the right conferred by the said sub-clause in the interests of the sovereignty and integrity of India, the security of the State, friendly relations with the foreign States, public order, decency or morality or in relation to contempt of court, defamation or incitement of an offence. The grounds upon which reasonable restrictions can be placed upon the freedom of speech and expression are designed firstly to ensure that the said right is not exercised in such a manner as to threaten the sovereignty and integrity of India, security of the State, friendly relations with the foreign States, public order, decency or morality. Similarly, the said right cannot be so exercised as to amount to contempt of court, defamation or incitement of an offence. Existing laws providing such restrictions are saved and the State is free to make laws in future imposing such restrictions. The grounds aforesaid are conceived in the interest of ensuring and maintaining conditions in which the said right can meaningfully and peacefully be exercised by the citizens of this country."

66. Hence, in our view, right of a voter to know the biodata of a candidate is the foundation of democracy. The old dictum — let the people have the truth and the freedom to discuss it and all will go well with the Government — should prevail.

67. The true test for deciding the validity of the Act is — whether it takes away or abridges fundamental rights of the citizens. If there is direct abridgement of the fundamental right of freedom of speech and expression, the law would be invalid.

68. Before parting with the case, there is one aspect which is to be dealt with. After the judgment in *Association for Democratic Reforms case* [(2002) 5 SCC 294] the Election Commission gave certain directions in implementation of the judgment by its Order No. 3/ER/2002/JS-II/Vol-III, dated 28-6-2002. In the course of arguments, learned Solicitor-General as well as learned Senior Counsel appearing for the intervener (BJP) pointed out that Direction 4 is beyond the competence of the Election Commission and moreover, it is not necessary to give effect to the judgment of this Court. The said direction reads as follows :

> *"Furnishing of any wrong or incomplete information or suppression of any material information by any candidate in or from the said affidavit may also result in the rejection of his nomination paper where such wrong or incomplete information or suppression of material information is considered by the Returning Officer to be a defect of substantial character, apart from inviting penal consequences under the Indian Penal Code for furnishing wrong information to a public servant or suppression of material facts before him :*
>
> *Provided that only such information shall be considered to be wrong or incomplete or amounting to suppression of material information as is capable of easy verification by the Returning Officer by reference to documentary proof adduced before him in the summary inquiry conducted by him at the time of scrutiny of nominations under Section 36(2) of the Representation of the People Act, 1951, and only the information so verified shall be taken into account by him for further consideration of the question whether the same is a defect of substantial character."*

69. While no exception can be taken to the insistence of affidavit with regard to the matters specified in the judgment in *Association for Democratic Reforms case* [(2002) 5 SCC 294] the direction to reject the nomination paper for furnishing wrong information or concealing material information and providing for a summary enquiry at the time of scrutiny of the nominations, cannot be justified. In the case of assets and liabilities, it would be very difficult for the Returning Officer to consider the truth or otherwise of the details furnished with reference to the "documentary proof". Very often, in such matters the documentary proof may not be clinching and the candidate concerned may be handicapped to rebut the allegation then and there. If sufficient time is provided, he may be able to produce proof to contradict the objector's version. It is true that the aforesaid directions issued by the Election Commission are not under challenge but at the same time prima facie it appears that the Election Commission is required to revise its instructions in the light of directions issued in *Association for Democratic Reforms case* [(2002) 5 SCC 294] and as provided under the Representation of the People Act and its Third Amendment.

70. Finally, after the amendment application was granted, the following additional contentions were raised :

> 1. Notice should be issued to the Attorney-General as vires of the Act is challenged.

> 2. Parliament in its wisdom and after due deliberation has amended the Act and has also incorporated the directions issued by this Court in its earlier judgment in *Association for Democratic Reforms* including the direction for declaration of assets and liabilities of every elected candidate for a House of Parliament. They are also required to declare assets of their spouse and dependent children.

71. The contention that notice is required to be issued to the Attorney-General as vires of the Act is challenged, is of no substance because "Union of India" is the party-respondent and on its behalf learned Solicitor-General is appearing before the Court. He has forcefully raised the contentions which were required to be raised at the time of hearing of the matter. So, service of notice to the learned Attorney-General would be nothing but empty formality and the contention is raised for the sake of raising such contention.

72. Further, we have also reproduced certain recommendations of the National Commission to Review the Working of the Constitution in the earlier paragraphs and have also relied upon the same. In the Report, the Commission has recommended that any person charged with any offence punishable with imprisonment for a maximum term of five years or more, should be disqualified for being chosen as, or for being, a Member of Parliament or Legislature of a State on the expiry of a period of one year from the date the charges were framed against him by the court in that offence. The Commission has also recommended that every candidate at the time of election must declare his assets and liabilities along with those of his close relatives and all candidates should be required under law to declare their assets and liabilities by an affidavit and the details so given by them should be made public. Again, the legislators should be required under law to submit their returns about their liabilities every year and a final statement in this regard at the end of their term of office. Many such other recommendations are reproduced in earlier paragraphs.

73. With regard to the second contention, it has already been dealt with in previous paragraphs.

74. What emerges from the above discussion can be summarised thus :

> (A) The legislature can remove the basis of a decision rendered by a competent court thereby rendering that decision ineffective but the legislature has no power to ask the instrumentalities of the State to disobey or disregard the decisions given by the court. A declaration that an order made by a court of law is void is normally a part of the judicial function. The legislature cannot declare that decision rendered by the Court is not binding or is of no effect.
>
> It is true that the legislature is entitled to change the law with retrospective effect which forms the basis of a judicial decision. This exercise of power is subject to constitutional provision, therefore, it cannot enact a law which is violative of fundamental right.
>
> (B) Section 33-B which provides that notwithstanding anything contained in

the judgment of any court or directions issued by the Election Commission, no candidate shall be liable to disclose or furnish any such information in respect of his election which is not required to be disclosed or furnished under the Act or the rules made thereunder, is on the face of it beyond the legislative competence, as this Court has held that the voter has a fundamental right under Article 19(1)(a) to know the antecedents of a candidate for various reasons recorded in the earlier judgment as well as in this judgment.

The Amended Act does not wholly cover the directions issued by this Court. On the contrary, it provides that a candidate would not be bound to furnish certain information as directed by this Court.

(C) The judgment rendered by this Court in *Association for Democratic Reforms* [(2002) 5 SCC 294] has attained finality, therefore, there is no question of interpreting constitutional provision which calls for reference under Article 145(3).

(D) The contention that as there is no specific fundamental right conferred on a voter by any statutory provision to know the antecedents of a candidate, the directions given by this Court are against the statutory provisions is, on the face of it, without any substance. In an election petition challenging the validity of an election of a particular candidate, the statutory provisions would govern respective rights of the parties. However, voters' fundamental right to know the antecedents of a candidate is independent of statutory rights under the election law. A voter is first citizen of this country and apart from statutory rights, he is having fundamental rights conferred by the Constitution. Members of a democratic society should be sufficiently informed so that they may cast their votes intelligently in favour of persons who are to govern them. Right to vote would be meaningless unless the citizens are well informed about the antecedents of a candidate. There can be little doubt that exposure to public gaze and scrutiny is one of the surest means to cleanse our democratic governing system and to have competent legislatures.

(E) It is established that fundamental rights themselves have no fixed content, most of them are empty vessels into which each generation must pour its content in the light of its experience. The attempt of the Court should be to expand the reach and ambit of the fundamental rights by process of judicial interpretation. During the last more than half a decade, it has been so done by this Court consistently. There cannot be any distinction between the fundamental rights mentioned in Chapter III of the Constitution and the declaration of such rights on the basis of the judgments rendered by this Court.

75. In the result, Section 33-B of the Amended Act is held to be illegal, null and void. However, this judgment would not have any retrospective effect but would be prospective. Writ petitions stand disposed of accordingly.

P. Venkatarama Reddi, J.

76. The width and amplitude of the right to information about the candidates contesting elections to Parliament or the State Legislature in the context of the citizen's right to vote broadly falls for consideration in these writ petitions under Article 32 of the Constitution. While I respectfully agree with the conclusion that Section 33-B of the Representation of the People Act, 1951 does not pass the test of constitutionality, I have come across a limited area of disagreement on certain aspects, especially pertaining to the extent of disclosures that could be insisted upon by the Court in the light of legislation on the subject. Moreover, the importance and intricacies of the subject-matter and the virgin ground trodden by this Court in *Union of India v. Association for Democratic Reforms* [(2002) 5 SCC 294] to bring the right to information of the voter within the sweep of Article 19(1)(a) has impelled me to elucidate and clarify certain crucial aspects. Hence, this separate opinion.

I. (1) Freedom of expression and right to information

77. In the Constitution of our democratic Republic, among the fundamental freedoms, freedom of speech and expression shines radiantly in the firmament of Part III. We must take legitimate pride that this cherished freedom has grown from strength to strength in the post-independence era. It has been constantly nourished and shaped to new dimensions in tune with the contemporary needs by the constitutional courts. Barring a few aberrations, the Executive government and the Political Parties too have not lagged behind in safeguarding this valuable right which is the insignia of the democratic culture of a nation. Nurtured by this right, Press and electronic media have emerged as powerful instruments to mould the public opinion and to educate, entertain and enlighten the public.

78. Freedom of speech and expression, just as the equality clause and the guarantee of life and liberty, has been very broadly construed by this Court right from the 1950s. It has been variously described as a 'basic human right', 'a natural right' and the like. It embraces within its scope the freedom of propagation and interchange of ideas, dissemination of information which would help formation of one's opinion and viewpoint and debates on matters of public concern. The importance which our Constitution-makers wanted to attach to this freedom is evident from the fact that reasonable restrictions on that right could be placed by law only on the limited grounds specified in Article 19(2), not to speak of inherent limitations of the right.

79. In due course of time, several species of rights unenumerated in Article 19(1)(a) have branched off from the genus of the article through the process of interpretation by this apex Court. One such right is the 'right to information'. Perhaps, the first decision which has adverted to this right is *State of U.P. v. Raj Narain* [(1975) 4 SCC 428]. "The right to know", it was observed by Mathew, J. "which is derived from the concept of freedom of speech, though not absolute, is a factor which should make one wary, when secrecy is claimed for transactions which can, at any rate, have no repercussion on public security". It was said very aptly:

"*74. In a Government of responsibility like ours, where all the agents of the public must be responsible for their conduct, there can be but few secrets. The people of this country have a right to know every public act, everything that is done in a public way, by their public functionaries.*"

80. The next milestone which showed the way for concretizing this right is the decision in *S.P. Gupta v. Union of India* [(1981) Supp. SCC 87] in which this Court dealt with the issue of High Court Judges' transfer. Bhagwati, J. observed :

"*The concept of an open government is the direct emanation from the right to know which seems to be implicit in the right of free speech and expression guaranteed under Article 19(1)(a). Therefore, disclosure of information in regard to the functioning of Government must be the rule and secrecy an exception....*"

81. Peoples' right to know about governmental affairs was emphasized in the following words :

"*No democratic Government can survive without accountability and the basic postulate of accountability is that the people should have information about the functioning of the Government. It is only if people know how Government is functioning that they can fulfil the role which democracy assigns to them and make democracy a really effective participatory democracy.*"

82. These two decisions have recognized that the right of the citizens to obtain information on matters relating to public acts flows from the fundamental right enshrined in Article 19(1)(a). The pertinent observations made by the learned Judges in these two cases were in the context of the question whether the privilege under Section 123 of the Evidence Act could be claimed by the State in respect of the Blue Book in the first case i.e. *Raj Narain case* [(1975) 4 SCC 428] and the file throwing light on the consultation process with the Chief Justice, in the second case. Though the scope and ambit of Article 19(1)(a) vis-à-vis the right to information did not directly arise for consideration in those two landmark decisions, the observations quoted supra have a certain amount of relevance in evaluating the nature and character of the right.

83. Then, we have the decision in *Dinesh Trivedi v. Union of India* [(1997) 4 SCC 306] . This Court was confronted with the issue whether background papers and investigatory reports which were referred to in Vohra Committee's Report could be compelled to be made public. The following observations of Ahmadi, C.J. are quite pertinent :

"*16. In modern Constitutional democracies, it is axiomatic that citizens have a right to know about the affairs of the Government which, having been elected by them, seeks to formulate sound policies of governance aimed at their welfare. However, like all other rights, even this right has recognized limitations; it is, by no means, absolute.*"

84. The proposition expressed by Mathew, J. in *Raj Narain case* [(1975) 4 SCC 428] was quoted with approval.

85. The next decision which deserves reference is the case of *Secretary, Ministry of I&B* v. *Cricket Association of Bengal* [(1995) 2 SCC 161]. Has an organizer or producer of any event a right to get the event telecast through an agency of his choice, whether national or foreign? That was the primary question decided in that case. It was highlighted that the right to impart and receive information is a part of the fundamental right under Article 19(1)(a) of the Constitution. On this point, Sawant, J. had this to say at para 122(ii) :

> *"122. (ii) The right to impart and receive information is a species of the right of freedom of speech and expression guaranteed by Article 19(1)(a) of the Constitution. A citizen has a fundamental right to use the best means of imparting and receiving information and as such to have an access to telecasting for the purpose. However, this right to have an access to telecasting has limitations on account of the use of the public property...."*

86. Jeevan Reddy, J. spoke more or less in the same voice :

> *"3. (b) The right of free speech and expression includes the right to receive and impart information. For ensuring the free speech right of the citizens of this country, it is necessary that the citizens have the benefit of plurality of views and a range of opinions on all public issues. A successful democracy posits an 'aware' citizenry. Diversity of opinions, views, ideas and ideologies is essential to enable the citizens to arrive at informed judgment on all issues touching them."*

87. A conspectus of these cases would reveal that the right to receive and impart information was considered in the context of privilege pleaded by the State in relation to confidential documents relating to public affairs and the freedom of electronic media in broadcasting/telecasting certain events.

I. (2) Right to information in the context of the voter's right to know the details of contesting candidates and the right of the media and others to enlighten the voter

88. For the first time in *Union of India v. Association for Democratic Reforms* [(2002) 5 SCC 294] which is the forerunner to the present controversy, the right to know about the candidate standing for election has been brought within the sweep of Article 19(1)(a). There can be no doubt that by doing so, a new dimension has been given to the right embodied in Article 19(1)(a) through a creative approach dictated by the need to improve and refine the political process of election. In carving out this right, the Court had not traversed a beaten track but took a fresh path. It must be noted that the right to information evolved by this Court in the said case is qualitatively different from the right to get information about public affairs or the right to receive information through the press and electronic media, though to a certain extent, there may be overlapping. The right to information of the voter/citizen is sought to be enforced against an individual who intends to become a public figure and the information relates to his personal matters. Secondly, that right cannot materialize without the State's intervention. The State or its instrumentality has to compel a subject to make the information available to the public, by means of legislation or orders having the force of law. With respect, I am unable to share the view that it stands on the same footing as right to telecast and the right to view sports and games or other items of entertainment through television (vide observations at Paragraph 38 of *Association for Democratic Reforms case* [(2002) 5 SCC 294]). One more observation at Paragraph 30 to the effect that "the decision making process of a voter would include his right to know about public functionaries who are required to be elected by him" needs explanation. Till a candidate gets elected and enters the House, it would not be appropriate to refer to him as a public functionary. Therefore, the right to know about a public act done by a public functionary to which we find reference in *Raj Narain case* [(1975) 4 SCC 428] is not the same thing as the right to know about the antecedents of the candidate contesting the election. Nevertheless, the conclusion reached by the Court that the voter has such a right and that the right falls within the realm of freedom of speech and expression guaranteed by Article 19(1)(a) can be justified on good and substantial grounds. To this aspect, I will advert a little later. Before that, I would like to say that it would have been in the fitness of things if the case (*UOI v. Association for Democratic Reforms*) was referred to the Constitution Bench as per the mandate of Article 145(3) for the reason that a new dimension has been added to the concept of freedom of expression so as to bring within its ambit a new species of right to information. Apparently, no such request was made at the hearing and all parties invited the decision of the three-Judge Bench. The law has been laid down therein elevating the right to secure information about a contesting candidate to the position of a fundamental right. That decision has been duly taken note of by Parliament and acted upon by the Election Commission. It has attained finality. At this stage, it would not be appropriate to set the clock back and refer the matter to the Constitution Bench to test the correctness of the view taken in that case. I agree with my learned Brother Shah, J. in this respect. However, I would prefer to give reasons of my own – may not be very different from what the learned Judge had expressed, to demonstrate that the proposition laid down by this Court rests on a firm Constitutional basis.

89. I shall now proceed to elucidate as to how the right to know the details about the contesting candidate should be regarded as a part of the freedom of expression guaranteed by Article 19(1)(a). This issue has to be viewed from more than one angle – from the point of view of the voter, the public viz. representatives of the press, organizations such as the petitioners which are interested in taking up public issues and thirdly, from the point of view of the persons seeking election to the legislative bodies.

90. The trite saying that "democracy is for the people, of the people and by the people" has to be remembered forever. In a democratic republic, it is the will of the people that is paramount and becomes the basis of the authority of the Government. The will is expressed in periodic elections based on universal adult suffrage held by means of secret ballot. It is through the ballot that the voter expresses his choice or preference for a candidate. "Voting is formal expression of will or opinion by the person entitled to exercise the right on the subject or issue", as observed by this Court in *Lily Thomas v. Speaker, Lok Sabha* [(1993) 4 SCC 234] quoting from Black's Law Dictionary. The citizens of the country are enabled to take part in the Government through their chosen representatives. In a Parliamentary democracy like ours, the Government of the day is responsible to the people through their elected representatives. The elected representative acts or is supposed to act as a live link between the people and the

Government. The people's representatives fill the role of law-makers and custodians of the Government. People look to them for ventilation and redressal of their grievances. They are the focal point of the will and authority of the people at large. The moment they put in papers for contesting the election, they are subjected to public gaze and public scrutiny. The character, strength and weakness of the candidate is widely debated. Nothing is therefore more important for sustenance of democratic polity than the voter making an intelligent and rational choice of his or her representative. For this, the voter should be in a position to effectively formulate his/her opinion and to ultimately express that opinion through ballot by casting the vote. The concomitant of the right to vote which is the basic postulate of democracy is thus twofold: first, formulation of opinion about the candidates and second, the expression of choice by casting the vote in favour of the preferred candidate at the polling booth. The first step is complementary to the other. Many a voter will be handicapped in formulating the opinion and making a proper choice of the candidate unless the essential information regarding the candidate is available. The voter/citizen should have at least the basic information about the contesting candidate, such as his involvement in serious criminal offences. To scuttle the flow of information — relevant and essential — would affect the electorate's ability to evaluate the candidate. Not only that, the information relating to the candidates will pave the way for public debate on the merits and demerits of the candidates. When once there is public disclosure of the relevant details concerning the candidates, the press, as a media of mass communication and voluntary organizations vigilant enough to channel the public opinion on right lines will be able to disseminate the information and thereby enlighten and alert the public at large regarding the adverse antecedents of a candidate. It will go a long way in promoting the freedom of speech and expression. That goal would be accomplished in two ways. It will help the voter who is interested in seeking and receiving information about the candidate to form an opinion according to his or her conscience and best of judgment and secondly, it will facilitate the press and voluntary organizations in imparting information on a matter of vital public concern. An informed voter — whether he acquires information directly by keeping track of disclosures or through the press and other channels of communication — will be able to fulfil his responsibility in a more satisfactory manner. An enlightened and informed citizenry would undoubtedly enhance democratic values. Thus, the availability of proper and relevant information about the candidate fosters and promotes the freedom of speech and expression both from the point of view of imparting and receiving the information. In turn, it would lead to the preservation of the integrity of electoral process which is so essential for the growth of democracy. Though I do not go to the extent of remarking that the election will be a farce if the candidates' antecedents are not known to the voters, I would say that such information will certainly be conducive to fairness in election process and integrity in public life. The disclosure of information would facilitate and augment the freedom of expression both from the point of view of the voter as well as the media through which the information is publicized and openly debated.

90. The problem can be approached from another angle. As observed by this Court in *Association for Democratic Reforms case* [(2002) 5 SCC 294] a voter "speaks out or expresses by casting vote". Freedom of expression, as contemplated by Article 19(1)(a) which in many respects overlaps and coincides with freedom of speech, has manifold meanings. It need not and ought not to be confined to expressing something in words orally or in writing. The act of manifesting by action or language is one of the meanings given in Ramanatha Aiyar's Law Lexicon (edited by Justice Y.V. Chandrachud). Even a manifestation of an emotion, feeling etc. without words would amount to expression. The example given in Collin's Dictionary of English Language (1983 Reprint) is: "tears are an expression of grief", is quite apposite. Another shade of meaning is: "a look on the face that indicates mood or emotion; e.g.: a joyful expression". Communication of emotion and display of talent through music, painting etc. is also a sort of expression. Having regard to the comprehensive meaning of the phrase "expression", voting can be legitimately regarded as a form of expression. Ballot is the instrument by which the voter expresses his choice between candidates or in respect to propositions; and his "vote" is his choice or election, as expressed by his ballot (vide 'A Dictionary of Modern Legal Usage'; 2nd Edition, by Garner Bryan A.). "Opinion expressed, resolution or decision carried, by voting" is one of the meanings given to the expression "vote" in the New Oxford Illustrated Dictionary. It is well settled and it needs no emphasis that the fundamental right of freedom of speech and expression should be broadly construed and it has been so construed all these years. In the light of this, the dictum of the Court that the voter "speaks out or expresses by casting a vote" is apt and well founded. I would only reiterate and say that freedom of voting by expressing preference for a candidate is nothing but freedom of expressing oneself in relation to a matter of prime concern to the country and the voter himself.

I. (3) Right to vote is a constitutional right though not a fundamental right but right to make choice by means of ballot is part of freedom of expression

91. The right to vote for the candidate of one's choice is of the essence of democratic polity. This right is recognized by our Constitution and it is given effect to in specific form by the Representation of the People Act. The Constituent Assembly Debates reveal that the idea to treat the voting right as a fundamental right was dropped; nevertheless, it was decided to provide for it elsewhere in the Constitution. This move found its expression in Article 326 which enjoins that "the elections to the House of the People and to the Legislative Assembly of every State shall be on the basis of adult suffrage; that is to say, every person who is a citizen of India and who is not less than 21* years of age, and is not otherwise disqualified under the Constitution or law on the ground of non-residence, unsoundness of mind, crime, corrupt or illegal practice — shall be entitled to be registered as voter at such election" (*Now 18 years). However, case after case starting from *Ponnuswami case* [(1952) SCR 218] characterized it as a statutory right. "The right to vote or stand as a candidate for election", it was observed in *Ponnuswami case* [(1952) SCR 218] "is not a civil right but is a creature of statute or special law and must be subject to the limitations imposed by it." It was further elaborated in the following words :

> *"Strictly speaking, it is the sole right of the legislature to examine and determine all matters relating to the election of its own members, and if the legislature takes it out of its own hands and vests in a special tribunal an entirely new and unknown jurisdiction, that special jurisdiction should be exercised in accordance with the law which creates it."*

92. In *Jyoti Basu v. Debi Ghosal* [1982 (3) SCR 318] this Court again pointed out in no uncertain terms that: "A right to elect, fundamental though it is to democracy, is, anomalously enough, neither a fundamental right nor a common law right. It is pure and simple a statutory right." With great reverence to the eminent Judges, I would like to clarify that the right to vote, if not a fundamental right, is certainly a constitutional right. The right originates from the Constitution and in accordance with the constitutional mandate contained in Article 326, the right has been shaped by the statute, namely the RP Act. That, in my understanding, is the correct legal position as regards the nature of the right to vote in elections to the House of the People and Legislative Assemblies. It is not very accurate to describe it as a statutory right, pure and simple. Even with this clarification, the argument of the learned Solicitor General that the right to vote not being a fundamental right, the information which at best facilitates meaningful exercise of that right cannot be read as an integral part of any fundamental right, remains to be squarely met. Here, a distinction has to be drawn between the conferment of the right to vote on fulfilment of requisite criteria and the culmination of that right in the final act of expressing choice towards a particular candidate by means of ballot. Though the initial right cannot be placed on the pedestal of a fundamental right, but, at the stage when the voter goes to the polling booth and casts his vote, his freedom to express arises. The casting of vote in favour of one or the other candidate tantamounts to expression of his opinion and preference and that final stage in the exercise of voting right marks the accomplishment of freedom of expression of the voter. That is where Article 19(1)(a) is attracted. Freedom of voting as distinct from right to vote is thus a species of freedom of expression and therefore carries with it the auxiliary and complementary rights such as right to secure information about the candidate which are conducive to the freedom. None of the decisions of this Court wherein the proposition that the right to vote is a pure and simple statutory right was declared and reiterated, considered the question whether the citizen's freedom of expression is or is not involved when a citizen entitled to vote casts his vote in favour of one or the other candidate. The issues that arose in *Ponnuswami case* [(1952) SCR 218] and various cases cited by the learned Solicitor-General fall broadly within the realm of procedural or remedial aspects of challenging the election or the nomination of a candidate. None of these decisions, in my view, go counter to the proposition accepted by us that the fundamental right of freedom of expression sets in when a voter actually casts his vote. I, therefore, find no merit in the submission made by the learned Solicitor-General that these writ petitions have to be referred to a larger Bench in view of the apparent conflict. As already stated, the factual matrix and legal issues involved in those cases were different and the view, we are taking, does not go counter to the actual ratio of the said decisions rendered by the eminent Judges of this Court.

93. Reliance has been placed by the learned Solicitor General on the Constitution Bench decision in *Jamuna Prasad Mukhariya v. Lachhi Ram* [(1955) 1 SCR 608]. That was a case of special appeal to this Court against the decision of an Election Tribunal. Apart from assailing the finding of the Tribunal on the aspect of "corrupt practice", Sections 123(5) and 124(5) (as they stood then) of the RP Act were challenged as ultra vires Article 19(1)(a). The former provision declared the character assassination of a candidate as a major corrupt practice and the latter provision made an appeal to vote on the ground of caste a minor corrupt practice. The contention that these provisions impinged on the freedom of speech and expression was unhesitatingly rejected. The Court observed that those provisions did not stop a man from speaking. They merely prescribed conditions which must be observed if a citizen wanted to enter Parliament. It was further observed that the right to stand as a candidate and contest an election is a special right created by the statute and can only be exercised on the conditions laid down by the statute. In that context, the Court made an observation that the fundamental right chapter had no bearing on the right to contest the election which is created by the statute and the appellant had no fundamental right to be elected as a Member of Parliament. If a person wants to get elected, he must observe the rules laid down by law. So holding, those sections were held to be *intra vires*. I do not think that this decision which dealt with the contesting candidate's rights and obligations has any bearing on the freedom of expression of the voter and the public in general in the context of elections. The remark that "the fundamental right chapter has no bearing on a right like this created by statute" cannot be divorced from the context in which it was made.

94. The learned senior counsel appearing for one of the interveners (BJP) has advanced the contention that if the right to information is culled out from Article 19(1)(a) and read as an integral part of that right, it is fraught with dangerous consequences inasmuch as the grounds of reasonable restrictions which could be imposed are by far limited and therefore, the Government may be constrained to part with certain sensitive informations which would not be in public interest to disclose. This raises the larger question whether apart from the heads of restriction envisaged by sub-article (2) of Article 19, certain inherent limitations should not be read into the article, if it becomes necessary to do so in national or societal interest. The discussion on this aspect finds its echo in the separate opinion of Jeevan Reddy, J. in *Cricket Association case* [(1995) 2 SCC 161]. The learned Judge was of the view that the freedom of speech and expression cannot be so exercised as to endanger the interest of the nation or the interest of the society, even if the expression 'national interest' or 'public interest' has not been used in Article 19(2). It was pointed out that such implied limitation has been read into the First Amendment of the US Constitution which guarantees the freedom of speech and expression in unqualified terms.

95. The following observations of the US Supreme Court in *Gitlow v. New York* [(1924) 69 L.Ed. 1138] are very relevant in this context :

> *"It is a fundamental principle, long established, that the freedom of speech and of the press which is secured by the Constitution does not confer an absolute right to speak or publish, without responsibility, whatever one may choose, or an unrestricted and unbridled license that gives immunity for every possible use of language, and prevents the punishment of those who abuse this freedom."*

96. Whenever the rare situations of the kind anticipated by the learned counsel arise, the Constitution and the courts are not helpless in checking the misuse and abuse of the freedom. Such a check need not necessarily be found strictly within the confines of Article 19(2).

II. Sections 33-A and 33-B of the Representation of the People (3rd Amendment) Act, 2002 – whether Section 33-A by itself effectively secures the voter's/citizen's right to information – whether Section 33-B is unconstitutional?

II. (1) Sections 33-A & 33-B of the Representation of the People (3rd Amendment) Act :

97. Now I turn my attention to the discussion of the core question, that is to say, whether the impugned legislation falls foul of Article 19(1)(a) for limiting the area of disclosure and whether Parliament acted beyond its competence in deviating from the directives given by this Court to the Election Commission in *Democratic Reforms Associationcase* [(2002) 5 SCC 294]. By virtue of the Representation of the People (Amendment) Act, 2002 the only information which a prospective contestant is required to furnish apart from the information which he is obliged to disclose under the existing provisions is the information on two points: (i) whether he is accused of any offence punishable with imprisonment for two years or more in a pending case in which a charge has been framed; and (ii) whether he has been convicted of an offence (other than the offence referred to in sub-sections (1) to (3) of Section 8) and sentenced to imprisonment for one year or more. On other points spelt out in this Court's judgment, the candidate is not liable to furnish any information and that is so, notwithstanding anything contained in any judgment or order of a court or any direction, order or instruction issued by the Election Commission. Omission to furnish the information as per the mandate of Section 33-B and furnishing false information in that behalf is made punishable. That is the sum and substance of the two provisions, namely, Sections 33A and 33B.

98. The plain effect of the embargo contained in Section 33-B is to nullify substantially the directives issued by the Election Commission pursuant to the judgment of this Court. At present, the instructions issued by the Election Commission could only operate in respect of the items specified in Section 33A and nothing more. It is for this reason that Section 33B has been challenged as ultra vires the Constitution both on the ground that it affects the fundamental right of the voter/citizen to get adequate information about the candidate and that Parliament is incompetent to nullify the judgment of this Court. I shall briefly notice the rival contentions on this crucial issue.

II. (2) Contentions

99. Petitioners' contention is that the legislation on the subject of disclosure of particulars of candidates should adopt in entirety the directives issued by this Court to the Election Commission in the pre-ordinance period. Any dilution or deviation of those norms or directives would necessarily violate the fundamental right guaranteed by Article 19(1)(a) as interpreted by this Court and therefore the law, as enacted by Parliament, infringes the said guarantee. This contention has apparently been accepted by my learned Brother M.B. Shah, J. The other view point presented on behalf of the Union of India and one of the interveners is that the freedom of the legislature in identifying and evolving the specific areas in which such information should be made public cannot be curtailed by reference to the ad hoc directives given by this Court in the pre-Ordinance period and the legislative wisdom of Parliament, especially in election matters, cannot be questioned. This is the position even if the right to know about the candidate is conceded to be part of Article 19(1)(a). It is for Parliament to decide to what extent and how far the information should be made available. In any case, it is submitted that the Court's verdict has been duly taken note of by Parliament and certain provisions have been made to promote the right to information vis-à-vis the contesting candidates. Section 33-B is only a part of this exercise and it does not go counter to Article 19(1)(a) even though the scope of public disclosures has been limited to one important aspect only.

II. (3) Broad points for consideration

100. A liberal but not a constricted approach in the matter of disclosure of information in relation to candidates seeking election is no doubt a desideratum. The wholesale adoption of the Court's diktats on the various items of information while enacting the legislation would have received public approbation and would have been welcomed by the public. It would have been in tune with the recommendations of various commissions and even the statements made by eminent and responsible political personalities. However, the fact remains that Parliament in its discretion did not go the whole hog, but chose to limiting the scope of mandated disclosures to only one of the important aspects highlighted in the judgment. The question remains to be considered whether in doing so, Parliament outstepped its limits and enacted a law in violation of the guarantee enshrined in Article 19(1)(a) of the Constitution. The allied question is whether Parliament has no option but to scrupulously adopt the directives given by this Court to the Election Commission. Is it open to Parliament to independently view the issue and formulate the parameters and contents of disclosure, though it has the effect of diluting or diminishing the scope of disclosures which, in the perception of the Court, were desirable? In considering these questions of far-reaching importance from the constitutional angle, it is necessary to have a clear idea of the ratio and implications of this Court's judgment in *Association for Democratic Reforms case* [(2002) 5 SCC 294].

II. (4) Analysis of the judgment in Assn. for Democratic Reforms case [Ed.: See full text at 2003 Current Central Legislation, Pt. II, at p. 3] —whether and how far the directives given therein have an impact on the parliamentary legislation — approach of the Court in testing the legislation.

101. The first proposition laid down by this Court in the said case is that a citizen/voter has the right to know about the antecedents of the contesting candidate and that right is a part of the fundamental right under Article 19(1)(a). In this context, M.B. Shah, J. observed that :

> "*...Voter's speech or expression in case of election would include casting of votes, that is to say, voter speaks out or expresses by casting vote.*"

102. It was then pointed out that the information about the candidate to be selected is essential as it would be conducive to transparency and purity in the process of election. The next question considered was how best to enforce that right. The Court having noticed that there was a void in the field in the sense that it was not covered by any legislative provision, gave directions to the Election Commission to fill the vacuum by requiring the candidate to furnish information on the specified aspects while filing the nomination paper. Five items of information which the Election Commission should call for from the prospective candidates were spelt out by the Court. Two of them relate to criminal background of the candidate and pendency of criminal cases against him. Points 3 & 4 relate to assets and liabilities of the candidate and his/her family. The last one is about the educational qualifications of the candidate. The legal basis and the justification for issuing such directives to the Commission has been stated thus (vide paragraphs 19 & 20) :

> *"19. At the outset, we would say that it is not possible for this Court to give any directions for amending the Act or the statutory Rules. It is for Parliament to amend the Act and the Rules. It is also established law that no direction can be given, which would be contrary to the Act and the Rules.*
>
> *xxx*
>
> *20. However, it is equally settled that in case when the Act or Rules are silent on a particular subject and the authority implementing the same has constitutional or statutory power to implement it, the Court can necessarily issue directions or orders on the said subject to fill the vacuum or void till the suitable law is enacted."*

Again, at paragraph 49 it was emphasized :

> *"It is to be stated that the Election Commission has from time to time issued instructions/orders to meet with the situation where the field is unoccupied by the legislation. Hence, the norms and modalities to carry out and give effect to the aforesaid directions should be drawn up properly by the Election Commission as early as possible."*

103. Thus, the Court was conscious of the fact that the Election Commission could act in the matter only so long as the field is not covered by legislation. The Court also felt that the vacuum or void should be suitably filled so that the right to information concerning a candidate would soon become a reality. In other words, till Parliament applied its mind and came forward with appropriate legislation to give effect to the right available to a voter-citizen, the Court felt that the said goal has to be translated into action through the media of the Election Commission, which is endowed with 'residuary power' to regulate the election process in the best interests of the electorate. Instead of leaving it to the Commission and with a view to give quietus to the possible controversies that might arise, the Court considered it expedient to spell out five points (broadly falling into three categories) on which the information has to be called for from the contesting candidate. In the very nature of things, the directives given by the Court were intended to operate only till the law was made by the legislature and in that sense 'pro tempore' in nature. The five directives cannot be considered to be rigid theorems — inflexible and immutable, but only reflect the perception and tentative thinking of the Court at a point of time when the legislature did not address itself to the question.

104. When the Parliament, in the aftermath of the verdict of this Court, deliberated and thought it fit to secure the right to information to a citizen only to a limited extent (having a bearing on criminal antecedents), a fresh look has to be necessarily taken by the Court and the validity of the law made has to be tested on a clean slate. It must be remembered that the right to get information which is a corollary to the fundamental right to free speech and expression has no fixed connotation. Its contours and parameters cannot be precisely defined and the Court in my understanding, never meant to do so. It is often a matter of perception and approach. How far to go and where to stop? These are the questions to be pondered over by the legislature and the Constitutional Court called upon to decide the question of validity of the legislation. For instance, many voters/citizens may like to have more complete information—a sort of biodata of the candidate starting from his school days such as his academic career, the properties which he had before and after entering into politics, the details of his income and tax payments for the last one decade and sources of acquisition of his and his family's wealth. Can it be said that all such information which will no doubt enable the voter and public to have a comprehensive idea of the contesting candidate, should be disclosed by a prospective candidate and that the failure to provide for it by law would infringe the fundamental right under Article 19(1)(a)? The preponderance of view would be that it is not reasonable to compel a candidate to make disclosures affecting his privacy to that extent in the guise of effectuating the right to information. A line has to be drawn somewhere. While there cannot be a lip service to the valuable right to information, it should not be stretched too far. At the same time, the essence and substratum of the right has to be preserved and promoted, when once it is brought within the fold of fundamental right. A balanced but not a rigid approach, is needed in identifying and defining the parameters of the right which the voter/citizen has. The standards to be applied to disclosures vis-à-vis public affairs and governance and the disclosures relating to personal life and biodata of a candidate cannot be the same. The measure or yardstick will be somewhat different. It should not be forgotten that the candidates' right to privacy is one of the many factors that could be kept in view, though that right is always subject to overriding public interest.

105. In my view, the points of disclosure spelt out by this Court in *Association for Democratic Reforms case* [(2002) 5 SCC 294] should serve as broad indicators or parameters in enacting the legislation for the purpose of securing the right to information about the candidate. The paradigms set by the Court, though pro tempore in nature as clarified supra, are entitled to due weight. If the legislature in utter disregard of the indicators enunciated by this Court proceeds to make a legislation providing only for a semblance or pittance of information or omits to provide for disclosure on certain essential points, the law would then fail to pass the muster of Article 19(1)(a). Though certain amount of deviation from the aspects of disclosure spelt out by this Court is not impermissible, a substantial departure cannot be countenanced. The legislative provision should be such as to promote the right to information to a reasonable extent, if not to the fullest extent on details of concern to the voters and citizens at large. While enacting the legislation, the legislature has to ensure that the fundamental right to know about the candidate is reasonably secured and information which is crucial, by any objective standards, is not denied. It is for the Constitutional Court in exercise of its judicial review power to judge whether the areas of disclosure carved out by the legislature are reasonably adequate to safeguard the citizens' right to information. The Court has to take a holistic view and adopt a balanced approach, keeping in view the twin principles that the citizens' right to information to know about the personal details of a candidate is not an unlimited right and that at any rate, it has no fixed concept and the legislature has freedom to choose between two reasonable alternatives. It is not a proper approach to test the validity of legislation only from the standpoint whether the legislation implicitly and word to word gives effect to the directives issued by the Court as an ad hoc measure when the field was unoccupied by legislation. Once legislation is made, this Court has to make an independent assessment in the process of evaluating whether the items of information statutorily ordained are reasonably adequate to secure the right of information to the voter so as to facilitate him to form a fairly clear opinion on the merits and demerits of the candidates. In embarking on this exercise, as already stated, this Court's directives on the points of disclosure even if they be tentative or ad hoc in nature, cannot be brushed aside, but should be given due weight. But, I reiterate that the shape of the legislation need not be solely controlled by the directives issued to the Election Commission to meet an ad hoc situation. As I said earlier, the right to information cannot be placed in straitjacket formulae and the perceptions regarding the extent and amplitude of this right are bound to vary.

III. Section 33-B is unconstitutional

III. (1) The right to information cannot be frozen and stagnated

106. In my view, the Constitutional validity of Section 33B has to be judged from the above angle and perspective. Considered in that light, I agree with the conclusion of M.B. Shah, J. that Section 33B does not pass the test of constitutionality. The reasons are more than one. Firstly, when the right to secure information about a contesting candidate is recognized as an integral part of fundamental right as it ought to be, it follows that its ambit, amplitude and parameters cannot be chained and circumscribed for all times to come by declaring that no information, other than that specifically laid down in the Act, should be required to be given. When the legislation delimiting the areas of disclosure was enacted, it may be that Parliament felt that the disclosure on other aspects was not necessary for the time being. Assuming that the guarantee of right to information is not violated by making a departure from the paradigms set by the Court, it is not open to Parliament to stop all further disclosures concerning the candidate in future. In other words, a blanket ban on dissemination of information other than that spelt out in the enactment, irrespective of the need of the hour and the future exigencies and expedients is, in my view, impermissible. It must be remembered that the concept of freedom of speech and expression does not remain static. The felt necessities of the times coupled with experiences drawn from the past may give rise to the need to insist on additional information on the aspects not provided for by law. New situations and the march of events may demand the flow of additional facets of information. The right to information should be allowed to grow rather than being frozen and stagnated; but the mandate of Section 33B prefaced by the non obstante clause impedes the flow of such information conducive to the freedom of expression. In the face of the prohibition under Section 33B, the Election Commission which is entrusted with the function of monitoring and supervising the election process will have to sit back with a sense of helplessness in spite of the pressing need for insisting on additional information. Even the Court may at times feel handicapped in taking necessary remedial steps to enforce the right to information. In my view, the legislative injunction curtailing the nature of information to be furnished by the contesting candidates only to the specific matters provided for by the legislation and nothing more would emasculate the fundamental right to freedom of expression of which the right to information is a part. The very objective of recognizing the right to information as part of the fundamental right under Article 19(1)(a) in order to ensure free and fair elections would be frustrated if the ban prescribed by Section 33B is taken to its logical effect.

III. (2) Impugned legislation fails to effectuate right to information on certain vital aspects

107. The second reason why Section 33B should be condemned is that by blocking the ambit of disclosures only to what has been specifically provided for by the amendment, Parliament failed to give effect to one of the vital aspects of information viz. disclosure of assets and liabilities and thus failed in substantial measure to give effect to the right to information as a part of the freedom of expression. The right to information which is now provided for by the legislature no doubt relates to one of the essential points but in ignoring the other essential aspect relating to assets and liabilities as discussed hereinafter, Parliament has unduly restricted the ambit of information which the citizens should have and thereby impinged on the guarantee enshrined in Article 19(1)(a).

III. (3) How far the principle that the legislature cannot encroach upon the judicial sphere applies

108. It is a settled principle of constitutional jurisprudence that the only way to render a judicial decision ineffective is to enact a valid law by way of amendment or otherwise fundamentally altering the basis of the judgment either prospectively or retrospectively. The legislature cannot overrule or supersede a judgment of the Court without lawfully removing the defect or infirmity pointed out by the Court because it is obvious that the legislature cannot trench on the judicial power vested in the courts. Relying on this principle, it is contended that the decision of the Apex Constitutional Court cannot be set at naught in the manner in which it has been done by the impugned legislation. As a sequel, it is further contended that the question of altering the basis of judgment or curing the defect does not arise in the instant case as Parliament cannot pass a law in curtailment of fundamental right recognized, amplified and enforced by this Court.

109. The contention that the fundamental basis of the decision in *Association for Democratic Reforms case* [(2002) 5 SCC 294] has not at all been altered by Parliament, does not appeal to me. I have discussed at length the real scope and ratio of the judgment and the nature and character of directives given by this Court to the Election Commission. As observed earlier, those directions are pro tempore in nature when there was a vacuum in the field. When once Parliament stepped in and passed the legislation providing for right of information, maybe on certain limited aspects, the void must be deemed to have been filled up and the judgment works itself out, though the proposition laid down and observations made in the context of Article 19(1)(a) on the need to secure information to the citizens will hold good. Now the new legislation has to be tested on the touchstone of Article 19(1)(a). Of course, in doing so, the decision of this Court should be given due weight and there cannot be a marked departure from the items of information considered essential by this Court to effectuate the fundamental right to information. Viewed in this light, it must be held that Parliament did not by law provide for disclosure of information on certain crucial points such as assets and liabilities and at the same time, placed an embargo on calling for further informations by enacting Section 33-B. That is where Section 33-B of the impugned Amendment Act does not pass the muster of Article 19(1)(*a*), as interpreted by this Court.

IV. Right to information with reference to specific aspects

110. I shall now discuss the specifics of the problem. With a view to promote the right to information, this Court gave certain directives to the Election Commission which, as I have already clarified, were ad hoc in nature. The Election Commission was directed to call for details from the contesting candidates broadly on three points, namely, (i) criminal record, (ii) assets and liabilities, and (iii) educational qualification. The Third Amendment to the RP Act which was preceded by an ordinance provided for disclosure of information. How far the Third Amendment to the Representation of the People Act, 2002 safeguards the right of information which is a part of the guaranteed right under Article 19(1)(a), is the question to be considered now with specific reference to each of the three points spelt out in the judgment of this Court in *Association for Democratic Reforms case* [(2002) 5 SCC 294].

IV. (1) Criminal background and pending criminal cases against candidates — Section 33-A of the RP (3rd Amendment) Act

111. As regards the first aspect, namely, criminal record, the directives in *Association for Democratic Reforms case* [(2002) 5 SCC 294] are two fold :

> *"(i) whether the candidate is convicted/acquitted/discharged of any criminal offence in the past — if any, whether he is punished with imprisonment or fine and*
>
> *(ii) prior to six months of filing of nomination, whether the candidate is an accused in any pending case, of any offence punishable with imprisonment for two years or more, and in which charge is framed or cognizance is taken by the court of law."*

As regards the second directive, the Parliament has substantially proceeded on the same lines and made it obligatory for the candidate to furnish information as to whether he is accused of any offence punishable with imprisonment for two years or more in a pending case in which a charge has been framed by the competent court. However, the case in which cognizance has been taken but charge has not been framed is not covered by Clause (i) of Section 33A(I). The Parliament having taken the right step of compelling disclosure of the pendency of cases relating to major offences, there is no good reason why it failed to provide for the disclosure of the cases of the same nature of which cognizance has been taken by the Court. It is common knowledge that on account of a variety of reasons such as the delaying tactics of one or the other accused and inadequacies of the prosecuting machinery, framing of formal charges gets delayed considerably, especially in serious cases where committal procedure has to be gone through. On that account, the voter/citizen shall not be denied information regarding cognizance taken by the Court of an offence punishable with imprisonment for two years or more. The citizen's right to information, when once it is recognized to be part of the fundamental right under Article 19(1)(a), cannot be truncated in the manner in which it has been done. Clause (i) of Section 33A(I) therefore falls short of the avowed goal to effectuate the right of information on a vital aspect. Cases in which cognizance has been taken should therefore be comprehended within the area of information accessible to the voters/citizens, in addition to what is provided for in Clause (i) of Section 33A. Coming to clause (ii) of Section 33A(I), the Parliament broadly followed the pattern shown by the Court itself. This Court thought it fit to draw a line between major/serious offences and minor/non-serious offences while giving direction No.2 (vide Para 48). If so, the legislative thinking that this distinction should also hold good in regard to past cases cannot be faulted on the ground that the said clause fails to provide adequate information about the candidate. If Parliament felt that the convictions and sentences of the long past relating to petty/non-serious offences need not be made available to the electorate, it cannot be definitely said that the valuable right to information becomes a casualty. Very often, such offences by and large may not involve moral turpitude. It is not uncommon, as one of the learned senior counsel pointed out that the political personalities are prosecuted for politically related activities such as holding demonstrations and visited with the punishment of fine or short imprisonment. Information regarding such instances may not be of real importance to the electorate in judging the worth of the relative merits of the candidates. At any rate, it is a matter of perception and balancing of various factors, as observed supra. The legislative judgment cannot be faulted merely for the reason that the pro tempore directions of this Court have not been scrupulously followed. As regards acquittals, it is reasonable to take the view that such information will not be of much relevance inasmuch as acquittal prima facie implies that the accused is not connected with the crime or the prosecution has no legs to stand. It is not reasonable to expect that from the factum of prosecution resulting in acquittal, the voters/citizens would be able to judge the candidate better. On the other hand, such information in general has the potential to send misleading signals about the honesty and integrity of the candidate.

112. I am therefore of the view that as regards past criminal record, what Parliament has provided for is fairly adequate.

113. One more aspect which needs a brief comment is the exclusion of offences referred to in sub-Sections (1) and (2) of Section 8 of the RP Act, 1951. Section 8 deals with disqualification on conviction for certain offences. Those offences are of serious nature from the point of view of national and societal interest. Even the existing provisions viz. Rule 4-A inserted by the Conduct of Elections (Amendment) Rules, 2002 makes a provision for disclosure of such offences in the nomination form. Hence, such offences have been excluded from the ambit of Clause (ii) of Section 33A.

IV. (2) Assets and liabilities

114. Disclosure of assets and liabilities is another thorny issue. If the right to information is to be meaningful and if it is to serve its avowed purpose, I am of the considered view that the candidate entering the electoral contest should be required to disclose the assets and liabilities (barring articles of household use). A member of Parliament or State Legislature is an elected representative occupying high public office and at the same time, he is a 'public servant' within the meaning of the Prevention of Corruption Act as ruled by this Court in the case of *P.V. Narasimha Rao v. State* [(1998) 4 SCC 636267]. They are the repositories of public trust. They have public duties to perform. It is borne out by experience that by virtue of the office they hold there is a real potential for misuse. The public awareness of financial position of the candidate will go a long way in forming an opinion whether the candidate, after election to the office had amassed wealth either in his own name or in the name of family members viz., spouse and dependent children. At the time when the candidate seeks re-election, the citizens/voters can have a comparative idea of the assets before and after the election so as to assess whether the high public office had possibly been used for self-aggrandizement. Incidentally, the disclosure will serve as a check against misuse of power for making quick money, a malady which nobody can deny, has been pervading the political spectrum of our democratic nation. As regards liabilities, the disclosure will enable the voter to know, inter alia, whether the candidate has outstanding dues payable to public financial institutions or the Government. Such information has a relevant bearing on the antecedents and the propensities of the candidate in his dealings with public money. 'Assets and liabilities' is one of the important aspects to which extensive reference has been made in *Association for Democratic Reforms case* [(2002) 5 SCC 294]. The Court did consider it, after an elaborate discussion, as a vital piece of information as far as the voter is concerned. But, unfortunately, the observations made by this Court in this regard have a been given a short shrift by Parliament with little realization that they have a significant bearing on the right to get information from the contesting candidates and such information is necessary to give effect to the freedom of expression.

115. As regards the purpose of disclosure of assets and liabilities, I would like to make it clear that it is not meant to evaluate whether the candidate is financially sound or has sufficient money to spend in the election. Poor or rich are alike entitled to contest the election. Every citizen has equal accessibility in the public arena. If the information is meant to mobilize public opinion in favour of an affluent/financially sound candidate, the tenet of socialistic democracy and the concept of equality so firmly embedded in our Constitution will be distorted. I cannot also share the view that this information on assets would enable the public to verify whether unaccounted money played a part in contesting the election. So long as Explanation-I to Section 77 of the RP Act, 1951 stands and the contributions can legitimately come from any source, it is not possible for a citizen/voter to cause a verification to be made on those lines. In my opinion, the real purposes of seeking information in regard to assets and liabilities are those which I adverted to in the preceding paragraph. It may serve other purposes also, but, I have confined myself to the relevancy of such disclosure vis-à-vis right to information only.

116. It has been contended with much force that the right to information made available to the voters/citizens by judicial interpretation has to be balanced with the right of privacy of the spouse of the contesting candidate and any insistence on the disclosure of assets and liabilities of the spouse invades his/her right to privacy which is implied in Article 21. After giving anxious consideration to this argument, I am unable to uphold the same. In this context, I would like to recall the apt words of Mathew, J., in *Gobind v. State of M.P.* [(1975) 2 SCC 148]. While analysing the right to privacy as an ingredient of Article 21, it was observed :

> *"There can be no doubt that privacy-dignity claims deserve to be examined with care and to be denied only when an important countervailing interest is shown to be superior."*
>
> (emphasis supplied)

It was then said succinctly :

> *"If the court does find that a claimed right is entitled to protection as a fundamental privacy right, a law infringing it must satisfy the compelling State interest test. Then the question would be whether a State interest is of such paramount importance as would justify an infringement of the right."*

It was further explained :

> *"Privacy primarily concerns the individual. It therefore relates to and overlaps with the concept of liberty. The most serious advocate of privacy must confess that there are serious problems of defining the essence and scope of the right. Privacy interest in autonomy must also be placed in the context of other rights and values."*

117. By calling upon the contesting candidate to disclose the assets and liabilities of his/her spouse, the fundamental right to information of a voter/citizen is thereby promoted. When there is a competition between the right to privacy of an individual and the right to information of the citizens, the former right has to be subordinated to the latter right as it serves the larger public interest. The right to know about the candidate who intends to become a public figure and a representative of the people would not be effective and real if only truncated information of the assets and liabilities is given. It cannot be denied that the family relationship and social order in our country is such that the husband and wife look to the properties held by them as belonging to the family for all practical purposes, though in the eye of law the properties may distinctly belong to each of them. By and large, there exists a sort of unity of interest in the properties held by spouses. The property being kept in the name of the spouse benami is not unknown in our country. In this situation, it could be said that a countervailing or paramount interest is involved in requiring a candidate who chooses to subject himself/herself to public gaze and scrutiny to furnish the details of assets and liabilities of the spouse as well. That is one way of looking at the problem. More important, it is to be noted that Parliament itself accepted in principle that not only the assets of the elected candidates but also his or her spouse and dependent children should be disclosed to the constitutional authority and the right of privacy should not come in the way of such disclosure; but, the hitch lies in the fact that the disclosure has to be made to the Speaker or Chairman of the House after he or she is elected. No provision has been made for giving access to the details filed with the presiding officer of the House. By doing so, Parliament has omitted to give effect to the principle, which it rightly accepted as a step in aid to promote integrity in public life. Having accepted the need to insist on disclosure of assets and liabilities of the elected candidate together with those of other family members, Parliament refrained from making a provision for furnishing the information at the time of filing the nomination. This has resulted in jeopardizing the right to information implicitly guaranteed by Article 19(1)(a). Therefore, the provision made in Section 75A regarding declaration of assets and liabilities of the elected candidates to the presiding officer has failed to effectuate the right to information and the freedom of expression of the voters/citizens.

IV. (3) Educational qualifications

118. The last item left for discussion is about educational qualifications. In my view, the disclosure of information regarding educational qualifications of a candidate is not an essential component of the right to information flowing from Article 19(1)(a). By not providing for disclosure of educational qualifications, it cannot be said that Parliament violated the guarantee of Article 19(1)(a). Consistent with the principle of adult suffrage, the Constitution has not prescribed any educational qualification for being Member of the House of the People or Legislative Assembly. That apart, I am inclined to think that the information relating to educational qualifications of contesting candidates does not serve any useful purpose in the present context and scenario. It is a well-known fact that barring a few exceptions, most of the candidates elected to Parliament or the State Legislatures are fairly educated even if they are not graduates or postgraduates. To think of illiterate candidates is based on a factually incorrect assumption. To say that well-educated persons such as those having graduate and postgraduate qualifications will be able to serve the people better and conduct themselves in a better way inside and outside the House is nothing but overlooking the stark realities. The experience and events in public life and the legislatures have demonstrated that the dividing line between the well educated and less educated from the point of view of his/her calibre and culture is rather thin. Much depends on the character of the individual, the sense of devotion to duty and the sense of concern to the welfare of the people. These characteristics are not the monopoly of well-educated persons. I do not think that it is necessary to supply information to the voter to facilitate him to indulge in an infructuous exercise of comparing the educational qualifications of the candidates. It may be that certain candidates having exceptionally high qualifications in specialized field may prove useful to the society, but it is natural to expect that such candidates would voluntarily come forward with an account of their own academic and other talents as a part of their election programme. Viewed from any angle, the information regarding educational qualifications is not a vital and useful piece of information to the voter, in ultimate analysis. At any rate, two views are reasonably possible. Therefore, it is not possible to hold that Parliament should have necessarily made the provision for disclosure of information regarding educational qualifications of the candidates.

V. Conclusions

119. Finally, the summary of my conclusions :

> (1) Securing information on the basic details concerning the candidates contesting for elections to Parliament or the State Legislature promotes freedom of expression and therefore the right to information forms an integral part of Article 19(1)(a). This right to information is, however, qualitatively different from the right to get information about public affairs or the right to receive information through the Press and electronic media, though, to a certain extent, there may be overlapping.

(2) The right to vote at the elections to the House of the People or Legislative Assembly is a constitutional right but not merely a statutory right; freedom of voting as distinct from right to vote is a facet of the fundamental right enshrined in Article 19(1)(a). The casting of vote in favour of one or the other candidate marks the accomplishment of freedom of expression of the voter.

(3) The directives given by this Court in *Union of India v. Association for Democratic Reforms* [(2002) 5 SCC 294] were intended to operate only till the law was made by the legislature and in that sense 'pro tempore' in nature. Once legislation is made, the Court has to make an independent assessment in order to evaluate whether the items of information statutorily ordained are reasonably adequate to secure the right of information available to the voter/citizen. In embarking on this exercise, the points of disclosure indicated by this Court, even if they be tentative or ad hoc in nature, should be given due weight and substantial departure therefrom cannot be countenanced.

(4) The Court has to take a holistic view and adopt a balanced approach in examining the legislation providing for right to information and laying down the parameters of that right.

(5) Section 33B inserted by the Representation of the People (3rd Amendment) Act, 2002 does not pass the test of constitutionality, firstly, for the reason that it imposes a blanket ban on dissemination of information other than that spelt out in the enactment irrespective of the need of the hour and the future exigencies and expedients and secondly, for the reason that the ban operates despite the fact that the disclosure of information now provided for is deficient and inadequate.

(6) The right to information provided for by Parliament under Section 33A in regard to the pending criminal cases and past involvement in such cases is reasonably adequate to safeguard the right to information vested in the voter/citizen. However, there is no good reason for excluding the pending cases in which cognizance has been taken by the Court from the ambit of disclosure.

(7) The provision made in Section 75A regarding declaration of assets and liabilities of the elected candidates to the Speaker or the Chairman of the House has failed to effectuate the right to information and the freedom of expression of the voters/citizens. Having accepted the need to insist on disclosure of assets and liabilities of the elected candidate together with those of the spouse or dependent children, Parliament ought to have made a provision for furnishing this information at the time of filing the nomination. Failure to do so has resulted in the violation of guarantee under Article 19(1)(a).

(8) The failure to provide for disclosure of educational qualification does not, in practical terms, infringe the freedom of expression.

(9) The Election Commission has to issue revised instructions to ensure implementation of Section 33A subject to what is laid down in this judgment regarding the cases in which cognizance has been taken. The Election Commission's orders related to disclosure of assets and liabilities will still hold good and continue to be operative. However, direction No.4 of para 14 insofar as verification of assets and liabilities by means of summary enquiry and rejection of nomination paper on the ground of furnishing wrong information or suppressing material information should not be enforced.

120. Accordingly, the writ petitions stand disposed of without costs.

Dharmadhikari, J.

121. I have carefully gone through the well-considered separate opinions of Brothers M.B. Shah and P.V. Reddi, JJ. Both the learned Judges have come to a common conclusion that Section 33-B inserted in the Representation of the People Act, 1951 by Amendment Ordinance 4 of 2002, which on repeal is succeeded by the Third Amendment Act of 2002, is liable to be declared invalid being violative of Article 19(1)(a) of the Constitution. I am in respectful agreement with the above conclusion reached in common by both the learned Brothers. I would, however, like to supplement the above conclusion.

122. The reports of the advisory commissions set up one after the other by the Government to which a reference has been made by Brother Shah, J., highlight the present political scenario where money power and muscle power have substantially polluted and perverted the democratic processes in India. To control the ill-effects of money power and muscle power the commissions recommend that election system should be overhauled and drastically changed lest democracy would become a teasing illusion to common citizens of this country. Not only a half-hearted attempt in the direction of reform of the election system is to be taken, as has been done by the present legislation by amending some provisions of the Act here and there, but a much improved election system is required to be evolved to make the election process both transparent and accountable so that influence of tainted money and physical force of criminals do not make democracy a farce — the citizen's fundamental "right to information" should be recognised and fully effectuated. This freedom of a citizen to participate and choose a candidate at an election is distinct from exercise of his right as a voter which is to be regulated by statutory law on the election like the RP Act.

123. Making of law for election reform is undoubtedly a subject exclusively of the legislature. Based on the decision of this Court in the case of *Association for Democratic Reforms* [(2002) 5 SCC 294] and the directions made therein to the Election Commission, the Amendment Act under consideration has made an attempt to fill the void in law but the void has not been filled fully and does not satisfy the requirements for exercise of fundamental freedom of the citizen to participate in election as a well-informed voter.

124. Democracy based on "free and fair elections" is considered as a basic feature of the Constitution in the case of *Kesavananda Bharati* [(2002) 5 SCC 294]. Lack of adequate legislative will to fill the vacuum in law for reforming the election process in accordance with the law declared by this Court in the case of *Association for Democratic Reforms* [(2002) 5 SCC 294] obligates this Court as an important organ in constitutional process to intervene.

125. In my opinion, this Court is obliged by the Constitution to intervene because the legislative field, even after the passing of the Ordinance and the Amendment Act, leaves a vacuum. This Court in the case of *Association for Democratic Reforms* [(2002) 5 SCC 294] has determined the ambit of fundamental "right of information" to a voter. The law, as it stands today after amendment, is deficient in ensuring "free and fair elections". This Court has, therefore, found it necessary to strike down Section 33B of the Amendment Act so as to revive the law declared by this Court in the case of *Association for Democratic Reforms* [(2002) 5 SCC 294].

126. With these words, I agree with Conclusions (A) to (E) in the opinion of Brother Shah, J. and Conclusions (1), (2), (4), (5), (6), (7) and (9) in the opinion of Brother P.V. Reddi, J.

127. With utmost respect, I am unable to agree with Conclusions (3) and (8) in the opinion of Brother P.V. Reddi, J., as on those aspects, I have expressed my respectful agreement with Brother Shah, J.

In the Supreme Court of India

Writ Petition (Civil) No. 161 of 2004
People's Union for Civil Liberties (PUCL) & Anr. v. Union of India & Anr.[4]

Date of Judgement : 27.09.2013

Bench : P. Sathasivam, C.J. and Ranjana P. Desai and Ranjan Gogoi, JJ.

[This case pertains to the right of a voter to exercise his vote for "None Of The Above (NOTA)". PUCL had taken up this issue before the Supreme Court under Article 32 of the Constitution. The Court accepted the Petition filed by PUCL and held that in a vibrant democracy, the voter must be given an opportunity to choose None Of The Above (NOTA) button which will indeed compel political parties to nominate a sound candidate. It further said that giving right to a voter not to vote for any candidate while protecting his right of secrecy was extremely important in a democracy. This judgment is landmark because it brought in effective NOTA right to the voter.]

Judgment

P. Sathasivam, C.J.

1. The present writ petition, under Article 32 of the Constitution of India, has been filed by the petitioners herein challenging the constitutional validity of Rules 41(2) and (3) and 49-O of the Conduct of Elections Rules, 1961 (in short "the Rules") to the extent that these provisions violate the secrecy of voting which is fundamental to the free and fair elections and is required to be maintained as per Section 128 of the Representation of the People Act, 1951 (in short "the RP Act") and Rules 39 and 49-M of the Rules.

2. The petitioners herein have preferred this petition for the issuance of a writ or direction(s) of like nature on the ground that though the abovesaid rules viz. Rules 41(2) and (3) and 49-O, recognise the right of a voter not to vote but still the secrecy of his having not voted is not maintained in its implementation and thus the impugned rules, to the extent of such violation of the right to secrecy, are not only ultra vires to the said Rules but also violative of Articles 19(1)(a) and 21 of the Constitution of India besides International Covenants.

4. (2013) 10 SCC 1

3. In the above backdrop, the petitioners herein prayed for declaring Rules 41(2) and (3) and 49-O of the Rules *ultra vires* and unconstitutional and also prayed for a direction to the Election Commission of India, Respondent No. 2 herein, to provide necessary provision in the ballot papers as well as in the electronic voting machines for the protection of the right of not to vote in order to keep the exercise of such right a secret under the existing RP Act/the Rules or under Article 324 of the Constitution.

4. On 23.02.2009, a Division Bench of this Court, on an objection with regard to maintainability of the writ petition on the ground that right to vote is not a fundamental right but is a statutory right, after considering *Union of India v. Association for Democratic Reforms* (2002) 5 SCC 294 and *People's Union for Civil Liberties v. Union of India*(2003) 4 SCC 399 held that even though the judgment in *Kuldip Nayar v. Union of India* (2006) 7 SCC 1 did not overrule or discard the ratio laid down in the judgments mentioned above, however, it creates a doubt in this regard, and referred the matter to a larger Bench to arrive at a decision.

5. One Centre for Consumer Education and Association for Democratic Reforms has filed applications for impleadment in this Writ Petition. Impleadment applications are allowed.

6. Heard Mr. Rajinder Sachhar, learned Senior Counsel for the petitioners; Mr. P.P. Malhotra, learned Additional Solicitor General for the Union of India, Respondent No. 1 herein; Ms. Meenakshi Arora, learned counsel for the Election Commission of India, Respondent No. 2 herein; Ms. Kamini Jaiswal and Mr. Raghenth Basant, learned counsel for the impleading parties.

Contentions

7. Mr. Rajinder Sachhar, learned Senior Counsel for the petitioners, by taking us through various provisions, particularly, Section 128 of the RP Act as well as Rules 39, 41, 49-M and 49-O of the Rules submitted that in terms of Rule 41(2) of the Rules, an elector has a right not to vote but still the secrecy of his having not voted is not maintained under Rules 41(2) and (3) thereof. He further pointed out that similarly according to Rule 49-O of the Rules, the right of a voter who decides not to vote has been accepted but the secrecy is not maintained. According to him, in case an elector decides not to record his vote, a remark to this effect shall be made against the said entry in Form 17-A by the Presiding Officer and the signature or thumb impression of the elector shall be obtained against such remark. Hence, if a voter decides not to vote, his record will be maintained by the Presiding Officer which will thereby disclose that he has decided not to vote. The main substance of the arguments of the learned Senior Counsel for the petitioners is that though the right not to vote is recognised by Rules 41 and 49-O of the Rules and is also a part of the freedom of expression of a voter, if a voter chooses to exercise the said right, it has to be kept secret. The learned Senior Counsel further submitted that both the above provisions, to the extent of such violation of the secrecy clause are not only ultra vires but also contrary to Section 128 of the RP Act, Rules 39 and 49-M of the Rules as well as Articles 19(1)(a) and 21 of the Constitution.

8. On the other hand, Mr. P.P. Malhotra, learned Additional Solicitor General appearing for the Union of India submitted that the right to vote is neither a fundamental right nor a constitutional right nor a common law right but is a pure and simple statutory right. He asserted that neither the RP Act nor the Constitution of India declares the right to vote as anything more than a statutory right and hence the present writ petition is not maintainable. He further pointed out that in view of the decision of the Constitution Bench in *Kuldip Nayar* [(2006) 7 SCC 1], the reference for deciding the same by a larger Bench was unnecessary. He further pointed out that in view of the above decision, the earlier two decisions of this Court viz. *Association for Democratic Reforms* [(2002) 5 SCC 294] and *People's Union for Civil Liberties* [(2003) 4 SCC 399], stood impliedly overruled, hence, on this ground also reference to a larger Bench was not required. He further pointed out that though the power of the Election Commission under Article 324 of the Constitution is wide enough, but still the same can, in no manner, be construed as to cover those areas, which are already covered by the statutory provisions. He further pointed out that even from the existing provisions, it is clear that secrecy of ballot is a principle which has been formulated to ensure that in no case it shall be known to the candidates or their representatives that in whose favour a particular voter has voted so that he can exercise his right to vote freely and fearlessly. He also pointed out that the right of secrecy has been extended to only those voters who have exercised their right to vote and the same, in no manner, can be extended to those who have not voted at all. Finally, he submitted that since Section 2(d) of the RP Act specifically defines "election" to mean an election to fill a seat, it cannot be construed as an election not to fill a seat.

9. Ms. Meenakshi Arora, learned counsel appearing for the Election Commission of India, Respondent No. 2 herein, by pointing out various provisions both from the RP Act and the Rules submitted that inasmuch as secrecy is an essential feature of "free and fair elections", Rules 41(2) and (3) and 49-O of the Rules violate the requirement of secrecy.

10. Ms. Kamini Jaiswal and Mr. Raghenth Basant, learned counsel appearing for the impleading parties, while agreeing with the stand of the petitioners as well as the Election Commission of India, prayed that necessary directions may be issued for providing another button viz. "None of the Above (NOTA)" in the electronic voting machines (EVMs) so that the voters who come to the polling booth and decide not to vote for any of the candidates, are able to exercise their right not to vote while maintaining their right of secrecy.

11. We have carefully considered the rival submissions and perused the relevant provisions of the RP Act and the Rules.

Discussion

12. In order to answer the above contentions, it is vital to refer to the relevant provisions of the RP Act and the Rules. Sections 79(d) and 128 of the RP Act read as under :

> *"79. **(d)** - 'electoral right' means the right of a person to stand or not to stand as, or to withdraw or not to withdraw from being, a candidate, or to vote or refrain from voting at an election.*
>
> ***128.Maintenance of secrecy of voting.**—(1) Every officer, clerk, agent or other person who performs any duty in connection with the recording or counting of votes at an election shall maintain, and aid in maintaining, the*

secrecy of the voting and shall not (except for some purpose authorised by or under any law) communicate to any person any information calculated to violate such secrecy :

Provided that the provisions of this sub-section shall not apply to such officer, clerk, agent or other person who performs any such duty at an election to fill a seat or seats in the Council of States.

(2) Any person who contravenes the provisions of sub-section (1) shall be punishable with imprisonment for a term which may extend to three months or with fine or with both."

Rules 39(1), 41, 49-M and 49-O of the Rules read as under :

"39. Maintenance of secrecy of voting by electors within polling station and voting procedure.*—(1) Every elector to whom a ballot paper has been issued under Rule 38 or under any other provision of these Rules, shall maintain secrecy of voting within the polling station and for that purpose observe the voting procedure hereinafter laid down.*

41. Spoilt and returned ballot papers.*—(1) An elector who has inadvertently dealt with his ballot paper in such manner that it cannot be conveniently used as a ballot paper may, on returning it to the Presiding Officer and on satisfying him of the inadvertence, be given another ballot paper, and the ballot paper so returned and the counterfoil of such ballot paper shall be marked 'Spoilt: cancelled' by the Presiding Officer.*

(2) If an elector after obtaining a ballot paper decides not to use it, he shall return it to the Presiding Officer, and the ballot paper so returned and the counterfoil of such ballot paper shall be marked as 'Returned: cancelled' by the Presiding Officer.

(3) All ballot papers cancelled under sub-rule (1) or sub-rule (2) shall be kept in a separate packet.

49M. Maintenance of secrecy of voting by electors within the polling station and voting procedures.*—(1) Every elector who has been permitted to vote under Rule 49-L shall maintain secrecy of voting within the polling station and for that purpose observe the voting procedure hereinafter laid down.*

(2) Immediately on being permitted to vote the elector shall proceed to the Presiding Officer or the polling officer in charge of the control unit of the voting machine who shall, by pressing the appropriate button on the control unit, activate the balloting unit; for recording of elector's vote.

(3) The elector shall thereafter forthwith—

(a) proceed to the voting compartment;

(b) record his vote by pressing the button on the balloting unit against the name and symbol of the candidate for whom he intends to vote; and

(c) come out of the voting compartment and leave the polling station.

(4) Every elector shall vote without undue delay.

(5) No elector shall be allowed to enter the voting compartment when another elector is inside it.

(6) If an elector who has been permitted to vote under Rule 49-L or Rule 49-P refuses after warning given by the Presiding Officer to observe the procedure laid down in sub-rule (3) of the said Rules, the Presiding Officer or a polling officer under the direction of the Presiding Officer shall not allow such elector to vote.

(7) Where an elector is not allowed to vote under sub-rule (6), a remark to the effect that voting procedure has been violated shall be made against the elector's name in the register of voters in Form 17-A by the Presiding Officer under his signature.

49-O. Elector deciding not to vote.—*If an elector, after his electoral roll number has been duly entered in the register of voters in Form 17-A and has put his signature or thumb impression thereon as required under sub-rule (1) of Rule 49-L decided not to record his vote, a remark to this effect shall be made against the said entry in Form 17-A by the Presiding Officer and the signature or thumb impression of the elector shall be obtained against such remark."*

13. Apart from the above provisions, it is also relevant to refer to Article 21(3) of the Universal Declaration of Human Rights and Article 25(b) of the International Covenant on Civil and Political Rights, which read as under :

*"**21(3)** The will of the people shall be the basis of the authority of government; this will shall be expressed in periodic and genuine elections which shall be by universal and equal suffrage and shall be held by secret vote or by equivalent free voting procedures."*

*"**25.** Every citizen shall have the right and the opportunity, without any of the distinctions mentioned in Article 2 and without unreasonable restrictions :*

Sl. No.	Sl. no. of elector in the electoral roll	Details of the document produced by the elector in proof of his/her identification	Signature/Thumb impression of the elector	Remarks
(1)	(2)	(3)	(4)	(5)
1.				
2.				
3.				
4.				

*(a)*** *** ***;*

(b) To vote and to be elected at genuine periodic elections which shall be by universal and equal suffrage and shall be held by secret ballot, guaranteeing the free expression of the will of the electors;"

14. Articles 19(1)(a) and 21 of the Constitution, which are also pertinent for this matter, are as under:

*"**19. Protection of certain rights regarding freedom of speech, etc.**—(1) All citizens shall have the right—*

(a) to freedom of speech and expression;

xxxxx

***21. Protection of life and personal liberty.**—No person shall be deprived ofhis life or personal liberty except according to procedure established by law."*

15. From the above provisions, it is clear that in case an elector decides not to record his vote, a remark to this effect shall be made in Form 17-A by the Presiding Officer and the signature or thumb impression of the elector shall be obtained against such remark. Form 17-A reads as under :

*"**FORM 17-A***
(See Rule 49-L)
REGISTER OF VOTERS
Election to the House of the People/Legislative Assembly of the State/Union Territory .... from .... Constituency No. and name of Polling Station .... Part No. of electoral roll...........

etc.

Signature of the Presiding Officer"

16. Before elaborating the contentions relating to the above provisions with reference to the secrecy of voting, let us first consider the issue of maintainability of the Writ Petition as raised by the Union of India. In the present Writ Petition, which is of the year 2004, the petitioners have prayed for the following reliefs :

> *"(i) declaring that Rules 41(2) and (3) and 49-O of the Conduct of Elections Rules, 1961 are ultra vires and unconstitutional to the extent they violate secrecy of vote;*
>
> *(ii) direct the Election Commission under the existing Representation of the People Act, 1951 and the Conduct of Elections Rules, 1961 and/or under Article 324 to provide necessary provision in the ballot papers and the voting machines for protection of right not to vote and to keep the exercise of such right secret;"*

17. It is relevant to point out that initially the present Writ Petition came up for hearing before a Bench of two-Judges. During the course of hearing, an objection was raised with regard to the maintainability of the writ petition under Article 32 on the ground that the right claimed by the petitioners is not a fundamental right as enshrined in Part III of the Constitution. It is the categorical objection of the Union of India that inasmuch as the writ petition under Article 32 would lie to this Court only for the violation of the fundamental rights and since the right to vote is not a fundamental right, the present writ petition under Article 32 is not maintainable. It is the specific stand of the Union of India that right to vote is not a fundamental right but merely a statutory right. It is further pointed out that this Court in paras 40 and 41 of the referral order dated 23.02.2009, reported in (2009) 3 SCC 200, observed that since in *Kuldip Nayar* [(2006) 7 SCC 1], the judgments of this Court in *Association for Democratic Reforms* [(2002) 5 SCC 294] and *People's Union for Civil Liberties*[(2003) 4 SCC 399] have not been specifically overruled which tend to create a doubt whether the right to vote is a fundamental right or not and referred the same to a larger Bench stating that the issue requires clarity. In view of the reference, we have to decide :

(i) Whether there is any doubt or confusion with regard to the right of a voter in *Kuldip Nayar* [(2006) 7 SCC 1];

(ii) Whether earlier two judgments viz. *Association for Democratic Reforms* [(2002) 5 SCC 294] and *People's Union for Civil Liberties* [(2003) 4 SCC 399] referred to by the Constitution Bench in *Kuldip Nayar* [(2006) 7 SCC 1] stand impliedly overruled.

18. Though Mr. Malhotra relied on a large number of decisions, we are of the view that there is no need to refer to those decisions except a reference to the decision of this Court in *Kuldip Nayar* [(2006) 7 SCC 1], *Association for Democratic Reforms* [(2002) 5 SCC 294] and *People's Union for Civil Liberties* [(2003) 4 SCC 399] .

19. A three-Judge Bench of this Court comprising M.B. Shah, P. Venkatarama Reddi and D.M. Dharmadhikari, JJ. expressed separate but concurring opinions in *People's Union for Civil Liberties* [(2003) 4 SCC 399] . In para 97, Reddi, J. made an observation as to the right to vote being a constitutional right if not a fundamental right which reads as under :

"97. In Jyoti Basu v. Debi Ghosal [(1982) 3 SCR 318] this Court again pointed out in no uncertain terms that :

> *'8. A right to elect, fundamental though it is to democracy, is, anomalously enough, neither a fundamental right nor a common law right. It is pure and simple, a statutory right.'*

With great reverence to the eminent Judges, I would like to clarify that the right to vote, if not a fundamental right, is certainly a constitutional right. The right originates from the Constitution and in accordance with the constitutional mandate contained in Article 326, the right has been shaped by the statute, namely, the RP Act. That, in my understanding, is the correct legal position as regards the nature of the right to vote in elections to the House of the People and Legislative Assemblies. It is not very accurate to describe it as a statutory right, pure and simple. Even with this clarification, the argument of the learned Solicitor General that the right to vote not being a fundamental right, the information which at best facilitates meaningful exercise of that right cannot be read as an integral part of any fundamental right, remains to be squarely met."

Similarly, in para 123, point No. 2 Reddi, J., held as under :

> *"(2) The right to vote at the elections to the House of the People or Legislative Assembly is a constitutional right but not merely a statutory right; freedom of voting as distinct from right to vote is a facet of the fundamental right enshrined in Article 19(1)(a). The casting of vote in favour of one or the other candidate marks the accomplishment of freedom of expression of the voter."*

Except the above two paragraphs, this aspect has nowhere been discussed or elaborated wherein all the three Judges, in their separate but concurring judgments, have taken the pains to specifically distinguish between the right to vote and freedom of voting as a species of freedom of expression. In succinct, the ratio of the judgment was that though the right to vote is a statutory right but the decision taken by a voter after verifying the credentials of the candidate either to vote or not is his right of expression under Article 19(1)(a) of the Constitution.

***20.** As a result, the judgments in Association for Democratic Reforms [(2002) 5 SCC 294] and People's Union for Civil Liberties [(2003) 4 SCC 399] have not disturbed the position that right to vote is a statutory right. Both the judgments have only added that the right to know the background of a candidate is a fundamental right of a voter so that he can take a rational decision of expressing himself while exercising the statutory right to vote. In People's Union for Civil Liberties [(2003) 4 SCC 399], Shah, J. in para 78D, held as under :*

> *"...However, voters' fundamental right to know the antecedents of a candidate is independent of statutory rights under the election law. A voter is first citizen of this country and apart from statutory rights, he is having fundamental rights conferred by the Constitution..."*

P. Venkatarama Reddi, J., in para 97, held as under :

"...Though the initial right cannot be placed on the pedestal of a fundamental right, but, at the stage when the voter goes to the polling booth and casts his vote, his freedom to express arises. The casting of vote in favour of one or the other candidate tantamounts to expression of his opinion and preference and that final stage in the exercise of voting right marks the accomplishment of freedom of expression of the voter. That is where Article 19(1)(a) is attracted. Freedom of voting as distinct from right to vote is thus a species of freedom of expression and therefore carries with it the auxiliary and complementary rights such as right to secure information about the candidate which are conducive to the freedom..."

Dharmadhikari, J., in para 127, held as under :

"...This freedom of a citizen to participate and choose a candidate at an election is distinct from exercise of his right as a voter which is to be regulated by statutory law on the election like the RP Act..."

In view of the above, para 362 in *Kuldip Nayar* [(2006) 7 SCC 1] does not hold to the contrary, which reads as under :

"We do not agree with the above submission. It is clear that a fine distinction was drawn between the right to vote and the freedom of voting as a species of freedom of expression, while reiterating the view in Jyoti Basu v. Debi Ghosal that a right to elect, fundamental though it is to democracy, is neither a fundamental right nor a common law right, but pure and simple, a statutory right."

21. After a careful perusal of the verdicts of this Court in *Kuldip Nayar* [(2006) 7 SCC 1], *Association for Democratic Reforms* [(2002) 5 SCC 294] and *People's Union for Civil Liberties* [(2003) 4 SCC 399], we are of the considered view that *Kuldip Nayar* [(2006) 7 SCC 1] does not overrule the other two decisions rather it only reaffirms what has already been said by the aforesaid two decisions. The said paragraphs recognise that right to vote is a statutory right and also in *People's Union for Civil Liberties* [(2003) 4 SCC 399] it was held that "a fine distinction was drawn between the right to vote and the freedom of voting as a species of freedom of expression". Therefore, it cannot be said that *Kuldip Nayar* [(2006) 7 SCC 1] has observed anything to the contrary. In view of the whole debate of whether these two decisions were overruled or discarded because of the opening line in para 362 of *Kuldip Nayar* [(2006) 7 SCC 1] i.e., "we do not agree with the above submissions..." we are of the opinion that this line must be read as a whole and not in isolation. The contention of the petitioners in *Kuldip Nayar* [(2006) 7 SCC 1] was that majority view in *People's Union for Civil Liberties* [(2003) 4 SCC 399] held that right to vote is a constitutional right besides that it is also a facet of the fundamental right under Article 19(1)(a) of the Constitution. It is this contention on which the Constitution Bench did not agree too in the opening line in para 362 and thereafter went on to clarify that in fact in *People's Union for Civil Liberties* [(2003) 4 SCC 399], a fine distinction was drawn between the right to vote and the freedom of voting as a species of freedom of expression. Thus, there is no contradiction as to the fact that right to vote is neither a fundamental right nor a constitutional right but a pure and simple statutory right. The same has been settled in a catena of cases and it is clearly not an issue in dispute in the present case. With the above observation, we hold that there is no doubt or confusion persisting in the Constitution Bench judgment of this Court in *Kuldip Nayar* [(2006) 7 SCC 1] and the decisions in *Association for Democratic Reforms* [(2002) 5 SCC 294] and *People's Union for Civil Liberties (PUCL)* [(2003) 4 SCC 399] do not stand impliedly overruled.

Whether the present writ petition under Article 32 is maintainable

22. In the earlier part of our judgment, we have quoted the reliefs prayed for by the petitioners in the writ petition. Mr. Malhotra, learned Additional Solicitor General, by citing various decisions submitted that since the right to vote is not a fundamental right but is merely a statutory right, hence, the present writ petition under Article 32 is not maintainable and is liable to be dismissed. He referred to the following decisions of this Court in *N.P. Ponnuswami v. Returning Officer* [1952 SCR 218], *Jamuna Prasad Mukhariya v. Lachhi Ram* [1955 (1) SCR 608], *University of Delhi v. Anand Vardhan Chandal* [(2000) 10 SCC 648], *Kuldip Nayar* [(2006) 7 SCC 1] and *K. Krishna Murthy (Dr.) v. Union of India* [(2010) 7 SCC 202] , wherein it has been held that the right to vote is not a fundamental right but is merely a statutory right.

23. In *K.K. Kochunni v. State of Madras* [1959 (2) Supp SCR 316], this Court held that the right to move before this Court under Article 32, when a fundamental right has been breached, is a substantive fundamental right by itself. In a series of cases, this Court has held that it is the duty of this Court to enforce the guaranteed fundamental rights. (Vide *Daryao v. State of U.P.* [1962 (1) SCR 574])

24. The decision taken by a voter after verifying the credentials of the candidate either to vote or not is a form of expression under Article 19(1)(a) of the Constitution. The fundamental right under Article 19(1)(a) read with the statutory right under Section 79(d) of the RP Act is violated unreasonably if right not to vote effectively is denied and secrecy is breached. This is how Articles 14 and 19(1)(a) are required to be read for deciding the issue raised in this writ petition. The casting of the vote is a facet of the right of expression of an individual and the said right is provided under Article 19(1)(a) of the Constitution of India (Vide: *Association for Democratic Reforms* [(2002) 5 SCC 294] and *People's Union for Civil Liberties* [(2003) 4 SCC 399]). Therefore, any violation of the said rights gives the aggrieved person the right to approach this Court under Article 32 of the Constitution of India. In view of the abovesaid decisions as well as the observations of the Constitution Bench in *Kuldip Nayar* [(2006) 7 SCC 1], a prima facie case exists for the exercise of jurisdiction of this Court under Article 32.

25. Apart from the above, we would not be justified in asking the petitioners to approach the High Court to vindicate their grievance by way of a writ petition under Article 226 of the Constitution of India at this juncture. Considering the reliefs prayed for which relate to the right of a voter and applicable to all eligible voters, it may not be appropriate to direct the petitioners to go to each and every High Court and seek appropriate relief. Accordingly, apart from our conclusion on the legal issue, in view of the fact that the writ petition is pending before this Court for the last more than nine years, it may not be proper to reject the same on the ground, as pleaded by the learned ASG. For the reasons mentioned above, we reject the said contention and hold that this Court is competent to hear the issues raised in this writ petition filed under Article 32 of the Constitution.

Discussion about the relief prayed for in the writ petition

26. We have already quoted the relevant provisions, particularly, Section 128 of the RP Act and Rules 39, 41, 49-M and 49-O of the Rules. It is clear from the above provisions that secrecy of casting vote is duly recognised and is necessary for strengthening democracy. We are of the opinion that paras 441, 442 and 452 to 454 of the decision of the Constitution Bench in *Kuldip Nayar* [(2006) 7 SCC 1] are relevant for this purpose which are extracted hereinbelow :

> *"441. Voting at elections to the Council of States cannot be compared with a general election. In a general election, the electors have to vote in a secret manner without fear that their votes would be disclosed to anyone or would result in victimisation. There is no party affiliation and hence the choice is entirely with the voter. This is not the case when elections are held to the Council of States as the electors are elected Members of the Legislative Assemblies who in turn have party affiliations.*
>
> *442. The electoral systems world over contemplate variations. No one yardstick can be applied to an electoral system. The question whether election is direct or indirect and for which House members are to be chosen is a relevant aspect. All over the world in democracies, Members of the House of Representatives are chosen directly by popular vote. Secrecy there is a must and insisted upon; in representative democracy, particularly to the Upper Chamber, indirect means of election adopted on party lines is well-accepted practice.*
>
> *452. Parliamentary democracy and multi-party system are an inherent part of the basic structure of the Indian Constitution. It is the political parties that set up candidates at an election who are predominantly elected as Members of the State Legislatures. The context in which general elections are held, secrecy of the vote is necessary in order to maintain the purity of the electoral system. Every voter has a right to vote in a free and fair manner and not disclose to any person how he has voted. But here we are concerned with a voter who is elected on the ticket of a political party. In this view, the context entirely changes.*
>
> *453. That the concept of 'constituency-based representation' is different from 'proportional representation' has been eloquently brought out in United Democratic Movement v. President of the Republic of South Africa [(2003) 1 SA 495] where the question before the Supreme Court was: whether 'floor crossing' was fundamental to the Constitution of South Africa. In this judgment the concept of proportional representation vis-à-vis*

constituency-based representation is highlighted....

454. The distinguishing feature between 'constituency-based representation' and 'proportional representation' in a representative democracy is that in the case of the list system of proportional representation, members are elected on party lines. They are subject to party discipline. They are liable to be expelled for breach of discipline. Therefore, to give effect to the concept of proportional representation, Parliament can suggest 'open ballot'. In such a case, it cannot be said that 'free and fair elections' would stand defeated by 'open ballot'. As stated above, in a constituency-based election it is the people who vote whereas in proportional representation it is the elector who votes. This distinction is indicated also in the Australian judgment in R. v. Jones [(1972) 128 CLR 221 (Aust)]. ***In constituency-based representation, 'secrecy' is the basis*** *whereas in the case of proportional representation in a representative democracy the basis can be 'open ballot' and it would not violate the concept of 'free and fair elections', which concept is one of the pillars of democracy."*

27. The above discussion in the cited paragraphs makes it clear that in direct elections to the Lok Sabha or State Legislatures, maintenance of secrecy is a must and is insisted upon all over the world in democracies where direct elections are involved to ensure that a voter casts his vote without any fear of being victimised if his vote is disclosed.

28. After referring to Section 128 of the RP Act and Rule 39 of the Rules, this Court in*S. Raghbir Singh Gill v. S. Gurcharan Singh Tohra* [1980 (Supp) SCC 53] held as under :

"14. ...Secrecy of ballot can be appropriately styled as a postulate of constitutional democracy. It enshrines a vital principle of parliamentary institutions set up under the Constitution. It subserves a very vital public interest in that an elector or a voter should be absolutely free in exercise of his franchise untrammelled by any constraint which includes constraint as to the disclosure. A remote or distinct possibility that at some point a voter may under a compulsion of law be forced to disclose for whom he has voted would act as a positive constraint and check on his freedom to exercise his franchise in the manner he freely chooses to exercise. Therefore, it can be said with confidence that this postulate of constitutional democracy rests on public policy."

29. In the earlier part of this judgment, we have referred to Article 21(3) of the Universal Declaration of Human Rights and Article 25(b) of the International Covenant on Civil and Political Rights, which also recognise the right of secrecy.

30. With regard to the first prayer of the petitioners viz. extension of principle of secrecy of ballot to those voters who decide not to vote, Mr. Malhotra, learned ASG, submitted that the principle of secrecy of ballot is extended only to those voters who have cast their votes in favour of one or the other candidates, but the same, in no manner, can be read as extended to even those voters who have not voted in the election. He further pointed out that the principle of secrecy of ballot presupposes validly cast vote and the object of secrecy is to assure a voter to allow him to cast his vote without any fear and in no manner it will be disclosed that in whose favour he has voted or he will not be compelled to disclose in whose favour he voted. The pith and substance of his argument is that secrecy of ballot is a principle which has been formulated to ensure a voter (who has exercised his right to vote) that in no case it shall be known to the candidates or their representatives that in whose favour a particular voter has voted so that he can exercise his right to vote freely and fearlessly. The stand of the Union of India as projected by the learned ASG is that the principle of secrecy of ballot is extended only to those voters who have cast their vote and the same in no manner can be extended to those who have not voted at all.

31. Right to vote as well as right not to vote have been statutorily recognised under Section 79(d) of the RP Act and Rules 41(2) and (3) and 49-O of the Rules respectively. Whether a voter decides to cast his vote or decides not to cast his vote, in both cases, secrecy has to be maintained. It cannot be said that if a voter decides to cast his vote, secrecy will be maintained under Section 128 of the RP Act read with Rules 39 and 49-M of the Rules and if in case a voter decides not to cast his vote, secrecy will not be maintained. Therefore, a part of Rule 49-O read with Form 17-A, which treats a voter who decides not to cast his vote differently and allows the secrecy to be violated, is arbitrary, unreasonable and violative of Article 19 and is also ultra vires Sections 79(d) and 128 of the RP Act.

32. As regards the question as to whether the right of expression under Article 19 stands infringed when secrecy of the poll is not maintained, it is useful to refer *S. Raghbir Singh* [1980 (Supp) SCC 53] wherein this Court deliberated on the interpretation of Section 94 of the RP Act which mandates that no elector can be compelled as a witness to disclose his vote. In that case, this Court found that the "secrecy of ballots constitutes a postulate of constitutional democracy... A remote or distinct possibility that the voter at some point of time may under a compulsion of law be forced to disclose for whom he has voted would act as a positive constraint and check on his freedom to exercise his franchise in the manner he freely chooses to exercise". Secrecy of ballot, thus, was held to be a privilege granted in public interest to an individual. It is pertinent to note that in the said case, the issue of the disclosure by an elector of his vote arose in the first place because there was an allegation that the postal ballot of an MLA was tampered with to secure the victory of one of the candidates to the Rajya Sabha. Therefore, seemingly there was a conflict between the "fair vote" and "secret ballot".

33. In *Kuldip Nayar* [(2006) 7 SCC 1] this Court held that though secrecy of ballots is a vital principle for ensuring free and fair elections, the higher principle is free and fair elections. However, in the same case, this Court made a copious distinction between "constituency-based representation" and "proportional representation". It was held that while in the former, secrecy is the basis, in the latter the system of open ballot and it would not be violative of "free and fair elections". In the said case *R.* v. *Jones* [(1972) 128 CLR 221 (Aust)], and *United Democratic Movement v. President of the Republic of South Africa* [(2003) 1 SA 495] were also cited with approval.

34. Therefore, in view of the decisions of this Court in *S. Raghbir Singh Gill* [1980 (Supp) SCC 53] and *Kuldip Nayar* [(2006) 7 SCC 1], the policy is clear that secrecy principle is integral to free and fair elections which can be removed only when it can be shown that there is any conflict between secrecy and the "higher principle" of free elections. The instant case concerns elections to the Central and State Legislatures that are undoubtedly "constituency based". No discernible public interest shall be served by disclosing the elector's vote or his identity. Therefore, secrecy is an essential feature of the "free and fair elections" and Rule 49-O undoubtedly violates that requirement.

35. In *Lily Thomas v. Speaker, Lok Sabha* [(1993) 4 SCC 234] this Court held that *"voting is a formal expression of will or opinion by the person entitled to exercise the right on the subject or issue in question" and that "right to vote means right to exercise the right in favour of or against the motion or resolution. Such a right implies right to remain neutral as well".*

36. In view of the same, this Court also referred to the Practice and Procedure of Parliament for voting which provides for three buttons viz. AYES, NOES and ABSTAIN whereby a member can abstain or refuse from expressing his opinion by casting vote in favour or against the motion. The constitutional interpretation given by this Court was based on inherent philosophy of parliamentary sovereignty.

37. A perusal of Section 79(d) of the RP Act, Rules 41(2) and (3) and Rule 49-O of the Rules makes it clear that a right not to vote has been recognised both under the RP Act and the Rules. A positive "right not to vote" is a part of expression of a voter in a parliamentary democracy and it has to be recognised and given effect to in the same manner as "right to vote". A voter may refrain from voting at an election for several reasons including the reason that he does not consider any of the candidates in the field worthy of his vote. One of the ways of such expression may be to abstain from voting, which is not an ideal option for a conscientious and responsible citizen. Thus, the only way by which it can be made effectual is by providing a button in the EVMs to express that right. This is the basic requirement if the lasting values in a healthy democracy have to be sustained, which the Election Commission has not only recognised but has also asserted.

38. The Law Commission of India, in its 170th Report relating to Reform of the Electoral Laws recommended for implementation of the concept of negative vote and also pointed out its advantages.

39. In India, elections traditionally have been held with ballot papers. As explained by the Election Commission, from 1998 onwards, the electronic voting machines (EVMs) were introduced on a large scale. Formerly, under the ballot paper system, it was possible to secretly cast a neutral/negative vote by going to the polling booth, marking presence and dropping one's ballot in the ballot box without making any mark on the same. However, under the system of EVMs, such secret neutral voting is not possible, in view of the provision of Rule 49-B of the Rules and the design of the EVM and other related voting procedures. Rule 49-B of the Rules mandates that the names of the candidates shall be arranged on the balloting unit in the same order in which they appear in the list of contesting candidates and there is no provision for a neutral button.

40. It was further clarified by the Election Commission that EVM comprises of two units i.e. control and balloting units, which are interconnected by a cable. While the balloting unit is placed in a screened enclosure where an elector may cast his vote in secrecy, the control unit remains under the charge of the Presiding Officer and so placed that all polling agents and others present have an unhindered view of all the operations. The balloting unit, placed inside the screened compartment at the polling station gets activated for recording votes only when the button marked "Ballot" on the control unit is pressed by the Presiding Officer/Polling Officer-in-charge. Once the ballot button is pressed, the control unit emanates red light while the ballot unit which has been activated to receive the vote emanates green light. Once an elector casts his vote by pressing balloting button against the candidate of his choice, he can see a red light glow against the name and symbol of that candidate and a high-pitched beep sound emanates from the machine. Upon such casting of vote, the balloting unit is blocked, green light emanates on the control unit, which is in public gaze, and the high-pitched beep sound is heard by one and all. Thereafter, the EVM has to reactivate for the next elector by pressing "ballot button". However, should an elector choose not to cast his vote in favour of any of the candidates labelled on the EVM, and consequently, not press any of the labelled buttons, neither will the light on the control unit change from red to green nor will the beep sound emanate. Hence, all present in the poll booth at the relevant time will come to know that a vote has not been cast by the elector.

41. Rule 49-O of the Rules provides that if an elector, after his electoral roll number has been entered in the register of electors in Form 17-A, decides not to record his vote on the EVM, a remark to this effect shall be made against the said entry in Form 17-A by the Presiding Officer and signature/thumb impression of the elector shall be obtained against such remark. As is apparent, mechanism of casting vote through EVM and Rule 49-O compromise on the secrecy of the vote as the elector is not provided any privacy when the fact of the neutral/negative voting goes into record.

42. Rules 49A to 49X of the Rules come under Chapter II of Part IV of the Rules. Chapter II deals with voting by electronic voting machines only. Therefore, Rule 49-O, which talks about Form 17-A, is applicable only in cases of voting by EVMs. The said Chapter was introduced in the Rules by way of an amendment dated 24.03.1992. Voting by ballot papers is governed by Chapter I of Part IV of the Rules. Rule 39 talks about secrecy while voting by ballot and Rule 41 talks about ballot papers. However, as said earlier, in the case of voting by ballot paper, the candidate always had the option of not putting the cross mark against the names of any of the candidates and thereby record his disapproval for all the candidates in the fray. Even though such a ballot paper would be considered as an invalid vote, the voter still had the right not to vote for anybody without compromising on his/her right of secrecy. However, with the introduction of EVMs, the said option of not voting for anybody without compromising the right of secrecy is not available to the voter since the voting machines did not have "None of the Above" (NOTA) button.

43. It is also pointed out that in order to rectify this serious defect, on 10.12.2001, the Election Commission addressed a letter to the Secretary, Ministry of Law and Justice stating, *inter alia*, that the "electoral right" under Section 79(d) includes a right not to cast vote and sought to provide a panel in the EVMs so that an elector may indicate that he does not wish to vote for any of the aforementioned candidates. The letter also stated that such number of votes expressing dissatisfaction with all the candidates may be recorded in a result sheet. It is also brought to our notice that no action was taken on the said letter dated 10.12.2001.

44. The Election Commission further pointed out that in the larger interest of promoting democracy, a provision for "None of the Above" or "NOTA" button should be made in the EVMs/ballot papers. It is also highlighted that such an action, apart from promoting free and fair elections in a democracy, will provide an opportunity to the elector to express his dissent/disapproval against the contesting candidates and will have the benefit of reducing bogus voting.

45. Democracy and free elections are a part of the basic structure of the Constitution. In *Indira Nehru Gandhi v. Raj Narain* [1975 Supp 1 SCC 198], Khanna, J..held that democracy postulates that there should be periodic elections where the people should be in a position to re-elect their old representatives or change the representatives or elect in their place new representatives. It was also held that democracy can function only when elections are free and fair and the people are free to vote for the candidates of their choice. In the said case, Article 19 was not in issue and the observations were in the context of basic structure of the Constitution. Thereafter, this Court reiterated that democracy is the basic structure of the Constitution in *Mohinder Singh Gill* v. *Chief Election Commissioner* [(1978) 1 SCC 405] and *Kihoto Hollohan* v. *Zachillhu* [1992 (Supp) 2 SCC 651].

46. In order to protect the right in terms of Section 79(d) and Rule 49-O viz. "right not to vote", we are of the view that this Court is competent/well within its power to issue directions that secrecy of a voter who decides not to cast his vote has to be protected in the same manner as the statute has protected the right of a voter who decides to cast his vote in favour of a candidate. This Court is also justified in giving such directions in order to give effect to the right of expression under Article 19(1)(a) and to avoid any discrimination by directing the Election Commission to provide NOTA button in the EVMs.

47. With regard to the above, Mr. Malhotra, learned ASG, by drawing our attention to Section 62 of the RP Act, contended that this section enables a person to cast a vote and it has no scope for negative voting. Section 62(1) of the RP Act reads as under:

> "**62. Right to vote**.—(1) No person who is not, and except as expressly provided by this Act, every person who is, for the time being entered in the electoral roll of any constituency shall be entitled to vote in that constituency."

48. Mr. Malhotra, learned ASG has also pointed out that elections are conducted to fill a seat by electing a person by a positive voting in his favour and there is no concept of negative voting under the RP Act. According to him, the Act does not envisage that a voter has any right to cast a negative vote if he does not like any of the candidates. Referring to Section 2(*d*) of the RP Act, he asserted that election is only a means of choice or election between various candidates to fill a seat. Finally, he concluded that negative voting (NOTA) has no legal consequence and there shall be no motivation for the voters to travel to the polling booth and reject all the candidates, which would have the same effect of not going to the polling station at all.

49. However, correspondingly, we should also appreciate that the election is a mechanism which ultimately represents the will of the people. The essence of the electoral system should be to ensure freedom of voters to exercise their free choice. Article 19 guarantees all individuals the right to speak, criticise, and disagree on a particular issue. It stands on the spirit of tolerance and allows people to have diverse views, ideas and ideologies. Not allowing a person to cast vote negatively defeats the very freedom of expression and the right ensured in Article 21 i.e. the right to liberty.

50. Eventually, voters' participation explains the strength of the democracy. Lesser voter participation is the rejection of commitment to democracy slowly but definitely whereas larger participation is better for the democracy. But, there is no yardstick to determine what the correct and right voter participation is. If introducing a NOTA button can increase the participation of democracy then, in our cogent view, nothing should stop the same. The voters' participation in the election is indeed the participation in the democracy itself. Non-participation causes frustration and disinterest, which is not a healthy sign of a growing democracy like India.

Conclusion

51. Democracy being the basic feature of our constitutional set-up, there can be no two opinions that free and fair elections would alone guarantee the growth of a healthy democracy in the country. The "fair" denotes equal opportunity to all people. Universal adult suffrage conferred on the citizens of India by the Constitution has made it possible for these millions of individual voters to go to the polls and thus participate in the governance of our country. For democracy to survive, it is essential that the best available men should be chosen as people's representatives for proper governance of the country. This can be best achieved through men of high moral and ethical values, who win the elections on a positive vote. Thus in a vibrant democracy, the voter must be given an opportunity to choose none of the above (NOTA) button, which will indeed compel the political parties to nominate a sound candidate. This situation palpably tells us the dire need of negative voting.

52. No doubt, the right to vote is a statutory right but it is equally vital to recollect that this statutory right is the essence of democracy. Without this, democracy will fail to thrive. Therefore, even if the right to vote is statutory, the significance attached with the right is massive. Thus, it is necessary to keep in mind these facets while deciding the issue at hand.

53. Democracy is all about choice. This choice can be better expressed by giving the voters an opportunity to verbalise themselves unreservedly and by imposing least restrictions on their ability to make such a choice. By providing NOTA button in the EVMs, it will accelerate the effective political participation in the present state of democratic system and the voters in fact will be empowered. We are of the considered view that in bringing out this right to cast negative vote at a time when electioneering is in full swing, it will foster the purity of the electoral process and also fulfil one of its objective, namely, wide participation of people.

54. Free and fair election is a basic structure of the Constitution and necessarily includes within its ambit the right of an elector to cast his vote without fear of reprisal, duress or coercion. Protection of elector's identity and affording secrecy is therefore integral to free and fair elections and an arbitrary distinction between the voter who casts his vote and the voter who does not cast his vote is violative of Article 14. Thus, secrecy is required to be maintained for both categories of persons.

55. Giving right to a voter not to vote for any candidate while protecting his right of secrecy is extremely important in a democracy. Such an option gives the voter the right to express his disapproval with the kind of candidates that are being put up by the political parties. When the political parties will realise that a large number of people are expressing their disapproval with the candidates being put up by them, gradually there will be a systemic change and the political parties will be forced to accept the will of the people and field candidates who are known for their integrity.

56. The direction can also be supported by the fact that in the existing system a dissatisfied voter ordinarily does not turn up for voting which in turn provides a chance to unscrupulous elements to impersonate the dissatisfied voter and cast a vote, be it a negative one. Furthermore, a provision of negative voting would be in the interest of promoting democracy as it would send clear signals to political parties and their candidates as to what the electorate thinks about them.

57. As mentioned above, the voting machines in Parliament have three buttons, namely, AYES, NOES, and ABSTAIN. Therefore, it can be seen that an option has been given to the members to press the ABSTAIN button. Similarly, the NOTA button being sought for by the petitioners is exactly similar to the ABSTAIN button since by pressing the nota button the voter is in effect saying that he is abstaining from voting since he does not find any of the candidates to be worthy of his vote.

58. The mechanism of negative voting, thus, serves a very fundamental and essential part of a vibrant democracy. The following countries have provided for neutral/protest/negative voting in their electoral systems :

Sl. No.	Name of the country	Method of voting	Form of negative vote
1.	France	Electronic	NOTA
2.	Belgium	Electronic	NOTA
3.	Brazil	Ballot paper	NOTA
4.	Greece	Ballot paper	NOTA
5.	Ukraine	Ballot paper	NOTA
6.	Chile	Ballot paper	NOTA
7.	Bangladesh	Ballot paper	NOTA
8.	State of Nevada, USA	Ballot paper	NOTA
9.	Finland	Ballot paper	Blank vote and/or "write-in*"
10.	Sweden	Ballot paper	Blank vote and/or "write-in*"
11.	United States of America	Electronic/Ballot (Depending on State)	Blank vote and/or "write-in*"
12.	Colombia	Ballot paper	Blank vote
13.	Spain	Ballot paper	Blank vote

* 'Write-in'—The 'write-in' the form of negative voting allows a voter to cast a vote in favour of any fictional name/candidate.

59. The Election Commission also brought to the notice of this Court that the present electronic voting machines can be used in a constituency where the number of contesting candidates is up to 64. However, in the event of there being more than 64 candidates in the poll fray, the conventional system of ballot paper is resorted to. The learned counsel appearing for the Election Commission also asserted through supplementary written submission that the Election Commission of India is presently exploring the possibility of developing balloting unit with 200 panels. Therefore, it was submitted that if in case this Court decides to uphold the prayers of the petitioners herein, the additional panel on the balloting unit after the last panel containing the name and election symbol of the last contesting candidate can be utilised as the NOTA button. Further, it was explicitly asserted in the written submission that the provision for the above facility for a negative or neutral vote can be provided in the existing electronic voting machines without any additional cost or administrative effort or change in design or technology of the existing machines. For illustration, if there are 12 candidates contesting an election, the 13th panel on the balloting unit will contain the words like "None of the Above" and the ballot button against this panel will be kept open and the elector who does not wish to vote for any of the abovementioned 12 contesting candidates, can press the button against the 13th panel and his vote will be accordingly recorded by the control unit. At the time of the counting, the votes recorded against Serial Number 13 will indicate as to how many electors have decided not to vote for any candidate.

60. Taking note of the submissions of the Election Commission, we are of the view that the implementation of the NOTA button will not require much effort except for allotting the last panel in the EVM for the same.

61. In the light of the above discussion, we hold that Rules 41(2) and (3) and Rule 49-O of the Rules are ultra vires Section 128 of the RP Act and Article 19(1)(a) of the Constitution to the extent they violate secrecy of voting. In view of our conclusion, we direct the Election Commission to provide necessary provision in the ballot papers/EVMs and another button called "None of the Above" (NOTA) may be provided in EVMs so that the voters, who come to the polling booth and decide not to vote for any of the candidates in the fray, are able to exercise their right not to vote while maintaining their right of secrecy. Inasmuch as the Election Commission itself is in favour of the provision for NOTA in EVMs, we direct the Election Commission to implement the same either in a phased manner or at a time with the assistance of the Government of India. We also direct the Government of India to provide necessary help for implementation of the above direction. Besides, we also direct the Election Commission to undertake awareness programmes to educate the masses.

62. The writ petition is disposed of with the aforesaid directions.

In the Supreme Court of India

Writ Petition (Criminal) No. 612 of 1992
People's Union for Civil Liberties (PUCL) v. Union of India & Anr.[5]

Date of Judgement : 05.02.1997
Bench : B.P. Jeevan Reddy and Suhas C. Sen, JJ.

[PUCL had taken up the case of killing of two persons in a fake encounter by Imphal Police by filing a Writ Petition under Article 32 of the Constitution. The Supreme Court had directed conduct of an enquiry by the District and Sessions Judge, Churachandpur. In the enquiry report, the District and Sessions Judge found that two persons were shot dead by the police while in custody. The Supreme Court held that "administrative liquidation" is not a course open to the police under the Rule of Law. The Court found that it was a case of fake encounter and, therefore, awarded compensation of Rs. 1 lakh each to the families of the two deceased. PUCL was given cost of Rs. 10,000 for filing the Petition and pursuing it for nearly 5 years.]

Judgment

B.P. Jeevan Reddy, J.

1. People's Union for Civil Liberties has filed this writ petition under Article 32 of the Constitution of India for issuance of a writ of mandamus or other appropriate order or direction (1) to institute a judicial inquiry into the fake encounter by Imphal Police on 03.04.1991 in which two persons of Lunthilian Village were killed, (2) to direct appropriate action to be taken against the erring police officials and (3) to award compensation to the members of the families of the deceased. According to the petitioner, there was in truth no encounter but it was a case where certain villagers were caught by the police during the night of 03.04.1991, taken in a truck to a distan t place and two of them killed there. It is alleged that three other persons who were also caught and taken away along with two deceased persons were kept in police custody for a number of days and taken to Mizoram. They were released on bail only on 22.07.1991. It is further submitted that Hamar Peoples' Convention is a political party active in Mizoram. It is not an unlawful organization. Even according to the news released by

5. (1997) 3 SCC 433

the said organization, it was a case of deliberate killing. Though representations were made to the Chief Minister of Manipur and other officials, no action was taken. Along with the writ petition, affidavit of the persons who were taken into custody along with the deceased, taken in a truck and kept in custody for a number of days, were filed. Affidavits of the wives of the deceased were also filed setting out the miserable condition of their families after the death of their respective husbands. On notice being given, a counter-affidavit was filed by the Joint Secretary (Home), Government of Manipur denying the allegations. The allegation of "fake encounter" was denied. It was submitted that there was genuine cross-firing between the police and the activists of Hamar Peoples' Convention during which the said two deaths took place. The report of the Superintendent of Police, Churachandpur was relied upon in support of the said averment. It was submitted that Hamar Peoples' Convention was indulging in illegal and terrorist activities and in acts disturbing the public order. Particulars of several FIRs issued in respect of crimes committed by them under different police stations in that area were set out. The truth and correctness of the supporting affidavits was also disputed. Along with the counter-affidavit, copies of post-mortem reports were filed.

2. After hearing the counsel for both the parties, this Court directed, by its order dated 30.05.1995, that the learned District and Sessions Judge, Churachandpur shall make an inquiry into the alleged incident and submit his report as to what exactly happened on that day. Subsequently, that inquiry was entrusted to the learned District and Sessions Judge, Manipur (West), who has submitted his report dated 08.04.1996. The learned District and Sessions Judge has concluded that :

> *"there was no encounter in the night between 03.04.1991 and 04.04.1991 at Nungthulien Village. The two deceased, namely, Lalbeiklien and Saikaplien were shot dead by the police while in custody on 04.04.1991".*

The State of Manipur has filed its objections to the report along with certain documents which according to them purport to disprove the correctness of finding recorded by the learned District and Sessions Judge.

3. We have heard the counsel for the parties. We are not satisfied that there are any reasons for not accepting the report of the learned District and Sessions Judge which means that the said two deceased persons were taken into custody on the night of 03.04.1991, taken in a truck to a long distance away and shot there. The question is what are the reliefs that should be granted in this writ petition?

4.It is submitted by Ms. S. Janani, the learned counsel for the State of Manipur, that Manipur is a disturbed area, that there are several terrorist groups operating in the State, that Hamar Peoples' Convention is one of such terrorist organizations, that they have been indulging in a number of crimes affecting the public order — indeed, affecting the security of the State. It is submitted that there have been regular encounters and exchange of fire between police and terrorists on a number of occasions. A number of citizens have suffered at the hands of terrorists and many people have been killed. The situation is not a normal one. Information was received by the police that terrorists were gathering in the house on that night and on the basis of that information, police conducted the raid. The raiding party was fortunate that the people inside the house including the deceased did not notice the police, in which case the police would have suffered serious casualties. The police party was successful in surprising the terrorists. There was exchange of fire resulting in the death of the terrorists.

5. In view of the fact that we have accepted the finding recorded by the learned District and Sessions Judge, it is not possible to accede to the contention of Ms. Janani insofar as the manner in which the incident had taken place. It is true that Manipur is a disturbed area, that there appears to be a good amount of terrorist activity affecting public order and, may be, even security of that State. It may also be that under these conditions, certain additional and unusual powers have to be given to the police to deal with terrorism. It may be necessary to fight terrorism with a strong hand which may involve vesting of good amount of discretion in the police officers or other paramilitary forces engaged in fighting them. If the version of the police with respect to the incident in question were true, there could have been no question of any interference by the court. Nobody can say that the police should wait till they are shot at. It is for the force on the spot to decide when to act, how to act and where to act. It is not for the court to say how the terrorists should be fought. We cannot be blind to the fact that even after fifty years of our independence, our territorial integrity is not fully secure. There are several types of separatist and terrorist activities in several parts of the country. They have to be subdued. Whether they should be fought politically or be dealt with by force is a matter of policy for the Government to determine. The courts may not be the appropriate forum to determine those questions. All this is beyond dispute. But the present case appears to be one where two persons along with some others were just seized from a hut, taken to a long distance away in a truck and shot there. This type of activity cannot certainly be countenanced by the courts even in the case of disturbed areas. If the police had information that terrorists were gathering at a particular place and if they had surprised them and arrested them, the proper course for them was to deal with them according to law. "Administrative liquidation" was certainly not a course open to them.

6. Shri Rajindar Sachar, learned counsel for the petitioner, submits that in view of the findings of the learned District and Sessions Judge, this is a proper case where this Court should order the prosecution of the police officials concerned and also award compensation to the families of the deceased.

7. In *Challa Ramkonda Reddy v. State of A.P.* [1989 AIR (AP) 235 : (1989) 2 Andh LT 1], a decision of the Division Bench of the Andhra Pradesh High Court, one of us (B.P. Jeevan Reddy, J.) dealt with the liability of the State where it deprives a citizen of his right to life guaranteed by Article 21. It was held :

> *"In our opinion, the right to life and liberty guaranteed by Article 21 is so fundamental and basic that no compromise is possible with this right. It is 'non-negotiable'. ... The State has no right to take any action which will deprive a citizen of the enjoyment of this basic right except in accordance with a law which is reasonable, fair and just."*

The decision also dealt with the question whether the plea of sovereign immunity is available in such a case. The following observations are relevant :

"The question, however, arises whether it is open to the State to deprive a citizen of his life and liberty otherwise than in accordance with the procedure prescribed by law and yet claim an immunity on the ground that the said deprivation of life occurred while the officers of the State were exercising the sovereign power of the State?

Can the fundamental right to life guaranteed by Article 21 be defeated by pleading the archaic defence of sovereign functions? Does it mean that the said theory clothes the State with the right to violate the fundamental right to life and liberty, guaranteed by Article 21? In other words, does the said concept constitute an exception to Article 21? We think not. Article 21 does not recognize any exception, and no such exception can be read into it by reference to clause (1) of Article 300. Where a citizen has been deprived of his life, or liberty, otherwise than in accordance with the procedure prescribed by law, it is no answer to say that the said deprivation was brought about while the officials of the State were acting in discharge of the sovereign functions of the State."

8. Reliance was placed in the said decision upon the decision of the Privy Council in *Maharaj v. Attorney General of Trinidad and Tobago* [(1978) 2 All E.R. 670 : 1978 (2) WLR 902 : [1979] A.C. 385, PC]. After setting out the relevant provisions of the Constitution of Trinidad and Tobago, it was pointed out that Section (1) of that Constitution corresponds inter alia to Section 21 of our Constitution, while Section 2 and Section 6 of that Constitution correspond to Articles 13 and 32/226 of our Constitution. Applying the reasoning of the Privy Council, it was held by the High Court :

"The fundamental rights are sacrosanct. They have been variously described as basic, inalienable and indefeasible. The founding-fathers incorporated the exceptions in the articles themselves — wherever they were found advisable, or appropriate. No such exception has been incorporated in Article 21, and we are not prepared to read the archaic concept of immunity of sovereign functions, incorporated in Article 300(1), as an exception to Article 21. True it is that the Constitution must be read as an integrated whole; but, since the right guaranteed by Article 21 is too fundamental and basic to admit of any compromise, we are not prepared to read any exception into it by a process of interpretation. We must presume that, if the founding-fathers intended to provide any exception, they would have said so specifically in Part III itself."

9. In *Nilabati Behera v. State of Orissa* [(1993) 2 SCC 746], this Court (J.S. Verma, Dr. A.S. Anand and N. Venkatachala, JJ.) held that award of compensation in a proceeding under Article 32 by the Supreme Court or under Article 226 by the High Court is a remedy available in public law based on strict liability for contravention of fundamental rights. It is held that the defence of sovereign immunity does not apply in such a case even though it may be available as a defence in private law in an action based on tort. It is held further that the award of damages by the Supreme Court or the High Court in a writ proceeding is distinct from and in addition to the remedy in private law for damages. It is one mode of enforcing the fundamental rights by this Court or High Court. Reliance is placed upon Article 9(5) of the International Covenant on Civil and Political Rights, 1966 which says,

> *"anyone who has been the victim of unlawful arrest or detention shall have an enforceable right to compensation".*

The two opinions rendered by J.S. Verma, J. and Dr. A.S. Anand, J. are unanimous on the aforesaid dicta. The same view has been reiterated very recently by a Bench comprising Kuldip Singh and Dr. A.S. Anand, JJ. in *D.K. Basu v. State of W.B.* [(1997) 1 SCC 416]. The observations in para 54 of the judgment are apposite and may be quoted :

> *"Thus, to sum up, it is now a well-accepted proposition in most of the jurisdictions, that monetary or pecuniary compensation is an appropriate and indeed an effective and sometimes perhaps the only suitable remedy for redressal of the established infringement of the fundamental right to life of a citizen by the public servants and the State is vicariously liable for their acts. The claim of the citizen is based on the principle of strict liability to which the defence of sovereign immunity is not available and the citizen must receive the amount of compensation from the State, which shall have the right to be indemnified by the wrongdoer. In the assessment of compensation, the emphasis has to be on the compensatory and not on punitive element. The objective is to apply balm to the wounds and not to punish the transgressor or the offender, as awarding appropriate punishment for the offence (irrespective of compensation) must be left to the criminal courts in which the offender is prosecuted, which the State, in law, is duty-bound to do. The award of compensation in the public law jurisdiction is also without prejudice to any other action like civil suit for damages which is lawfully available to the victim or the heirs of the deceased victim with respect to the same matter for the tortious act committed by the functionaries of the State. The quantum of compensation will, of course, depend upon the peculiar facts of each case and no strait-jacket formula can be evolved in that behalf. The relief to redress the wrong for the established invasion of the fundamental rights of the citizens, under the public law jurisdiction is, thus, in addition to the traditional remedies and not in derogation of them. The amount of compensation as awarded by the Court and paid by the State to redress the wrong done, may in a given case, be adjusted against any amount which may be awarded to the claimant by way of damages in a civil suit."*

10. The reference to and reliance upon Article 9(5) of the International Covenant on Civil and Political Rights, 1966 in *Nilabati Behera* [(1993) 2 SCC 746] raises an interesting question, viz., to what extent can the provisions of such international covenants/conventions be read into national laws. This issue has been the subject-matter of a recent decision in Australia, viz., *Minister for Immigration and Ethnic Affairs v. Teoh* [(1995) 69 Aus LJ 423]. The United Nations Convention on the Rights of the Child was ratified by the Commonwealth Executive in December 1990 and had force in Australia from 16.01.1991 pursuant to a declaration made on 22.12.1992 by the Attorney General pursuant to Section 47(1) of the Human Rights and Equal Opportunity Commission Act, 1986 to the effect that the said convention is an international instrument relating to human rights. Respondent Teoh, a Malaysian citizen was found to have imported and be in possession of heroin, for which he was convicted. A deportation order was passed on that basis. The Immigration Review Panel opined that deportation of Teoh would deprive his young children (who were Australian citizens) of their only financial support, landing them in bleak misery. Article 3 of the aforesaid Convention provides that :

> *"1. In all actions concerning children, whether undertaken by public or private social welfare institutions, courts of law, administrative authorities or legislative bodies, the best interests of the child shall be a primary consideration."*

Teoh invoked this article to ward off his deportation. The matter was carried to the High Court where the question of enforceability of the Convention by the national courts was thoroughly debated. Mason, C.J., speaking for himself and Dean, J., stated the position in the following words :

> *"It is well established that the provisions of an international treaty to which Australia is a party do not form part of Australian law unless those provisions have been validly incorporated into our municipal law by statute. (Chow Hung Ching v. King [1948 (77) CLR 449], CLR at p. 478; Bradley v. Commonwealth [1973 (128) CLR 557], CLR 582; Simsek v. Macphee [1982 (148) CLR 636], CLR at pp. 641-642; Koowarta v. Bjelke-Petersen [1982 (153) CLR 168], CLR at pp. 211-212, 224-225; Kioa v. West [1985 (159) CLR 550], CLR at p. 570; Dietrich v. Queen [1992 (177) CLR 292], CLR at p. 305; J.H. Rayner Ltd. v. Deptt. of Trade [(1990) 2 A.C. 418], A.C. at p. 550.) This principle has its foundation in the proposition that in our constitutional system the making and ratification of treaties fall within the province of the Executive in the exercise of its prerogative power whereas the making and the alteration of the law fall within the province of Parliament, not the Executive. (Simsek v. Macphee [1982 (148) CLR 636], CLR at pp. 641-642) So, a treaty which has not been incorporated into our municipal law cannot operate as a direct source of individual rights and obligations under that law. In this case, it is common ground that the provisions of the Convention have not been incorporated in this way. It is not suggested that the declaration made pursuant to Section 47(1) of the Human Rights and Equal Opportunity Commission Act has this effect.*
>
> *But the fact that the Convention has not been incorporated into Australian*

law does not mean that its ratification holds no significance for Australian law. Where a statute or subordinate legislation is ambiguous, the courts should favour that construction which accords with Australia's obligations under a treaty or international convention to which Australia is a party (Chu Kheng Lim v. Minister for Immigration [1992 (176) CLR 1], CLR at p. 38), at least in those cases in which the legislation is enacted after, or in contemplation of, entry into, or ratification of, the relevant international instrument. That is because Parliament, prima facie, intends to give effect to Australia's obligations under international law. It is accepted that a statute is to be interpreted and applied, as far as its language permits, so that it is in conformity and not in conflict with the established rules of international law (Polites v. Commonwealth [1945 (70) CLR 60], CLR at pp. 68-69, 77, 80-81)

Apart from influencing the construction of a statute or subordinate legislation, an international convention may play a part in the development by the courts of the common law. The provisions of an international convention to which Australia is a party, especially one which declares universal fundamental rights, may be used by the courts as a legitimate guide in developing the common law. [Mabo v. Queensland (No. 2) [1991 (175) CLR 1], CLR at p. 42, per Brennan, J. (with whom Mason C.J. and McHugh, J. agreed); Dietrich v. Queen [1992 (177) CLR 292] (CLR at p. 321), per Brennan J., at p. 360, per Toohey, J.; Jago v. District Court of New South Wales [(1988) 12 NSW LR 558] (NSWLR at p. 569), per Kirby, J.; Derbyshire County Council v. Times Newspapers Ltd. [1992 QB 770]] But the courts should act in this fashion with due circumspection when Parliament itself has not seen fit to incorporate the provisions of a convention into our domestic law. Judicial development of the common law must not be seen as a backdoor means of importing an unincorporated convention into Australian law. A cautious approach to the development of the common law by reference to international conventions would be consistent with the approach which the courts have hitherto adopted to the development of the common law by reference to statutory policy and statutory materials (Lamb v. Cotogno [1987 (164) CLR 1], CLR at pp. 11-12). Much will depend upon the nature of relevant provision, the extent to which it has been accepted by the international community, the purpose which it is intended to serve and its relationship to the existing principles of our domestic law."

11. Toohey, J. and Gaudron, J. broadly concurred with the above opinion. Toohey, J. spoke of such Conventions giving rise to legitimate expectation among the people that the Executive will honour the commitment while taking any action concerning children while Gaudron, J. relegated the Convention to a subsidiary position vis-à-vis Australian statute law. (McHugh, J. dissented altogether.)

12. The main criticism against reading such conventions and covenants into national laws is one pointed out by Mason, C.J. himself, viz., the ratification of these conventions and covenants is done, in most of the countries by the Executive acting alone and that the prerogative of making the law is that of Parliament alone; unless Parliament legislates, no law can come into existence. It is not clear whether our Parliament has approved the action of the Government of India ratifying the said 1966 Covenant. Indeed, it appears that at the time of ratification of the said Covenant in 1979, the Government of India had made a specific reservation to the effect that the Indian legal system does not recognize a right to compensation for victims of unlawful arrest or detention. This reservation has, of course, been held to be of little relevance now in view of the decision in *Nilabati Behera* [(1993) 2 SCC 746]. Assuming that it has, the question may yet arise whether such approval can be equated to legislation and invests the Covenant with the sanctity of a law made by Parliament. As pointed out by this Court in *S.R. Bommai v. Union of India* [(1994) 3 SCC 1], every action of Parliament cannot be equated to legislation. Legislation is no doubt the main function of Parliament but it also performs many other functions all of which do not amount to legislation. In our opinion, this aspect requires deeper scrutiny than has been possible in this case. For the present, it would suffice to state that the provisions of the covenant, which elucidate and go to effectuate the fundamental rights guaranteed by our Constitution, can certainly be relied upon by courts as facets of those fundamental rights and hence, enforceable as such. So far as multilateral treaties are concerned, the law is, of course, different – and definite. See United States Supreme Court decisions in *Elisa Chan v. Korean Airlines Ltd.* [104 L Ed 2d 113] and *Eastern Airlines v. Floyd* [113 L Ed 2d 569] and the House of Lords decision in *Equal Opportunities Commission v. Secy. of State for Employment* [1994 ICR 317] following its earlier decisions, including *Factortame Ltd. v. Secy. of State for Transport (No. 2)* [(1991) 1 AC 603].

13. Now coming to the facts of the case, we are of the opinion that award of compensation of Rs. 1,00,000 (Rupees one lakh only) to the families of each of the deceased would be appropriate and just. The same shall be paid by the Government of Manipur. The Collector/ District Magistrate, Churachandpur shall hand over the cheques to the respective families of the deceased, namely Lalbeiklien and Saikaplien, within two months from today. The writ petition is disposed of accordingly. The People's Union for Civil Liberties, which has filed this writ petition and pursued it all these years shall be entitled to its costs, assessed at Rs. 10,000 (Rupees ten thousand only) payable by the State of Manipur within the same period.

In the Supreme Court of India

Criminal Appeal No. 1255 of 1999
Criminal Appeal No. 1256 of 1999
Criminal Appeal No. 1367 of 1999
Writ Petition (Civil) No. 316 of 2008
Contempt Petition (Civil) No. 47 of 2011 in Writ Petition (Civil) No. 316 of 2008
Transferred Case (Civil) No. 27 of 2011

People's Union for Civil Liberties (PUCL) & Anr. v. State of Maharashtra & Ors.[6]

Date of Judgement : 23.09.2014

Bench: R.M. Lodha, CJI. And Rohinton Fali Nariman, J.

[This judgment arose from the Writ Petitions which were filed by PUCL before the Bombay High Court regarding nearly 99 encounters that had taken place. The Bombay High Court had issued several guidelines to be followed necessarily and mandatorily by the police in the State. As the High Court had not decided on the fake encounter committed by the police, PUCL had taken up the case before the Supreme Court. The Supreme Court gave several directions which are to be followed in the matter of investigation of police encounters. The Court directed that the requirements/norms must be strictly observed in all cases of death and grievous injury in police encounters by treating them as law declared under Article 141 of the Constitution.]

Order

R.M. Lodha, CJI.

1. On 03.09.2014, the arguments were heard on the question of the procedure to be followed in investigating police encounters. The present order is confined to the above question.

2. In the three writ petitions, which were filed by People's Union for Civil Liberties (for short, "PUCL") before the Bombay High Court, the issue of genuineness or otherwise of nearly 99 encounters between the Mumbai Police and the alleged criminals resulting in the death of about 135 persons between 1995 and 1997 was raised. *Inter alia*, the following prayers were made :

6. (2014) 10 SCC 635

i) directing Respondent Nos. 1 to 3 to furnish the particulars regarding the number of persons killed in last one year in police encounters, their names, addresses, the circumstances in which they were killed, the inquiries, if any, conducted with respect to the said killings and any other relevant information and the action taken, if any, by them;

ii) directing respondent No. 1 i.e. State of Maharashtra to register offence under Section 302 of the Penal Code, 1860 and other enactments against the police officers found prima facie responsible for the violations of fundamental rights and other provisions of the Penal Code and other relevant enactments;

iii) directing the 4th respondent viz. the Coroner of Mumbai to submit a detailed report and the details of action taken by him under the provisions of the Coroners Act, 1871;

iv) directing an appropriate authority to enquire into and report to this Court in all the police encounters that have taken place not only in the city of Mumbai but also in the entire State of Maharashtra in which persons have been killed or injured in police encounters;

v) directing the State of Maharashtra to constitute the Maharashtra State Human Rights Commission as provided under Section 21 and other provisions contained in the Human Rights Act, 1993,

vi) directing the State Government to frame appropriate guidelines governing planning and carrying out encounters for the purpose of protection of life and liberty guaranteed under Article 21 read with Article 14 of the Constitution of India.

3. It is not necessary to notice the facts of the three writ petitions in detail. Suffice it to say that while considering the above prayers, the High Court directed the following guidelines to be followed necessarily and mandatorily by the police in the State :

> *"1. Whenever the respondent police are on the receipt of intelligence or a tip-off about the criminal movements and activities pertaining to the commission of grave crime, it shall be entered into a case diary. If the receiving authority is the police officer of a particular police station, the relevant entry has to be made in the general diary and if the receiving authority is the higher police officer the relevant entry to the said effect has to be made by a separate diary kept and provided therefor and then pursue further in accordance with the procedural law.*
>
> *2. Regarding any encounter operation is over and persons are killed or injured and the same is reported to either orally or writing to the police in furtherance of Section 154 of the Criminal Procedure Code, it shall be registered in Crime Register of that particular police station and that*

further the said first information report along with copies to the higher officials and the court in original shall be sent with immediately without any delay whatsoever through proper channel so as to reach to the court without any delay at all. A report, as enjoined under Section 157(1) of the Criminal Procedure Code, shall also be followed necessarily by the police station concerned.

3. After setting the law in motion by registering the first information report in the crime register by the police officer concerned of the particular police station, the investigating staff of the police shall take such steps by deputing the man or men to get the scene of crime guarded so as to avoid or obliterate or disfigure the existing physical features of the scene of occurrence or the operation encounter. This guarding of the scene of occurrence shall continue till the inspection of occurrence takes place by the investigating staff of the police and preparation of spot panchnama and the recovery panchnama.

4. The police officer who takes part in the operation encounter or the investigating officer of the concerned police station, shall take all necessary efforts and arrangements to preserve fingerprints of the criminals or the dreaded gangster of the weapons who handled immediately after the said criminal was brought down to the ground and incapacitated and that the said fingerprints, if properly taken and preserved, must be sent to the chemical analyser for comparison of the fingerprints of the dead body to be taken.

5. The materials which are found on the scene of occurrence or the operation encounter and such of the materials including the bloodstained earth and bloodstained materials and the sample earth and other movable physical features, shall also be recovered by the investigating staff under the cover of recovery panchnama attested by the independent witnesses.

6. To fix the exact date and actual place of occurrence in which operation encounter has taken place, a rough sketch regarding the topography of the existing physical features of the said place shall be drawn by the police or the investigating staff of the police either by themselves or by the help of the staff of the Survey Department even during the spot panchnama is prepared.

7. The inquest examination shall be conducted by the investigating staff of the police on the spot itself without any delay and statements of the inquest witness are to be recorded under Section 161 of the Code of Criminal Procedure and the inquest panchnama shall be sent along with the above case record prepared along with the first information report without any delay whatsoever to the Court.

8. If the injured criminals during the operation encounter are found alive not only that they should be provided medical aid immediately but also arrangements and attempts shall be taken by the police to record their statements under Section 164 of the Criminal Procedure Code either by a Magistrate, if possible and if not, by the Medical Officer concerned duly attested by the hospital staff mentioning the time and factum that while recording such statements the injured were in a state of position that they will be able to give statements and the connected certificates by the doctors appended thereto.

9. After the examination of further witnesses and completing the investigation inclusive of securing the accused or accused persons, the police concerned is directed to send final report to the court of competent jurisdiction as required under Section 173 of the Criminal Procedure Code for further proceeding.

10. Either in sending the first information report or sending with the general diary entry referred in the guideline nos. 1 and 2, the police concerned shall avoid any iota of delay under any circumstances whatsoever so also rough sketch showing the topography of the scene and the recovery of the materials and the bloodstained materials with the sample earth and the bloodstained earth with the other documents viz. the spot panchnama, recovery panchnama — all seems very vital documents — the respondent police are also directed to send them to the court of jurisdiction concerned without any delay."

4. PUCL was not satisfied with the adequacy of the reliefs granted by the High Court and, consequently, it filed three SLPs against the judgment and order dated 25.02.1999. Few other matters have been connected with these three petitions.

5. After initial grant of leave, the matters came up for consideration before the two-Judge Bench on 05.11.2008. On that day, Mr. Prashant Bhushan, learned counsel appearing for the appellants placed before the Court the guidelines issued by the National Human Rights Commission (for short, "NHRC") and also his own suggestions. Looking at the gravity of the matter, the Court on that day directed issuance of notice to the Union of India, the States and the Union Territories for consideration of issuance of final directions/guidelines in the matter by this Court. After the notice was issued, the Union of India, States and Union Territories, have filed their affidavits.

6. On 28.08.2014, having regard to the importance of the matter, we appointed Mr. Gopal Sankaranarayanan as *amicus curiae* to assist the Court in the matter. Mr. Sankaranarayanan, learned counsel, after thorough research and study, placed before us his written submissions including the suggestions/guidelines.

7. Article 21 of the Constitution of India guarantees "right to live with human dignity". Any violation of human rights is viewed seriously by this Court as right to life is the most precious right guaranteed by Article 21 of the Constitution. The guarantee by Article 21 is available to every person and even the State has no authority to violate that right.

8. In *D.K. Basu v. State of West Bengal* [(1997) 1 SCC 416], this Court was concerned with custodial violence and deaths in police lock-ups. While framing the requirements to be followed in all cases of arrest or detention till legal provisions are made in that behalf, this Court issued certain directives as preventive measures. While doing so, the Court in para 29 (page 433 of the Report) made the following weighty observations :

> *"29. How do we check the abuse of police power? Transparency of action and accountability perhaps are two possible safeguards which this Court must insist upon. Attention is also required to be paid to properly develop work culture, training and orientation of the police force consistent with basic human values. Training methodology of the police needs restructuring. The force needs to be infused with basic human values and made sensitive to the constitutional ethos. Efforts must be made to change the attitude and approach of the police personnel handling investigations so that they do not sacrifice basic human values during interrogation and do not resort to questionable forms of interrogation. With a view to bring in transparency, the presence of the counsel of the arrestee at some point of time during the interrogation may deter the police from using third-degree methods during interrogation."*

9. The observations made by this Court in *Om Prakash and Ors.v. State of Jharkhand through the Secretary, Department of Home, Ranchi-1 and Anr.* [(2012) 12 SCC 72] (para 42, page 95 of the Report) are worth noticing :

> *"42. It is not the duty of the police officers to kill the accused merely because he is a dreaded criminal. Undoubtedly, the police have to arrest the accused and put them up for trial. This Court has repeatedly admonished trigger-happy police personnel, who liquidate criminals and project the incident as an encounter. Such killings must be deprecated. They are not recognised as legal by our criminal justice administration system. They amount to State-sponsored terrorism. But, one cannot be oblivious of the fact that there are cases where the police, who are performing their duty, are attacked and killed. There is a rise in such incidents and judicial notice must be taken of this fact. In such circumstances, while the police have to do their legal duty of arresting the criminals, they have also to protect themselves. The requirement of sanction to prosecute affords protection to the policemen, who are sometimes required to take drastic action against criminals to protect life and property of the people and to protect themselves against attack. Unless unimpeachable evidence is on record to establish that their action is indefensible, mala fide and vindictive, they cannot be subjected to prosecution. Sanction must be a precondition to their prosecution. It affords necessary protection to such police personnel. The plea regarding sanction can be raised at the inception."*

10. The statistics of the National Crime Records Bureau, 2013 are worth noticing. Table 14.2 under the title "Persons Killed Or Injured in Police Firing During 2013 (Event-Wise)" shows that there were 684 occasions of police firing classified as "Riot Control", "Anti-Dacoity Operations", "Against Extremists and Terrorists" and "Against Others" in 2013 and, in these police firings, 103 civilians were killed and 213 were injured and, as regards policemen, 47 were killed and 1158 were injured.

10.1 Table 15.1 gives details of police personnel killed across the country in 2013 in terrorist/extremists operations, dacoity operations or other raids by riotous mobs and by other criminals.

10.2 Table 16.1 catalogues the complaints/cases registered against police personnel during 2013. During the year 2013, 51120 complaints were received, of which 26640 were declared false or unsubstantiated. Of the rest, 14928 were dealt departmentally. Of this, 3896 were reported for regular departmental action while 799 were sent up for trials/charge-sheeted. In the completed trials, 53 were convicted. In departmental proceedings, 544 were dismissed from service and 3980 had been awarded major punishment.

10.3 Incidence of human rights violations by police during 2013 is indicated in Table 16.2. This Table lists only two fake encounters (both from Assam). The figure raises doubts about its correctness.

11. In some of the countries when a police firearms officer is involved in a shooting, there are strict guidelines and procedures in place to ensure that what has happened is thoroughly investigated. In India, unfortunately, such structured guidelines and procedures are not in place where police is involved in shooting and death of the subject occurs in such shooting. We are of the opinion that it is the constitutional duty of this Court to put in place certain guidelines adherence to which would help in bringing to justice the perpetrators of the crime who take law in their own hands.

12. Mr. Prashant Bhushan, learned counsel for PUCL has suggested the following guidelines :

> Whenever the police are in receipt of any intelligence or tip-off regarding criminal movements or activities pertaining to the commission of grave criminal offences, it shall be entered into a case diary. If the receiving authority is the police officer of a particular police station, the relevant entry must be made in the general diary and if the receiving authority is a police officer of higher rank, the relevant entry must be made in a separate diary kept and provided therefor and then be pursued further in accordance with the procedural law.
>
> A dedicated investigative team/separate cadre of police be formed/established which shall be attached to the NHRC/SHRC to investigate encounters and other matters of which NHRC/SHRC is seized. Till the time such dedicated team/police cadre is established, it is mandatory that the matters relating to encounter deaths/injuries are handed over for investigation to an independent investigating agency such as CBI/SHRC. NHRC/SHRC shall direct as to who will conduct the investigation.

Whenever a police party is involved in an encounter it shall immediately inform the NHRC/SHRC and the local police station of the encounter and shall seal off the premises to avoid any contamination till such investigative team of the NHRC/SHRC arrives subject to compliance with the other guidelines regarding the preservation of fingerprints etc.

When a police officer receives any information, either orally or in writing, in furtherance of section 154 of the Cr.P.C. regarding death or injuries caused in the course of an encounter operation between the Police party and others, he shall enter the information in the Crime Register or any other appropriate register of that particular police station and shall immediately send the Report (First Information Report) to the court without any further delay through a proper channel. The copies of the said report shall also be sent to the higher officials including the DGP of the State concerned and NHRC/SHRC. The DGP must also send his report with regard to such encounter death to NHRC. The DGP shall take disciplinary action against the officer-in-charge of the police station if he/she fails to send the report regarding the encounter death to NHRC and DGP. A report, as enjoined under Section 157(1) of the Criminal Procedure Code, shall also be followed necessarily by the police station concerned.

The independent investigating team shall take such steps by deputing the man or men to get the scene of crime guarded so as to avoid or obliterate or disfigure the existing physical features of the scene of occurrence or the operation encounter. This guarding of the scene of occurrence shall continue till the inspection of occurrence takes place by the aforesaid independent investigating team and preparation of spot panchnama and the recovery panchnama.

The police officer involved in the encounter operation and the independent investigating team, shall make all necessary efforts and arrangements immediately after the said criminal was brought down to the ground and incapacitated to preserve fingerprints of the criminals or the dreaded gangster, and those on the weapons handled during the course of the encounter. The said fingerprints, properly taken and preserved, must be sent to the chemical analyser for comparison of the fingerprints of the dead body to be taken.

The materials which are found on the scene of occurrence or the operation encounter and such of the materials including the bloodstained earth and bloodstained materials and the sample earth and other movable physical features, shall also be recovered by the independent investigating team under the cover of recovery panchnama attested by independent witnesses.

To fix the exact date and actual place of occurrence in which operation encounter has taken place, a rough sketch regarding the topography of the existing physical features of the said place shall be drawn by the aforesaid independent investigating team either by themselves or by the help of the staff of the Survey Department when the spot panchnama is prepared.

The inquest examination shall be conducted by aforesaid independent investigating team on the spot itself without any delay and statements of the inquest witnesses are to be recorded under section 161 of the Code of Criminal Procedure and the inquest panchnama shall be sent along with the above case-record prepared along with the first information report without any delay whatsoever to the Court.

A Magisterial Inquiry must invariably be held in all cases of death which occur in the course of police action. The next of kin of the deceased must invariably be associated in such inquiry.

In every case when a complaint is made against the police alleging commission of a criminal act on their part, which makes out a cognizable case of culpable homicide, an FIR to this effect must be registered under appropriate sections of I.P.C. Such case shall also be investigated by the aforesaid investigating team.

Prompt prosecution and disciplinary action must be initiated against all delinquent officers found guilty in the magisterial enquiry/the said investigation. Prosecution of such delinquent officers shall be conducted by the investigating agency. Such delinquent officers must be placed under suspension.

Question of granting of compensation to the dependants of the deceased would depend upon the facts and circumstances of each case and it shall be determined by NHRC. However, in every case of a person being killed by the police party in the course of an encounter, the compensation granted must necessarily be at least the same as that granted to the dependants of a police officer killed by terrorists in the course of duty by the Government.

No out-of-turn promotion, cash award or gallantry reward shall be bestowed on the officers concerned pursuant to their role in an encounter as this may be an incentive for officers to conduct encounters.

A six-monthly statement of all cases of deaths in police action in the State shall be sent by the Director General of Police to the Commission, so as to reach its office by the 15th day of January and July respectively. The statement may be sent in the following format along with post-mortem reports and inquest reports, wherever available and also the inquiry reports :

1. Date and place of occurrence.
2. Police station, District.
3. Circumstances leading to deaths:
   i. Self defence in encounter
   ii. In the course of dispersal of unlawful assembly
   iii. In the course of affecting arrest.
4. Brief facts of the incident
5. Criminal Case Number
6. Investigating Agency
7. Findings of the magisterial inquiry/enquiry by Senior Officers :
   a. disclosing in particular, names and designation of police officials, if found responsible for the death; and
   b. whether use of force was justified and action taken was lawful.

In order to ascertain the identity of persons killed in police encounter, their photographs and other details should be advertised on T.V., newspapers, etc.

With respect to the post mortem conducted after an encounter it is imperative that such a post-mortem is, at the least, conducted in the district level government hospital in the presence of at least three qualified doctors of which one must be a senior doctor. All such post-mortems must also necessarily be videotaped and copies of such videotapes preserved.

If the injured criminals during the operation encounter are found alive, not only that they should be provided medical aid immediately but also arrangements and attempts shall be taken by the independent investigative team to record their statements under Section 164 of the Criminal Procedure Code, either by a Magistrate, if possible and if not, by the Medical Officer concerned, duly attested by the hospital staff mentioning the time and factum that while recording such statements the injured were in a state of position that they will be able to give statements and the connected certificates by the doctors appended thereto.

After the examination of further witnesses and completing the investigation inclusive of securing the accused or accused persons, the independent investigative team is directed to send final report to the court of competent jurisdiction as required under Section 173 of the Criminal Procedure Code for further proceeding.

Either in sending the first information report or sending with the general diary entry referred in the guideline nos. 1 and 2, the concerned police / independent investigative team, shall avoid any iota of delay under any circumstances whatsoever so also rough sketch showing the topography of the scene and the recovery of materials and the bloodstained materials with the sample earth and the bloodstained earth with the other documents viz. the spot panchnama, recovery panchnama—all seems very vital documents—the respondent police are also directed to send them to the court of jurisdiction concerned without any delay.

13. The revised guidelines/procedures to be followed in cases of deaths caused in police action framed by NHRC read as under :

A. When the police officer in charge of a police station receives information about death in an encounter with the police, he shall enter that information in the appropriate register.

B. Where the police officers belonging to the same police station are members of the encounter party, whose action resulted in death, it is desirable that such cases are made over for investigation to some other independent investigating agency, such as State CBCID.

C. Whenever a specific complaint is made against the police alleging commission of a criminal act on their part, which makes out a cognizable case of culpable homicide, an FIR to this effect must be registered under appropriate sections of I.P.C. Such case shall be investigated by State CBCID or any other specialised investigation agency.

D. A magisterial enquiry must be held in all cases of death which occurs in the course of police action, as expeditiously as possible, preferably, within three months. The relatives of the deceased, eyewitnesses having information of the circumstances leading to encounter, police station records, etc. must be examined while conducting such enquiry.

E. Prompt prosecution and disciplinary action must be initiated against all delinquent officers found guilty in the magisterial enquiry/police investigation.

F. No out-of-turn promotion or instant gallantry rewards shall be bestowed on the officers concerned soon after the occurrence. It must be ensured at all cost that such rewards are given/recommended only when the gallantry of the officer concerned is established beyond doubt.

G. (a) All cases of deaths in police action in the States shall be reported to the Commission by the Senior Superintendent of Police/Superintendent of Police of the District within 48 hours of such death in the following format:

1. Date and place of occurrence
2. Police station, district
3. Circumstances leading to death :

(i) Self-defence in encounter
(ii) In the course of dispersal of unlawful assembly
(iii) In the course of effecting arrest
(iv) Any other circumstances

4. Brief facts of the incident
5. Criminal case No.
6. Investigating agency

(b) A second report must be sent in all cases of death in police action in the State by the Sr. Superintendent of Police/Superintendent of Police to the commission within three months providing following information :

1. Post mortem report
2. Inquest report
3. Findings of the magisterial enquiry/enquiry by senior officers disclosing :
   (i) Names and designation of police official, if found responsible for the death :
   (ii) Whether use of force was justified and action taken was lawful:
   (iii) Result of the forensic examination of 'handwash' of the deceased to ascertain the presence of residue of gun powder to justify exercise of right of self defence; and
   (iv) Report of the ballistic expert on examination of the weapons alleged to have been used by the deceased and his companions.

14. Union of India in its counter affidavit has given its comments to the guidelines framed by the High Court and so also to the guidelines suggested by the learned counsel for PUCL. Union of India has expressed its reservation on certain guidelines on diverse counts including the practical difficulties in their implementation. As regards the States and the Union Territories, their views are not uniform on the guidelines framed by the High Court and also the guidelines suggested by PUCL. In respect of some of the guidelines, some States and Union Territories have toed the line of the Union of India in not accepting the same on the ground of practical difficulties in their implementation. Few States have highlighted the procedure that is being followed by them when any death or encounter takes place. As regards investigation in such cases, some of the States have highlighted that the investigation of such cases cannot be done by officers / employees of the same police station and it is ensured that investigation of such cases is done by some higher officer. On the other hand, few States / Union Territories have stated that initial investigation may be conducted by the local police because local police is acquainted with the *modus operandi* of local criminals and crime.

15. Before we proceed further, we put on record our appreciation for the efforts of the learned *amicus curiae* in collating the guidelines framed by the High Court, guidelines suggested by PUCL and guidelines issued by NHRC and their acceptability or otherwise by the Union / States / Union Territories and his own comments.

16. Article 21 of the Constitution provides "no person shall be deprived of his life or personal liberty except according to procedure established by law." This Court has stated time and again that Article 21 confers sacred and cherished right under the Constitution which cannot be violated, except according to procedure established by law. Article 21 guarantees personal liberty to every single person in the country which includes the right to live with human dignity.

17. In line with the guarantee provided by Article 21 and other provisions in the Constitution of India, a number of statutory provisions also seek to protect personal liberty, dignity and basic human rights. In spite of constitutional and statutory provisions aimed at safeguarding the personal liberty and life of a citizen, the cases of death in police encounters continue to occur. This Court has been confronted with encounter cases from time to time. In *Chaitanya Kalbagh and Ors.v. State of U.P. and Ors.* [(1989) 2 SCC 314], this Court was concerned with a writ petition filed under Article 32 of the Constitution wherein the impartial investigation was sought for the alleged killing of 299 persons in the police encounters. The Court observed that in the facts and circumstances presented before it, there was an imperative need of ensuring that the guardians of law and order do in fact observe the code of discipline expected of them and that they function strictly as the protectors of innocent citizens."

18. In *R.S. Sodhi, Advocate v. State of U.P.* and Ors. [1994 Supp (1) SCC 143], a writ petition was brought to this Court under Article 32 of the Constitution relating to an incident in which 10 persons were reported to have been killed in what were described as "encounters" between the Punjab militants and the local police. The Court observed, "Whether the loss of lives was on account of a genuine or a fake encounter is a matter which has to be inquired into and investigated closely." The Court entrusted the investigation to the Central Bureau of Investigation (for short, "CBI") to ensure that the investigation did not lack credibility.

19. In *Satyavir Singh Rathi, Assistant Commissioner of Police and Ors. v. State through Central Bureau of Investigation* [(2011) 6 SCC 1], the matter before this Court arose from the First Information Report (for short, "FIR") registered against police personnel involved in a shoot-out for an offence punishable under Sections 302/34 of the Indian Penal Code (for short, "IPC"). In the complaint, it was alleged that the police officials had surrounded the car and had fired indiscriminately and without cause at the occupants, killing the two and causing grievous injuries to the third. This Court concurred with the High Court and the trial court on the conviction under Section 302 IPC and rejected the defence set up by the accused persons relying on Exception 3 in Section 300 IPC as it was found to be not in good faith or due discharge of their duty.

20. In *Prakash Kadam and Ors. v. Ramprasad Vishwanath Gupta and Anr.* [(2011) 6 SCC 189], the allegation was that the accused persons decided to eliminate the deceased in a false police encounter. The Court noted that this was a very serious case wherein *prima facie* some police officers and staff were engaged by some private persons to kill their opponent and the police officers and the staff acted as contract killers for them. The Court warned policemen that they would not be excused for committing murder in the name of "encounter" on the pretext that they were carrying out the orders of their superior officers or politicians. The Court said that the "encounter" philosophy is a criminal philosophy.

21. In *Om Prakash* [(2012) 12 SCC 72], the allegation against the accused persons was that the complainant's son was killed by them in a fake police encounter. The Court, however, held that the encounter was a genuine one though NHRC guideline for photography of the autopsy was not complied with.

22. A two-Judge Bench of this Court in *B.G. Verghese v. Union of India and Ors.* [(2013) 11 SCC 525] dealt with two writ petitions. In Writ Petition (Criminal) No. 31/2007, it was stated that during the years 2003-2006, 21 police encounter killings took place in the State of Gujarat. It was alleged that the so-called police encounters were fake and the persons were killed by the police officials in cold blood. In the writ petition a prayer was made for ordering an inquiry into all the cases of police encounters, which, according to the petitioner, were fake in order to establish the rule of law and to bring out the truth in each case. In the other Writ Petition (Criminal) No. 83/2007, the allegation related to the killing of one person in a police encounter. It was alleged that this too was an instance of fake encounter in which the victim was killed by the officers of the crime branch of police in cold blood and in a premeditated manner. The prayer was made in the writ petition to order an independent investigation by a special investigation team into all the fake encounters. During the pendency of the matter before this Court, the State of Gujarat had constituted a Monitoring Authority and Special Task Force for investigation of police encounters. Since the former Judge of this Court was appointed as Chairman of the Monitoring Authority, the Court requested the Chairman of the Monitoring Authority to look into all the cases of alleged fake encounters as enumerated in the two writ petitions and to have them thoroughly investigated so that full and complete truth comes to light in each case.

23. In *Rohtash Kumar v. State of Haryana through the Home Secretary, Government of Haryana, Civil Secretariat, Chandigarh and Ors.* [(2013) 14 SCC 290], again a two-Judge Bench of this Court was confronted with killing of a person in an encounter by the police officials. Having found that the death took place in the fake police encounter, the Court directed an independent investigating agency to conduct the investigation so that guilty could be brought to justice.

24. The above cases have been referred only by way of illustration to show that killings in police encounters require independent investigation. The killings in police encounters affect the credibility of the rule of law and the administration of the criminal justice system.

25. We are not oblivious of the fact that police in India has to perform a difficult and delicate task, particularly, when many hard-core criminals, like, extremists, terrorists, drug peddlers, smugglers who have organised gangs, have taken strong roots in the society but then such criminals must be dealt with by the police in an efficient and effective manner so as to bring them to justice by following the rule of law. We are of the view that it would be useful and effective to structure appropriate guidelines to restore faith of the people in police force. In a society governed by the rule of law, it is imperative that extra-judicial killings are properly and independently investigated so that justice may be done.

26. Learned *amicus curiae* submits that when a police encounter occurs, it is important that a complaint is registered; the evidence is preserved; independent and fair investigation takes place; victims are informed and inquest is conducted.

27. Sections 174, 175 and 176 of the Code of Criminal Procedure, 1973 (for short "Code") provide for Magisterial inquiries into cases of unnatural death. It is apposite to mention that a system for investigating the cause of death in cases of unusual or suspicious circumstances is in place in most countries. The system centres around the policy to have reassurance that unexplained deaths do not remain unexplained and that the perpetrator is tried by a competent court established by law.

28. Universal Declaration of Human Rights (UDHR) has framed certain general principles on the effective prevention and investigation of extra-legal, arbitrary and summary executions.

> 1. Requiring States to provide the investigative authority with sufficient power to compel any relevant parties including the official implicated to testify (Provision 10).
>
> 2. Obligating States to provide for an independent inquiry into alleged police misconduct through an appointed Commission when existing procedures are inadequate or when there are allegations of such inadequacies. The Commission members must be independent of individuals implicated in the incident (Provision 11).
>
> 3. Requiring that those conducting autopsies must be able to function independently and impartially (Provision 14).
>
> 4. Requiring States to protect those who witness or allege police misconduct and obligating States to remove the implicated officers from any involvement in the investigation (Provision 15).
>
> 5. Affording the victim's family and legal representative the right to request that an independent qualified representative be present during the autopsy of the victim's body (Provision 16).
>
> 6. Calling for the prompt submission of a written report on the investigation specifically detailing the methods utilised as well as the findings of fact and law resulting from the inquiry. It further requires that such reports be released to the public (Provision 17).
>
> 7. Recognising that those undertaking these investigations must "have at their disposal all the necessary budgetary and technical resources for effective investigation" into police killings.

The principles so framed by the UDHR are intended to guarantee independence while investigating police killings and help in preventing potential for abuse, corruption, ineffectiveness and neglect in investigation.

29. The United Nations Code of Conduct for Law Enforcement Officers (which includes all officers of the law, who exercise police powers) lays down that in the performance of duties, the Law Enforcement Officers shall respect and protect human dignity and maintain and uphold human rights of all persons. Basic human rights standards for good conduct by the Law Enforcement Officers by Amnesty International, *inter alia*, suggest, (1) Do not use force except when strictly necessary and to the minimum extent required under the circumstances and (2) do not carry out, order or cover up extra-judicial executions or "disappearances" and refuse to obey any order to do so.

30. Minnesota Protocol (Model protocol for a legal investigation of extra-legal, arbitrary and summary executions) establishes a long line of requisite steps. The Protocol sets the principles and medico legal standards for the investigation and prevention of extra legal, arbitrary and summary executions. The Protocol provides for in-depth guidance in a general way on the subjects (1) purpose of an inquiry (2) procedure for an inquiry (3) processing of the crime scene (4) processing of the evidence (5) avenues to investigation (6) personal testimony etc. In Section C of the Minnesota Protocol, a long list of requisite steps is suggested, some of which being :

1. the area in which evidence is located should be closed off to the public

2. photographs of the scene and physical evidence located at the scene should be taken in a prompt manner;

3. investigators should promptly record the condition of the body;

4. weapons such as guns, projectiles, bullets and cartridge cases should be taken and preserved;

5. tests for gunshot residue and trace metal detection should be performed on the victims' bodies and the police officers involved;

6. fingerprints of relevant persons should be preserved;

7. information should be obtained from witnesses;

8. all persons at the scene should be identified;

9. a report detailing the work of the investigators during their on-site visit should be kept and later disclosed;

10. evidence should be properly collected, handled, packaged, labelled, and placed in safekeeping to prevent contamination and loss of evidence.

31. In the light of the above discussion and having regard to the directions issued by the Bombay High Court, guidelines issued by NHRC, suggestions of the appellant - PUCL, *amicus curiae* and the affidavits filed by the Union of India, State Governments and the Union Territories, we think it appropriate to issue the following requirements to be followed in the matters of investigating police encounters in the cases of death as the standard procedure for thorough, effective and independent investigation :

(1) Whenever the police is in receipt of any intelligence or tip-off regarding criminal movements or activities pertaining to the commission of grave criminal offence, it shall be reduced into writing in some form (preferably into case diary) or in some electronic form. Such recording need not reveal details of the suspect or the location to which the party is headed. If such intelligence or tip-off is received by a higher authority, the same may be

noted in some form without revealing details of the suspect or the location.

(2)If pursuant to the tip-off or receipt of any intelligence, as above, encounter takes place and firearm is used by the police party and as a result of that, death occurs, an FIR to that effect shall be registered and the same shall be forwarded to the court under Section 157 of the Code without any delay. While forwarding the report under Section 157 of the Code, the procedure prescribed under Section 158 of the Code shall be followed.

(3)An independent investigation into the incident/encounter shall be conducted by the CID or police team of another police station under the supervision of a senior officer (at least a level above the head of the police party engaged in the encounter). The team conducting inquiry/investigation shall, at a minimum, seek :

(a) To identify the victim; colour photographs of the victim should be taken;

(b) To recover and preserve evidentiary material, including bloodstained earth, hair, fibres and threads, etc., related to the death;

(c) To identify scene witnesses with complete names, addresses and telephone numbers and obtain their statements (including the statements of police personnel involved) concerning the death;

(d) To determine the cause, manner, location (including preparation of rough sketch of topography of the scene and, if possible, photo/video of the scene and any physical evidence) and time of death as well as any pattern or practice that may have brought about the death;

(e) It must be ensured that intact fingerprints of deceased are sent for chemical analysis. Any other fingerprints should be located, developed, lifted and sent for chemical analysis;

(f) Post-mortem must be conducted by two doctors in the District Hospital, one of them, as far as possible, should be In-charge/ Head of the District Hospital. Post-mortem shall be video-graphed and preserved;

(g) Any evidence of weapons, such as guns, projectiles, bullets and cartridge cases, should be taken and preserved. Wherever applicable, tests for gunshot residue and trace metal detection should be performed.

(h) The cause of death should be found out, whether it was natural death, accidental death, suicide or homicide.

(4)A Magisterial inquiry under Section 176 of the Code must invariably be held in all cases of death which occur in the course of police firing and a report thereof must be sent to the Judicial Magistrate having jurisdiction under Section 190 of the Code.

(5)The involvement of NHRC is not necessary unless there is serious doubt about independent and impartial investigation. However, the information of the incident without any delay must be sent to NHRC or the State Human Rights Commission, as the case may be.

(6)The injured criminal/victim should be provided medical aid and his/her statement recorded by the Magistrate or Medical Officer with certificate of fitness.

(7)It should be ensured that there is no delay in sending FIR, diary entries, panchnamas, sketch, etc., to the concerned Court.

(8)After full investigation into the incident, the report should be sent to the competent court under Section 173 of the Code. The trial, pursuant to the chargesheet submitted by the investigating Officer, must be concluded expeditiously.

(9)In the event of death, the next of kin of the alleged criminal/victim must be informed at the earliest.

(10) Six monthly statements of all cases where deaths have occurred in police firing must be sent to NHRC by DGPs. It must be ensured that the six monthly statements reach to NHRC by 15th day of January and July, respectively. The statements may be sent in the following format along with post mortem, inquest and, wherever available, the inquiry reports :

- (i) Date and place of occurrence.
- (ii) Police Station, District.
- (iii) Circumstances leading to deaths:
  - (a) Self defence in encounter.
  - (b) In the course of dispersal of unlawful assembly.
  - (c) In the course of affecting arrest.
- (iv) Brief facts of the incident.
- (v) Criminal Case No.
- (vi) Investigating Agency.
- (vii) Findings of the Magisterial Inquiry/Inquiry by Senior Officers :
  - (a) disclosing, in particular, names and designation of police officials, if found responsible for the death; and

(b) whether use of force was justified and action taken was lawful.

(11)If on the conclusion of investigation the materials/evidence having come on record show that death had occurred by use of firearm amounting to offence under IPC, disciplinary action against such officer must be promptly initiated and he be placed under suspension.

(12)As regards compensation to be granted to the dependants of the victim who suffered death in a police encounter, the scheme provided under Section 357-A of the Code must be applied.

(13)The police officer(s) concerned must surrender his/her weapons for forensic and ballistic analysis, including any other material, as required by the investigating team, subject to the rights under Article 20 of the Constitution.

(14)An intimation about the incident must also be sent to the police officer's family and should the family need services of a lawyer / counselling, same must be offered.

(15)No out-of-turn promotion or instant gallantry rewards shall be bestowed on the officers concerned soon after the occurrence. It must be ensured at all cost that such rewards are given/recommended only when the gallantry of the officers concerned is established beyond doubt.

(16)If the family of the victim finds that the above procedure has not been followed or there exists a pattern of abuse or lack of independent investigation or impartiality by any of the functionaries as abovementioned, it may make a complaint to the Sessions Judge having territorial jurisdiction over the place of incident. Upon such complaint being made, the Sessions Judge concerned shall look into the merits of the complaint and address the grievances raised therein.

32. The above guidelines will also be applicable to grievous injury cases in police encounter, as far as possible.

33. Accordingly, we direct that the above requirements/norms must be strictly observed in all cases of death and grievous injury in police encounters by treating them as law declared under Article 141 of the Constitution of India.

In the Supreme Court of India

Writ Petition (Civil) No. 256 of 1991
People's Union for Civil Liberties (PUCL) v. Union of India & Anr.[7]

Date of Judgement : 18.12.1996

Bench : Kuldip Singh and S. Saghir Ahmad, JJ.

[In public interest, PUCL had filed a Petition under Article 32 of the Constitution narrating incidents of telephone tapping which violated Article 19(1)(a) and Article 21 of the Constitution. The Petition, among others, was based on report by the CBI "Tapping of politicians' phones" which was published in the March 1991 issue of the Mainstream. PUCL had emphasized the right of privacy being a part of Article 21 of the Constitution and had argued that prior judicial scrutiny is necessary before any order for telephone tapping is passed. The Court, however, issued certain directions in the absence of any guidelines being laid down under Section 5(2) of the Telegraph Act. The guidelines inter alia mandate that telephone tapping shall not be done except when there is an order by the Home Secretary, Government of India or by the Home Secretary of any State Government. In urgent cases, the said power will be delegated to officers not below the rank of Joint Secretary. There were several other directions given with regard to safeguarding the right of privacy of a person under the Constitution.]

Judgment

Kuldip Singh, J.

1. Telephone-tapping is a serious invasion of an individual's privacy. With the growth of highly sophisticated communication technology, the right to hold telephone conversation, in the privacy of one's home or office without interference, is increasingly susceptible to abuse. It is no doubt that every Government, howsoever democratic, exercises some degree of *sub rosa* operation as a part of its intelligence outfit but at the same time citizen's right to privacy has to be protected from being abused by the authorities of the day.

2. This petition — public interest — under Article 32 of the Constitution of India has been

7. (1997) 1 SCC 301.

filed by the People's Union of Civil Liberties, a voluntary organisation, highlighting the incidents of telephone-tapping in the recent past. The petitioner has challenged the constitutional validity of Section 5(2) of the Indian Telegraph Act, 1885 (the Act), in the alternative it is contended that the said provisions be suitably read down to include procedural safeguards to rule out arbitrariness and to prevent the indiscriminate telephone-tapping.

3. The writ petition was filed in the wake of the report on "Tapping of politicians' phones" by the Central Bureau of Investigation (CBI). Copy of the report as published in the *Mainstream*, Volume XXIX dated 26.03.1991 has been placed on record along with the rejoinder filed by the petitioner. The authenticity of the report has not been questioned by the learned counsel for the Union of India before us. Para 21 and 22 of the report are as under :

> *"21. Investigation has revealed the following lapses on the part of MTNL*
>
> *(i) In respect of 4 telephone numbers though they were shown to be under interception in the statement supplied by MTNL, the authorisation for putting the number under interception could not be provided. This shows that records have not been maintained properly.*
>
> *(ii) In respect of 279 telephone numbers, although authority letters from various authorised agencies were available, these numbers have not been shown in lists supplied by MTNL showing interception of telephones to the corresponding period. This shows that lists supplied were incomplete.*
>
> *(iii) In respect of 133 cases, interception of the phones were done beyond the authorised part. The GM(O), MTNL in his explanation has said that this was done in good faith on oral requests of the representatives of the competent authorities and that instructions have now been issued that interception beyond authorised periods will be done only on receipt of written requests.*
>
> *(iv) In respect of 111 cases, interception of telephones have exceeded 180 days' period and no permission of Government for keeping the telephone under interception beyond 180 days was taken.*
>
> *(v) The files pertaining to interception have not been maintained properly.*
>
> *22. Investigation has also revealed that various authorised agencies are not maintaining the files regarding interception of telephones properly. One agency is not maintaining even the logbooks of interception. The reasons for keeping a telephone number on watch have also not been maintained properly. The effectiveness of the results of observation have to be reported to the Government in quarterly returns which is also not being sent in time and does not contain all the relevant information. In the case of agencies other than IB, the returns are submitted to the MHA. The periodicity of maintenance of the records is not uniform. It has been found that whereas*

DRI keeps record for the last 5 years, in case of IB, as soon as the new quarterly statement is prepared, the old returns are destroyed for reasons of secrecy. The desirability of maintenance of uni-return and periodicity of these documents needs to be examined."

Section 5(2) of the Act is as under :

"5 (2) On the occurrence of any public emergency, or in the interest of the public safety, the Central Government or a State Government or any officer specially unauthorised in this behalf by the Central Government or a State Government may, if satisfied that it is necessary or expedient so to do in the interests of the sovereignty and integrity of India, the security of the State, friendly relations with foreign States or public order or for preventing incitement to the commission of an offence, for reasons to be recorded in writing, by order, direct that any message or class of messages to or from any person or class of persons, or relating to any particular subject, brought for transmission by or transmitted or received by any telegraph, shall not be transmitted, or shall be intercepted or detained, or shall be disclosed to the Government making the order or an officer thereof mentioned in the order :

Provided that press messages intended to be published in India of correspondents accredited to the Central Government or a State Government shall not be intercepted or detained, unless their transmission has been prohibited under this sub-section."

4. The above provisions clearly indicate that in the event of the occurrence of a public emergency or in the interest of the public safety, the Central Government or the State Government or any officer specially authorised on this behalf, can intercept messages if satisfied that it is necessary or expedient so to do in the interest of :

(i) The sovereignty and integrity of India.
(ii) The security of the State.
(iii) Friendly relations with foreign States.
(iv) Public order.
(v) For preventing incitement to the commission of an offence.

5. The CBI report indicates that under the above provisions of law, Director, Intelligence Bureau, Director, General Narcotics Control Bureau, Revenue Intelligence and Central Economic Intelligence Bureau and the Director, Enforcement Directorate have been authorised by the Central Government to do interception for the purposes indicated above. In addition, the State Governments generally give authorisation to the Police/Intelligence agencies to exercise the powers under the Act.

6. The Assistant Director General, Department of Telecom has filed counter-affidavit on behalf of the Union of India. The stand taken by the Union of India is as under :

"The allegation that the party in power at the Centre/State or officer authorised to tap the telephone by the Central/State Government could misuse this power is not correct. Tapping of telephone could be done only by the Central/State Government order by the officer specifically authorised by the Central/State Government on their behalf and it could be done only under certain conditions such as national emergency in the interest of public safety, security of State, public order etc. It is also necessary to record the reasons for tapping before tapping is resorted to. If the party, whose telephone is to be tapped is to be informed about this and also the reasons for tapping, it will defeat the very purpose of tapping of telephone. By the very sensitive nature of the work, it is absolutely necessary to maintain secrecy in the matter. In spite of safeguards, if there is alleged misuse of the powers regarding tapping of telephones by any authorised officer, the aggrieved party could represent to the State Government/Central Government and suitable action could be taken as may be necessary. Striking down the provision Section 5(2) of the Indian Telegraph Act, is not desirable as it will jeopardise public interest and security of the State."

7. Section 7(2)(b) of the Act which gives rule-making power to the Central Government is as under :

> *"7. Power to make rules for the conduct of telegraphs.—(1) The Central Government may, from time to time, by notification in the Official Gazette, make rules consistent with this Act for the conduct of all or any telegraphs established, maintained or worked by the Government or by the persons licensed under this Act.*
>
> (2) Rules under this section may provide for all or any of the following among other matters, that is to say :
>
> (a) xx xx
>
> (b) the precautions to be taken for preventing the improper interception or disclosure of messages."

8. No rules have been framed by the Central Government under the provisions quoted above.

9. Mr. Rajindar Sachar, Senior Advocate, assisted by Mr. Sanjay Parikh, vehemently contended that right to privacy is a fundamental right guaranteed under Article 19(1) and Article 21 of the Constitution of India. According to Mr. Sachar to save Section 5(2) of the Act from being declared unconstitutional, it is necessary to read down the said provision to provide adequate machinery to safeguard the right to privacy. Prior judicial sanction- ex parte in nature-according to Mr. Sachar, is the only safeguard, which can eliminate the element of arbitrariness or unreasonableness. Mr. Sachar contended that not only the substantive law but also the procedure provided therein has to be just, fair and reasonable.

10. While hearing the arguments on 06.09.1995, this Court passed the following order :

"Mr. Parikh is on his legs. He has assisted us in this matter for about half an hour. At this stage, Mr. Kapil Sibal and Dr. Dhavan, who are present in Court, stated that according to them the matter is important and they being responsible members of the Bar, are duty-bound to assist this Court in a matter like this. We appreciate the gesture. We permit them to intervene in this matter. They need a short adjournment to assist us.

The matter is adjourned to 11.10.1995."

11. While assisting this Court, Mr. Kapil Sibal at the outset stated that in the interest of the security and sovereignty of India and to deal with any other emergency situation for the protection of national interest, messages may indeed be intercepted. According to him the core question for determination is whether there are sufficient procedural safeguards to rule out arbitrary exercise of power under the Act. Mr. Sibal contended that Section 5(2) of the Act clearly lays down the conditions/situations which are sine qua non for the exercise of the power but the manner in which the said power can be exercised has not been provided. According to him procedural safeguards — short of prior judicial scrutiny — shall have to be read with Section 5(2) of the Act to save it from the vice of arbitrariness.

12. Both sides have relied upon the seven-Judge Bench judgment of this Court in *Kharak Singh v. State of U.P.* [(1964) 1 SCR 332]. The question for consideration before this Court was whether "surveillance" under Chapter XX of the U.P. Police Regulations constituted an infringement of any of the fundamental rights guaranteed by Part III of the Constitution. Regulation 236(b) which permitted surveillance by "domiciliary visits at night" was held to be violative of Article 21 on the ground that there was no "law" under which the said regulation could be justified.

13. The word "life" and the expression "personal liberty" in Article 21 were elaborately considered by this Court in *Kharak Singh case* [(1964) 1 SCR 332]. The majority read "right to privacy" as part of the right to life under Article 21 of the Constitution on the following reasoning :

"We have already extracted a passage from the judgment of Field, J. in Munn v. Illinois [(1877) 94 US 113] at p. 142, where the learned Judge pointed out that 'life' in the 5th and 14th Amendments of the U.S. Constitution corresponding to Article 21, means not merely the right to the continuance of a person's animal existence, but a right to the possession of each of his organs — his arms and legs etc. We do not entertain any doubt that the word 'life' in Article 21 bears the same signification. Is then the word 'personal liberty' to be construed as excluding from its purview an invasion on the part of the police of the sanctity of a man's home and an intrusion into his personal security and his right to sleep which is the normal comfort and a dire necessity for human existence even as an animal? It might not be inappropriate to refer here to the words of the preamble to the Constitution that it is designed to 'assure the dignity of the individual' and therefore of those cherished human values as the

means of ensuring his full development and evolution. We are referring to these objectives of the framers merely to draw attention to the concepts underlying the Constitution which would point to such vital words as 'personal liberty' having to be construed in a reasonable manner and to be attributed that sense which would promote and achieve those objectives and by no means to stretch the meaning of the phrase to square with any preconceived notions or doctrinaire constitutional theories. Frankfurter, J. observed in Wolf v. Colorado [(1949) 338 US 25] :

'The security of one's privacy against arbitrary intrusion by the police ... is basic to a free society. It is therefore implicit in 'the concept of ordered liberty' and as such enforceable against the States through the Due Process Clause. The knock at the door, whether by day or by night, as a prelude to a search, without authority of law but solely on the authority of the police, did not need the commentary of recent history to be condemned as inconsistent with the conception of human rights enshrined in the history and the basic constitutional documents of English-speaking peoples. ... We have no hesitation in saying that were a State affirmatively to sanction such police incursion into privacy it would run counter to the guaranty of the Fourteenth Amendment.'

Murphy, J. considered that such invasion was against 'the very essence of a scheme of ordered liberty'.

It is true that in the decision of the U.S. Supreme Court from which we have made these extracts, the Court had to consider also the impact of a violation of the Fourth Amendment which reads :

'The right of the people to be secure in their persons, houses, papers, and effects, against unreasonable searches and seizures, shall not be violated; and no warrants shall issue but upon probable cause, supported by oath or affirmation, and particularly describing the place to be searched, and the persons or things to be seized.'

and that our Constitution does not in terms confer any like constitutional guarantee. Nevertheless, these extracts would show that an unauthorised intrusion into a person's home and the disturbance caused to him thereby, is as it were the violation of a common law right of a man — an ultimate essential of ordered liberty, if not of the very concept of civilisation. An English Common Law maxim asserts that 'every man's house is his castle' and in Semayne case [(1604) 5 Co Rep 91 a], where this was applied, it was stated that 'the house of everyone is to him as his castle and fortress as well as for his defence against injury and violence as for his repose'. We are not unmindful of the fact that Semayne case [(1604) 5 Co Rep 91 a] was concerned with the law relating to executions in England, but the passage extracted has a validity quite apart from the context of the particular decision. It embodies an abiding principle which transcends mere protection of property rights and expounds a concept of 'personal liberty' which does not rest on any element of feudalism or on any theory of freedom which has ceased to be of value.

In our view clause (b) of Regulation 236 is plainly violative of Article 21 and as there is no 'law' on which the same could be justified it must be struck down as unconstitutional."

14. Subba Rao, J. (as the learned Judge then was), in his minority opinion also came to the conclusion that right to privacy was a part of Article 21 of the Constitution but went a step further and struck down Regulation 236 as a whole on the following reasoning :

> *"Further, the right to personal liberty takes in not only a right to be free from restrictions placed on his movements, but also free from encroachments on his private life. It is true our Constitution does not expressly declare a right to privacy as a fundamental right, but the said right is an essential ingredient of personal liberty. Every democratic country sanctifies domestic life; it is expected to give him rest, physical happiness, peace of mind and security. In the last resort, a person's house, where he lives with his family, is his 'castle': it is his rampart against encroachment on his personal liberty. The pregnant words of that famous Judge, Frankfurter J., in Wolf v. Colorado [(1949) 338 US 25], pointing out the importance of the security of one's privacy against arbitrary intrusion by the police, could have no less application to an Indian home as to an American one. If physical restraints on a person's movements affect his personal liberty, physical encroachments on his private life would affect it in a larger degree. Indeed, nothing is more deleterious to a man's physical happiness and health than a calculated interference with his privacy. We would, therefore, define the right of personal liberty in Article 21 as a right of an individual to be free from restrictions or encroachments on his person, whether those restrictions or encroachments are directly imposed or indirectly brought about by calculated measures. If so understood, all the acts of surveillance under Regulation 236 infringe the fundamental right of the petitioner under Article 21 of the Constitution."*

15. Article 21 of the Constitution has, therefore, been interpreted by all the seven learned Judges in Kharak Singh's *case* (majority and the minority opinions) to include that "right to privacy" as a part of the right to "protection of life and personal liberty" guaranteed under the said Article.

16. In Gobind v. State of M.P. [(1975) 2 SCC 148], a three-Judge Bench of this Court considered the constitutional validity of Regulations 855 and 856 of the Madhya Pradesh Police Regulations which provided surveillance by way of several measures indicated in the said regulations. This Court upheld the validity of the regulations by holding that Article 21 was not violated because the impugned regulations were "procedure established by law" in terms of the said Article.

17. In R. Rajagopal v. State of T.N. [(1994) 6 SCC 632], Jeevan Reddy, J. speaking for the

Court observed that in recent times right to privacy has acquired constitutional status. The learned Judge referred to Kharak Singh case[(1964) 1 SCR 332], Gobind's case [(1975) 2 SCC 148] and considered a large number of American and English cases and finally came to the conclusion that "the right to privacy is implicit in the right to life and liberty guaranteed to the citizens of this country by Article 21. It is a 'right to be let alone'." A citizen has a right "to safeguard the privacy of his own, his family, marriage, procreation, motherhood, child-bearing and education among other matters".

18. We have, therefore, no hesitation in holding that right to privacy is a part of the right to "life" and "personal liberty" enshrined under Article 21 of the Constitution. Once the facts in a given case constitute a right to privacy, Article 21 is attracted. The said right cannot be curtailed "except according to procedure established by law".

19. The right to privacy — by itself — has not been identified under the Constitution. As a concept it may be too broad and moralistic to define it judicially. Whether right to privacy can be claimed or has been infringed in a given case would depend on the facts of the said case. But the right to hold a telephone conversation in the privacy of one's home or office without interference can certainly be claimed as "right to privacy". Conversations on the telephone are often of an intimate and confidential character. Telephone conversation is part of a modern man's life. It is considered so important that more and more people are carrying mobile telephone instruments in their pockets. Telephone conversation is an important facet of a man's private life. Right to privacy would certainly include telephone conversation in the privacy of one's home or office. Telephone-tapping would, thus, infract Article 21 of the Constitution of India unless it is permitted under the procedure established by law.

20. Right to freedom of speech and expression is guaranteed under Article 19(1)(a) of the Constitution. This freedom means the right to express one's convictions and opinions freely by word of mouth, writing, printing, picture, or in any other manner. When a person is talking on telephone, he is exercising his right to freedom of speech and expression. Telephone-tapping, unless it comes within the grounds of restrictions under Article 19(2), would infract Article 19(1)(a) of the Constitution.

21. India is a signatory to the International Covenant on Civil and Political Rights, 1966. Article 17 of the said covenant is as under :

> *"Article 17*
>
> *1. No one shall be subject to arbitrary or unlawful interference with his privacy, family, human or correspondence, nor to lawful attacks on his honour and reputation.*
>
> *2. Everyone has the right to the protection of the law against such interference or attacks."*

22. Article 12 of the Universal Declaration of Human Rights, 1948, is almost in similar terms.

23. International law today is not confined to regulating the relations between the States. The scope continues to extend. Today, matters of social concern, such as health, education and economics apart from human rights fall within the ambit of International Regulations.

International law is more than ever aimed at individuals.

24. It is almost an accepted proposition of law, that the rules of customary international law which are not contrary to the municipal law shall be deemed to be incorporated in the domestic law.

25. Article 51 of the Constitution directs that the State shall endeavour to inter alia, foster respect for international law and treaty obligations in the dealings of organised peoples with one another. Relying upon the said Article, Sikri, C.J. in Kesavananda Bharati v. State of Kerala [(1973) Supp. SCR 1] observed as under :

> *"... it seems to me that, in view of Article 51 of the directive principles, this Court must interpret language of the Constitution, if not intractable, which is after all a municipal law, in the light of the United Nations Charter and the solemn declaration subscribed to by India."*

26. In A.D.M. v. Shivakant Shukla [(1976) 2 SCC 521], Khanna J. in his minority opinion observed as under :

> *"Equally well established is the rule of construction that if there be a conflict between the municipal law on one side and the international law or the provisions of any treaty obligations on the other, the courts would give effect to municipal law. If, however, two constructions of the municipal law are possible, the courts should lean in favour of adopting such construction as would make the provisions of the municipal law to be in harmony with the international law or treaty obligations. Every statute, according to this rule, is interpreted, so far as its language permits, so as not to be inconsistent with the comity of nations, or the established rules of international law, and the court will avoid a construction which would give rise to such inconsistency unless compelled to adopt it by plain and unambiguous language."*

27. In Jolly George Varghese v. Bank of Cochin [AIR 1980 SC 470] Krishna Iyer, J. posed the following question :

> *"From the perspective of international law the question posed is whether it is right to enforce a contractual liability by imprisoning a debtor in the teeth of Article 11 of the International Covenant on Civil and Political Rights. The Article reads :*
>
> > *No one shall be imprisoned merely on the ground of inability to fulfil a contractual obligation."*

28. The learned Judge interpreted Section 51 of the Code of Civil Procedure consistently with Article 11 of the International Covenant.

29. Article 17 of the International Covenant — quoted above — is not contrary to any part of our municipal law. Article 21 of the Constitution has, therefore, been interpreted in conformity with the international law.

30. Learned counsel assisting us in this case have not seriously challenged the constitutional vires of Section 5(2) of the Act. In this respect it would be useful to refer to the observations of this Court in Hukam Chand Shyam Lal v. Union of India [(1976) 2 SCC 128] :

> *"Section 5(1) if properly construed, does not confer unguided and unbridled power on the Central Government/State Government/specially authorised officer to take possession of any telegraph. Firstly, the occurrence of a 'public emergency' is the sine qua non for the exercise of power under this section. As a preliminary step to the exercise of further jurisdiction under this section the Government or the authority concerned must record its satisfaction as to the existence of such an emergency. Further, the existence of the emergency which is a prerequisite for the exercise of power under this section, must be a 'public emergency' and not any other kind of emergency. The expression 'public emergency' has not been defined in the statute, but contours broadly delineating its scope and features are discernible from the section which has to be read as a whole. In sub-section (1) the phrase 'occurrence of any public emergency' is connected with and is immediately followed by the phrase 'or in the interests of the public safety'. These two phrases appear to take colour from each other. In the first part of sub-section (2) those two phrases again occur in association with each other, and the context further clarifies with amplification that a public 'emergency' within the contemplation of this section is one which raises problems concerning the interest of the public safety, the sovereignty and integrity of India, the security of the State, friendly relations with foreign States or public order or the prevention of incitement to the commission of an offence. It is in the context of these matters that the appropriate authority has to form an opinion with regard to the occurrence of a 'public emergency' with a view to taking further action under this section. Economic emergency is not one of those matters expressly mentioned in the statute. Mere 'economic emergency' — as the High Court calls it — may not necessarily amount to a 'public emergency' and justify action under this section unless it raises problems relating to the matters indicated in the section."*

31. As mentioned above, the primary contention raised by the learned counsel is to lay down necessary safeguards to rule out the arbitrary exercise of power under the Act.

32. Section 5(2) of the Act permits the interception of messages in accordance with the provisions of the said section. "Occurrence of any public emergency" or "in the interest of public safety" are the sine qua non for the application of the provisions of Section 5(2) of the Act. Unless a public emergency has occurred or the interest of public safety demands, the authorities have no jurisdiction to exercise the powers under the said section. Public emergency would mean the prevailing of a sudden condition or state of affairs affecting the people at large calling for immediate action. The expression "public safety" means the state or condition of freedom from danger or risk for the people at large. When either of these two conditions are not in existence, the Central Government or a State Government or the authorised officer cannot resort to telephone-tapping even though there is satisfaction that it is necessary or expedient so to do in the interests of sovereignty and integrity of India etc. In other words, even if the Central Government is satisfied that it is necessary or expedient so to do in the interest of the sovereignty and integrity of India or the security of the State or friendly relations with sovereign States or public order or for preventing incitement to the commission of an offence, it cannot intercept the messages or resort to telephone-tapping unless a public emergency has occurred or the interest of public safety or the existence of the interest of public safety requires. Neither the occurrence of public emergency nor the interest of public safety are secretive conditions or situations. Either of the situations would be apparent to a reasonable person.

33. The first step under Section 5(2) of the Act, therefore, is the occurrence of any public emergency or the existence of a public safety interest. Thereafter, the competent authority under Section 5(2) of the Act is empowered to pass an order of interception after recording to its satisfaction that, it is necessary or expedient to do so in the interest of (i) sovereignty and integrity of India, (ii) the security of the State, (iii) friendly relations with foreign States, (iv) public order; or (v) for preventing incitement to the commission of an offence. When any of the five situations mentioned above require, then the said authority, to the satisfaction of the competent authority, may pass the order for interception of messages by recording reasons in writing for doing so.

34. The above analysis of Section 5(2) of the Act shows that so far the power to intercept messages/conversations with respect to the section clearly lays down the situations/conditions under which it can be exercised. But, the substantive law as laid down in Section 5(2) of the Act must have procedural backing so that the exercise of power is fair and reasonable. The said procedure itself must be just, fair and reasonable. It has been settled by this Court in Maneka Gandhi v. Union of India [(1978) 2 SCR 621], that the "procedure which deals with the modalities of regulating, restricting or even rejecting a fundamental right falling within Article 21 has to be fair, not foolish, carefully designed to effectuate, not to subvert, the substantive right itself". Thus, understood, "procedure" must rule out anything arbitrary, unconventional or bizarre. A valuable constitutional right can be canalised only by canalised processes.

35. We are of the view that there is considerable force in the contention of Mr. Rajindar Sachar, Mr. Kapil Sibal and Dr. Rajeev Dhavan that no procedure has been prescribed for the exercise of the power under Section 5(2) of the Act. It is not disputed that no rules have been framed under Section 7(2)(b) of the Act for providing the precautions to be taken for preventing the improper interception or disclosure of messages. In the absence of just and fair procedure for regulating the exercise of power under Section 5(2) of the Act, it is not possible to safeguard the rights of the citizens guaranteed under Articles 19(1)(a) and 21 of the Constitution of India. The CBI investigation has revealed several lapses in the execution of the orders passed under Section 5(2) of the Act. Paras 21 and 22 of the report have already been quoted in the earlier part of this judgment.

36. The Second Press Commission in paras 164, 165 and 166 of its report has commented on the "tapping of telephones" as under :

"Tapping of Telephones

164. It is felt in some quarters, not without reason, that not infrequently the Press in general and its editorial echelons in particular have to suffer tapping of telephones.

165. Tapping of telephones is a serious invasion of privacy. It is a variety of technological eavesdropping. Conversations on the telephone are often of an intimate and confidential character. The relevant statute, i.e., Indian Telegraph Act, 1885, a piece of ancient legislation, does not concern itself with tapping. Tapping cannot be regarded as a tort because the law as it stands today does not know of any general right to privacy.

166. This is hardly a satisfactory situation. There are instances where apprehensions of disclosure of sources of information as well as the character of information may result in constraints on freedom of information and consequential drying up of its source. We, therefore, recommend that telephones may not be tapped except in the interest of national security, public order, investigation of crime and similar objectives, under orders made in writing by the Minister concerned or an officer of rank to whom the power in that behalf is delegated. The order should disclose reasons. An order for tapping of telephones should expire after three months from the date of the order. Moreover, within a period of six weeks the order should come up for review before a Board constituted on the lines prescribed in statutes providing for preventive detention. It should be for the Board to decide whether tapping should continue any longer. The decision of the Board should be binding on the Government. It may be added that the Minister or his delegates will be competent to issue a fresh order for tapping of the telephone if circumstances call for it. The Telegraph Act should contain a clause to give effect to this recommendation."

37. While dealing with Section 5(2) of the Act, the Second Press Commission gave the following suggestions regarding "public emergency" and "interest of public safety" :

"160. It may be noticed that the public emergency mentioned in the sub-section is not an objective fact. Some public functionary must determine its existence and it is on the basis of the existence of a public emergency that an authorised official should exercise the power of withholding transmission of telegrams. We think that the appropriate Government should declare the existence of the public emergency by a notification warranting the exercise of this power and it is only after the issue of such a notification that the power of withholding telegraphic messages should be exercised by the delegated authority. When such a notification is issued, the principal officer of the telegraph office can be required to submit to the District

Magistrate, whom we consider to be the proper person to be the delegate for exercising this power, such telegrams brought for transmission which are likely to be prejudicial to the interest sought to be protected by the sub-section. Thereupon the District Magistrate should pass an order in writing withholding or allowing the transmission of the telegram. We are suggesting the safeguard of a prior notification declaring the existence of a public emergency because the power of interception is a drastic power and we are loath to leave the determination of the existence of a public emergency in the hands of a delegate.

We are of the view that whenever the power is exercised in the interest of public safety, it should, as far as possible, be exercised by the Minister concerned of the appropriate Government for one month at a time extendible by Government if the emergency continues. However, in exceptional circumstances the power can be delegated to the District Magistrate.

163. We also think that as soon as an order is passed by the District Magistrate withholding the transmission of a telegraphic message, it should be communicated to the Central or State Government, as the case may be, and also to the sender and the addressee of the telegram. The text of the order should be placed on the table of the respective State Legislatures after three months. We recommend that, as suggested by the Press Council of India in its annual report covering 1969, the officer in charge of a telegraph office should maintain a register giving particulars of the time of receipt, the sender and addressee of every telegram which he refers to the District Magistrate with recommendation of its withholding. Similarly, the District Magistrate should maintain a register of the time receipt, content and addressee of each telegram and record his decision thereon, together with the time of the decision. Data of this nature will help courts, if called upon, to determine the presence or absence of mala fide in the withholding of telegrams."

38. According to Mr. Sachar the only way to safeguard the right of privacy of an individual is that there should be a prior judicial scrutiny before any order for telephone-tapping is passed under Section 5(2) of the Act. He states that such judicial scrutiny may be ex parte. Mr. Sachar contended that the judicial scrutiny alone would take away the apprehension of arbitrariness or unreasonableness of the action. Mr. Kapil Sibal, on the other hand, has suggested various other safeguards — short of prior judicial scrutiny — based on the law on the subject in England as enacted by the Interception of the Communications Act, 1985.

39. We agree with Mr. Sibal that in the absence of any provision in the statute, it is not possible to provide for prior judicial scrutiny as a procedural safeguard. It is for the Central Government to make rules under Section 7 of the Act. Section 7(2)(b) specifically provides that the Central Government may make rules laying down the precautions to be taken for preventing the improper interception or disclosure of messages. The Act was enacted in the year 1885. The power to make rules under Section 7 of the Act has been there for over a century but the Central Government has not thought it proper to frame the necessary rules despite severe criticism of the manner in which the power under Section 5(2) has been exercised. It is entirely for the Central Government to make rules on the subject but till the time it is done, the right to privacy of an individual has to be safeguarded. In order to rule out arbitrariness in the exercise of power under Section 5(2) of the Act and till the time the Central Government lays down just, fair and reasonable procedure under Section 7(2)(b) of the Act, it is necessary to lay down procedural safeguards for the exercise of power under Section 5(2) of the Act so that the right to privacy of a person is protected.

40. We, therefore, order and direct as under :

1. An order for telephone-tapping in terms of Section 5(2) of the Act shall not be issued except by the Home Secretary, Government of India (Central Government) and Home Secretaries of the State Governments. In an urgent case the power may be delegated to an officer of the Home Department of the Government of India and the State Governments not below the rank of Joint Secretary. Copy of the order shall be sent to the Review Committee concerned within one week of the passing of the order.

2. The order shall require the person to whom it is addressed, to intercept in the course of their transmission by means of a public telecommunication system, such communications as are described in the order. The order may also require the person to whom it is addressed to disclose the intercepted material to such persons and in such manner as are described in the order.

3. The matters to be taken into account in considering whether an order is necessary under Section 5(2) of the Act and shall include the information which is considered necessary to acquire or could reasonably be acquired by other means.

4. The interception required under Section 5(2) of the Act shall be the interception of such communications as are sent to or from one or more addresses, specified in the order, being an address or addresses likely to be used for the transmission of communications to or from, from one particular person specified or described in the order or one particular set of premises specified or described in the order.

5. The order under Section 5(2) of the Act shall, unless renewed, cease to have effect at the end of the period of two months from the date of issue. The authority which issued the order may, at any time before the end of two month period renew the order if it considers that it is necessary to continue the order in terms of Section 5(2) of the Act. The total period for

the operation of the order shall not exceed six months.

6. The authority which issued the order shall maintain the following records :

(a) the intercepted communications;

(b) the extent to which the material is disclosed;

(c) the number of persons and their identity to whom any of the material is disclosed;

(d) the extent to which the material is copied; and

(e) the number of copies made of any of the material.

7. The use of the intercepted material shall be limited to the minimum; that is necessary in terms of Section 5(2) of the Act.

8. Each copy made of any of the intercepted material shall be destroyed as soon as its retention is no longer necessary in terms of Section 5(2) of the Act.

9. There shall be a Review Committee consisting of Cabinet Secretary, the Law Secretary and the Secretary, Telecommunication at the level of the Central Government. The Review Committee at the State level shall consist of Chief Secretary, Law Secretary and another member, other than the Home Secretary, appointed by the State Government.

(a) The Committee shall on its own, within two months of the passing of the order by the authority concerned, investigate whether there is or has been a relevant order under Section 5(2) of the Act. Where there is or has been an order, whether there has been any contravention of the provisions of Section 5(2) of the Act.

(b) If on an investigation the Committee concludes that there has been a contravention of the provisions of Section 5(2) of the Act, it shall set aside the order under scrutiny of the Committee. It shall further direct the destruction of the copies of the intercepted material.

(c) If on investigation, the Committee comes to the conclusion that there has been no contravention of the provisions of Section 5(2) of the Act, it shall record the finding to that effect.

41. The writ petition is disposed of. No costs.

In the Supreme Court of India

Writ Petition (Civil) No. 560 of 1994
People's Union for Civil Liberties (PUCL) v. Union of India & Ors.[8]

Date of Order : 26.03.1996

Bench : Kuldip Singh and Faizan Uddin, JJ.

[PUCL had filed this case based on the report given by "Campaign against Child Labour". According to this report, children below the age of 15 years were forced into bonded labour. One of the boys, aged about 8 years, was beaten to death. Out of 4 boys who were untraceable, 3 were recovered by the police. Regarding the 4th boy, the Maharashtra Police said that it was making efforts to trace him. The Supreme Court granted compensation of Rs. 2 lakhs to the boy whose brother was killed which was to be paid by the State of Maharashtra. The other 3 boys were granted compensation of Rs. 75,000 each to be paid by the State of Tamil Nadu. The Court recorded appreciation of the efforts made by PUCL.]

Order

1. This public interest petition under Article 32 of the Constitution of India is based on the report given by a non-governmental organisation called "Campaign against Child Labour". According to the said report, one Rajput used to travel to Madurai in Tamil Nadu for the purpose of procuring child labour by paying a paltry sum ranging between Rs. 500 to Rs. 1500 to the poor parents. The children aged below 15 years so procured were forced into bonded labour. It was further stated in the report that one of the boys, viz., Shiva Murugan, aged about 8 years was beaten to death by the said Rajput. As mentioned in this Court's order dated 18.03.1996, Rajput has already been convicted for murder by the trial court. The other four boys, viz., Raja Murugan (aged 8 years), Rajesh (aged 13 years), Muniyandi (aged 15 years) and Mukesh (aged 16 years) were not traceable after the occurrence, resulting in the death of Shiva Murugan. Under the directions of this Court, three boys, viz., Rajesh, Muniyandi and Mukesh have been traced by the Maharashtra Police. The fourth boy, Raja Murugan, who is the real brother of late Shiva Murugan is still untraced. As noticed by this Court, the Maharashtra Police is still making efforts to trace Raja Murugan.

2. Mr. Rajindar Sachar, learned counsel appearing for the petitioner, states that the parents

8. (1998) 8 SCC 485

of these boys are entitled to compensation. In support of his contention Mr. Sachar relies on *Nilabati Behera v. State of Orissa* [(1993) 2 SCC 746], Verma, J. speaking for this Court observed as under :

> *"17. It follows that 'a claim in public law for compensation' for contravention of human rights and fundamental freedoms, the protection of which is guaranteed in the Constitution, is an acknowledged remedy for enforcement and protection of such rights, and such a claim based on strict liability made by resorting to a constitutional remedy provided for the enforcement of a fundamental right is 'distinct from, and in addition to, the remedy in private law for damages for the tort' resulting from the contravention of the fundamental right. The defence of sovereign immunity being inapplicable, and alien to the concept of guarantee of fundamental rights, there can be no question of such a defence being available in the constitutional remedy. It is this principle which justifies award of monetary compensation for contravention of fundamental rights guaranteed by the Constitution, when that is the only practicable mode of redress available for the contravention made by the State or its servants in the purported exercise of their powers, and enforcement of the fundamental right is claimed by resort to the remedy in public law under the Constitution by recourse to Articles 32 and 226 of the Constitution. This is what was indicated in Rudul Sah v. State of Bihar [(1983) 4 SCC 441] and is the basis of the subsequent decisions in which compensation was awarded under Articles 32 and 226 of the Constitution, for contravention of fundamental rights."*

3. Mr. Sachar has further contended that under the Bonded Labour System (Abolition) Act, 1976, the State of Maharashtra is required to set up effective vigilance machinery to ensure that the children in the State are not exploited. He further contends that the trial court while convicting Rajput came to the conclusion that the District Magistrate and the Vigilance Committees which were set up under the above-mentioned Act were not functioning properly. Keeping in view the facts and circumstances of this case, we direct the State of Maharashtra to pay a sum of Rs. 2,00,000 (two lakhs) to Raja Murugan for himself and also for the death of his brother Shiva Murugan. Since Raja Murugan (a minor) is an orphan, the amount be deposited with the District Magistrate of the area where Raja Murugan lives. The District Magistrate shall deposit the amount in a scheduled bank. The total income so earned shall be divided into 12 months and be given to Raja Murugan every month till he attains majority. On attaining majority, he shall be entitled to receive the principal amount. This amount of Rs. 2,00,000 shall be paid by the State of Maharashtra.

4. So far as the other three boys Rajesh, Muniyandi and Mukesh are concerned, we direct that they be given Rs. 75,000 each as compensation which shall be given by the State of Tamil Nadu within two months. The amount shall be deposited with the District Magistrate concerned who shall deposit the same in a scheduled bank. Monthly interest be paid to the parents till the children attain majority when they shall be entitled to the principal amount.

5. The writ petition is disposed of. We place on record appreciation for Mr. Sanjay Parikh for assisting us in this case.

In the Supreme Court of India

Writ Petition (Civil) No. 105 of 2004
People's Union for Civil Liberties (PUCL) v. Union of India & Anr.[9]

Date of Judgement : 18.01.2005

Bench : Y.K. Sabharwal and D.M. Dharmadhikari, JJ.

[PUCL had challenged the appointment of a police officer as member of the National Human Right Commission (NHRC) under the provisions of Protection of Human Rights Act, 1993. The question before the Court was whether Section 3(2)(d) has to be read keeping in mind the Paris Principles and whether former members of the police force or members of any security force as a class were ineligible to become members of the Commission. Justice Y.K. Sabharwal allowed the Writ Petition by holding that the appointment of the police officer (in 2004) as member of NHRC was null and void. Justice D.M. Dharmadhikari gave a dissenting opinion. Therefore, the question was referred to a larger bench.]

Judgment

Y.K. Sabharwal, J.

1. The National Human Rights Commission (NHRC) is a high-powered statutory body to act as an instrument for the protection and promotion of human rights. The credibility of such an institution depends upon a high degree of public confidence. In the present case, the important question that has been raised is whether a former member of the police force is eligible to become a member of NHRC.

2. NHRC has been set up under provisions of the Protection of Human Rights Act, 1993 (for short 'the Act'). Its composition is provided for in Section 3(2) of the Act. The question for consideration in this petition is about the interpretation of Section 3(2)(d), which stipulates that the Commission shall consist of two members to be appointed from amongst persons having 'knowledge of, or practical experience in, matters relating to human rights'. The fundamental question is whether a Police officer would fall in the category stipulated under this provision and is appointment of such a person consistent with the language of the section and the true intendment of the Act. For determining this fundamental question, it is necessary to note, in

9. (2005) 2 SCC 436

brief, the background relating to the concept of Human Rights, the provisions of the Act and the scheme thereof. First the facts which led to the filing of the petition may be briefly noticed.

3. A vacancy arose in NHRC in November 2003. It was in respect of the appointment to be made under Section 3(2)(d). The Respondent No. 2, a Police Officer, retired as Director of Central Bureau of Investigation (CBI) in December 2003. Every appointment is required to be made after obtaining the recommendations of a Committee as postulated by Section 4 of the Act. The notice was sent to the Committee members on 13.02.2004, convening a meeting for 19.02.2004. It seems that on 19th February, the Home Secretary spoke to the Joint Secretary to the Leader of Opposition who informed him that the Leader of Opposition in the House of the People would not be able to attend the meeting but she has conveyed her approval for recommendation of the name of respondent No. 2. Likewise, the Speaker of the House of the People also expressed inability to attend the meeting but conveyed his approval to the appointment of respondent No. 2. So far the Leader of Opposition in the Council of States is concerned, his personal staff informed that being unwell and admitted in hospital, he would not be able to attend the meeting. A meeting was held on 19.02.2004 wherein it was decided to recommend the name of respondent No. 2 to be appointed as a member of the Commission. The Committee noticed that the Leader of Opposition in the House of the People and the Speaker had both conveyed their approval for the said recommendation. Thus on 19.02.2004, respondent No. 2 was selected to be appointed as a Member of NHRC.

4. The appointment has been challenged mainly on the ground of ineligibility of a police officer for being considered for appointment under the category contemplated by Section 3(2)(d). We may note that the challenge is based on the fundamental issue and not on any allegations of personal nature against respondent No. 2. The contention is that no one from police or security force is eligible to be a member of such a body and it is clear from the provisions of the Act, its scheme as also from the very concept which gave birth to the protection of Human Rights.

5. The Act has been enacted to provide for better protection of human rights and for matters connected therewith or incidental thereto. The Statement of Objects and Reasons notes that the human rights embodied in the International Covenant on Civil and Political Rights and the International Covenant on Economic, Social and Cultural Rights, adopted by the General Assembly of the United Nations on 16.12.1966, stand substantially protected by the Constitution of India. However, there has been growing concern in the country and abroad about issues relating to human rights. Having regard to this, changing social realities and emerging trends in the nature of crime and violence, the Government has been reviewing the existing laws, procedures and system of administration of justice, with a view to bringing about greater accountability and transparency in them, and devising efficient and effective methods of dealing with the situation. Taking into account the views of all concerned, the Act was enacted.

6. The "Human rights" means the rights relating to life, liberty, equality and dignity of the individual guaranteed by the Constitution or embodied in the International Covenants and enforceable by courts in India [Section 2(1)(d)]. "International Covenants" mean the International Covenant on Civil and Political Rights and the International Covenant on Economic, Social and Cultural Rights adopted by the General Assembly of the United Nations on 16.12.1966 [Section 2(1)(f)]. Besides, two members to be appointed from amongst persons having knowledge of or practical experience in, matters relating to human rights as provided in clause (d) of Section 3(2), it is stipulated that the Commission shall consist of (a) a Chairperson who shall have been a Chief Justice of the Supreme Court; (b) one member who is, or has been, a Judge of the Supreme Court; and (c) one member who is, or has been the Chief Justice of a High Court. A high powered Committee consisting of — (a) the Prime Minister; (b) Speaker of the House of the People; (c) Minister in charge of the Ministry of Home Affairs in the Government of India; (d) Leader of the Opposition in the House of the People; (e) Leader of the Opposition in the Council of States; and (f) Deputy Chairman of the Council of States, has been entrusted with the responsibility to make recommendations for appointment of Chairperson and other members, as provided in Section 4(1) of the Act. In the event of the occurrence of any vacancy in the office of the Chairperson, any one of the members can be authorised to act as the Chairperson until the appointment of a new Chairperson to fill such vacancy.

7. Section 11 of the Act provides that the Central Government shall make available to NHRC (a) an officer of the rank of Secretary to the Government of India who shall be the Secretary General of the Commission; and (b) such police and investigative staff under an officer not below the rank of a Director General of Police and such other officers and staff as may be necessary for the efficient performance of the function of the Commission.

8. The functions and powers of the Commission have been set out in Part III of the Act. Section 12 whereof, inter alia, provides that the Commission shall have power to review the safeguards provided by or under the Constitution or any other law for the time being in force for the protection of human rights and recommend measures for their effective implementation and study treaties and other international instruments on human rights and make recommendations for their effective implementation. The Commission is also empowered to require any person, subject to any privilege which may be claimed by that person under any law for the time being in force, to furnish information on such points or matters as, in the opinion of the Commission, may be useful for, or relevant to, the subject-matter of the inquiry and any person so required shall be deemed to be legally bound to furnish such information within the meaning of Sections 176 and 177 of the Penal Code [Section 13(2)].

9. The power to conduct any investigation pertaining to the inquiry has been provided for in Section 14 of the Act. Special investigation teams can be constituted for the purposes of investigation and prosecution of offences arising out of violation of human rights in the manner provided in Section 27 of the Act.

10. Chapter V deals with constitution of the State Human Rights Commission and matters related thereto including appointment of Chairperson and other members and functions of the said Commission.

11. The NHRC is a unique expert body in itself and has been augmented in *Paramjit Kaur v. State of Punjab* [(1999) 2 SCC 131]. The judgment sets out how the Chairman and other two members, postulated by clauses (a) to (c) of Section 3(2) of the Act, throughout their long tenure get opportunities to consider, expound and enforce the fundamental rights and how they are, in their own way, experts in the field.

12. Having noticed salient features of the Act, it can be seen that the aspect of investigation is only one part, which has been dealt with separately. The other part being the decision-making power and functions of the Commission is being dealt separately. Let us now note the development at the international level which ultimately led to the passing of the Act. The consideration at the international level on the establishment and functioning of national institutions can provide a backdrop to an understanding of the Act. Articles 1, 55, 56, 62, 68 and 76 of the UN Charter provide the basis for recognition, elaboration of the contents of the standards and the machinery for implementing the protection of human rights. The General Assembly of the United Nations on 10.09.1948 adopted a Universal Declaration of Human Rights. The International Covenant on Civil and Political Rights, the International Covenant on Economic, Social and Cultural Rights adopted by the General Assembly of the United Nations on 16.12.1966 form a bedrock of international recognition of human rights.

13. In the year 1991, the United Nations sponsored meetings of representatives of National Institutions in Paris wherein a detailed set of principles on the status of National Human Rights Institutions was developed. The principles developed therein are commonly known as 'Paris principles'. The Paris principles were subsequently endorsed by the United Nations Commission on Human Rights and the United Nations General Assembly. The six criteria of National Human Rights Institutions under the Paris principles are :

> *"(a) Independence guaranteed by the Statute or constitution.*
> *(b) Autonomy from Government.*
> *(c) Pluralism in membership.*
> *(d) Broad mandate based on human rights standards.*
> *(e) Adequate power of State.*
> *(f) Sufficient resources."*

14. The Paris Principles set out the principles relating to the status and functioning of national institutions for protection and promotion of human rights. In respect of composition and guarantees of independence and pluralism, it provides that :

> *"The composition of a national institution and the appointment of its members, whether by means of an election or otherwise, shall be established in accordance with a procedure which affords all necessary guarantees to ensure the pluralist representation of the social forces (of civilian society) involved in the protection and promotion of human rights, particularly by powers which will enable effective cooperation to be established with, or through the presence of, representatives of :*
>
> > *non-governmental organisations responsible for human rights and efforts to combat racial discrimination, trade unions, social and professional organisations concerned, for example, associations of lawyers, doctors, journalists and eminent scientists;*
> > *Trends in philosophical or religious thought;*
> > *Universities and qualified experts;*
> > *Parliament;*

Government departments (if they are included, these representatives should participate in the deliberations only in an advisory capacity)."

15. With regards to the structure of such institutions, the guidelines, inter alia, recommended that they would be so designed as to reflect in their composition, wide cross-sections of the nation thereby bringing all parts of that population into the decision-making process in regard to human rights.

16. India is a party to the aforesaid covenants. Indian Constitution guarantees essential human rights in the form of fundamental rights under Part III and also directive principles of State policy in Part IV which are fundamental in the governance of the country. Freedoms granted under Part III have been liberally construed by various pronouncements of this Court in the last half a century in favour of the subjects also, keeping in view the international covenants. The object has been to place citizens at a central stage and State being highly accountable.

17. The main question is whether Section 3(2)(d), is to be read keeping in view the Paris principles. If it is to be so, whether a former member of the Police force or member of any Security Forces as a class, are ineligible to become members of the Commission.

18. The investigation under the Act has been separately dealt with in the manner provided in Sections 11, 14 and 37. A Police officer may be a very good investigator. He may have vast experience in respect of the nature of commission of crime and consequentially its prevention. But, for the present purposes, what is relevant to be borne in mind is that a number of cases reported to NHRC relate to acts of omission and commission by the members of such forces. In this regard, reference can be made to NHRC Report for the year 2001-02. The report shows that a large number of cases relating to custodial deaths and police encounter deaths came up for inquiry and consideration before the Commission. The officers of these forces while being members of service necessarily come across such cases. An individual officer may be very good but something inbuilt in service as a class is the relevant consideration. The Commission has also to deal with types of cases, which officers had sometimes to defend, on account of nature of their service. Further, the knowledge or practical experience in relation to commission of crime, investigation and solving a crime which may show violation of human rights is one thing and the knowledge or experience relating to protection of life, liberty, equality and dignity of the individual guaranteed by the Constitution or embodied in the international covenants and enforceable by courts in India is altogether different. The requirement of the section is of latter and not former. *Paramjit Kaur case* [(1999) 2 SCC 131] gives an indication as to what type of knowledge or practical experience the Act has in contemplation in the matter of human rights, so as to make a person eligible to be appointed as a member of the Commission. We have to consider the eligibility of a person who has to become a part of the decision-making process of NHRC and not the process of investigation which the Commission may direct to be conducted. The exclusion of the category under consideration seems evident when seen as to who are included in the light of the Paris principles, namely, representatives of non-governmental organisations responsible for human rights and efforts to combat racial discrimination, trade unions, social and professional organisations concerned, for example, associations of lawyers, doctors, journalists, eminent scientists; trends in philosophical or religious thoughts; universities and qualified experts; and Parliament. Regarding the government departments, their representation in the deliberations is only in advisory capacity. The scheme of the Act is to protect and implement human rights including those envisaged in Article 21 of the Constitution and International Covenants. The functions include understanding and dissemination of knowledge on human rights. The members referred in Section 3(2)(d) are required to have the knowledge and practical experience in matters relating to human rights of the type expected from those covered under Sections 3(2)(a), (b) and (c). Reference may also be made to Section 7 which provides that in the event of the occurrence of any vacancy in the office of the Chairperson, any one of the members may be authorised to act as the Chairperson until the appointment of a new Chairperson. The person to be appointed under Section 3(2)(d) should also be one who can act as a Chairperson under the contingency contemplated by Section 7 of the Act.

19. The Union of India, in its counter-affidavit, has mentioned certain cases investigated by Respondent No. 2 during his tenure as a Police officer, which includes among others the Punjab Massacre case. It has also been stated that respondent No. 2 is a Vice-President (Asia) of Interpol, an international police organisation in which capacity, it is claimed, he is involved in developing mechanisms for police cooperation in investigation and prosecution of crimes across borders including terrorism, human safety and human trafficking, which are all offences against human rights. The Union of India in the counter-affidavit claims that :

> *"During the course of their careers, police officers garner in vast practical experience in police methodology, investigative techniques and other practical matters relating to human rights. It is submitted that such experience would inter alia aid the Commission in identifying cases of police malpractice and the Commission would be able to look behind cases of cover-up and attempts to shield guilty police officers. It is, therefore, submitted that Respondent No. 2 has adequate knowledge and practical experience in matters relating to human rights, qualifying him for appointment to the Commission under Section 3(2)(d) of the Act."*

20. The expertise in investigations cannot be confused with expertise in the matters relating to human rights. Two are entirely different. For investigation, police and investigating staff is available to the Commission. The Commission can also require any person to furnish information on such points or matters as may be useful for, or relevant to, the subject-matter of inquiry. It may utilise services of any officer or investigating agency as stipulated in Section 14 of the Act for the purpose of conducting any investigation pertaining to the inquiry. The Central Government is required to make available to the Commission such police and investigating staff under an officer not below the rank of Director General of Police and such other officers and staff as may be necessary for the efficient performance of the functions of the Commission.

21. While construing the provisions of the statute, the nature and object of the statute cannot be overlooked. In these matters, the aspect of public perception cannot be altogether overlooked. The statute of the nature under consideration is based on public confidence. It cannot be overlooked that notwithstanding the exemplary role of police and security forces, there have been many instances of excesses by the members of the forces leading to public unrest and deteriorating public faith. The issue is not whether all are fully true or not, but is what exists in the public mind and whether there is some justification.

22. An individual Police officer may be very good but his participation in decision-making as a member of the Commission is likely to give rise to a reasonable apprehension in the minds of the citizens that he may subconsciously influence the functioning of the Commission. Such reasonable perceptions of the affected parties are relevant considerations to ensure the continued public confidence in the credibility and impartiality of an institution like NHRC.

23. What has been said about the institution of the judiciary in *P.K. Ghosh v. J.G. Rajput* [(1995) 6 SCC 744], can also be applied for considering an institution like NHRC. It was said that the credibility in the functioning of justice-delivery system and the reasonable perception of the affected parties are relevant considerations to ensure the continuance of public confidence in the credibility and impartiality of the judiciary.

24. Assuming two constructions of Section 3(2)(d) are reasonably possible, the construction which promotes public confidence, advances the cause of human rights and seeks to fulfil the purpose of international instruments has to be preferred than the one which nullifies it. Ambiguity if any, in the statutory provision is required to be removed by judicial process to advance the cause of protection of human rights.

25. The observations in *P.N. Duda v. P. Shiv Shanker* [(1988) 3 SCC 167, that "After all it cannot be denied that predisposition or subtle prejudice or unconscious prejudice or what in Indian language is called 'sanskar' are inarticulate major premises in decision-making process" are quite apt in the present context.

26. On the aspect of subconscious mind, what Justice Frankfurter said for not participating in the decision of *Public Utilities Commission of the District of Columbia, Capital Transit Company & Washington Transit Radio, Inc. v. Franklin S. Pollak & Guy Martin* [343 US 451], is quite enlightening. It reads :

> *"The judicial process demands that a judge move within the framework of relevant legal rules and the covenanted modes of thought for ascertaining them. He must think dispassionately and submerge private feeling on every aspect of a case. There is a good deal of shallow talk that the judicial robe does not change the man within it. It does. The fact is that on the whole judges do lay aside private views in discharging their judicial functions. This is achieved through training, professional habits, self-discipline and that fortunate alchemy by which men are loyal to the obligation with which they are entrusted. But it is also true that reason cannot control the subconscious influence of feelings of which it is unaware. When there is ground for believing that such unconscious feelings may operate in the ultimate judgment, or may not unfairly lead others to believe they are operating, judges recuse themselves. They do not sit in judgment. They do this for a variety of reasons. The guiding consideration is that the administration of justice should reasonably appear to be disinterested as well as be so in fact."*
>
> (emphasis supplied)

27. The aforesaid passage has been quoted and endorsed in *Ranjit Thakur v. Union of India* [(1987) 4 SCC 611].

28. When a Police officer is a member of NHRC, the question to be asked is not of his bias but of the impression of a reasonable right minded person and the confidence the Commission would generate as a result of participation of a person of such a background.

29. The principles laid in the aforesaid decisions can be reasonably applied for considering the question in issue is in relation to NHRC which is headed by a person who held the position of the head of the judiciary and has the assistance of a former Chief Justice and Judge of the highest court of the country.

30. In respect of violations of human rights during investigation, in *D.K. Basu v. State of W.B.* [(1997) 1 SCC 416], grave concern was expressed by this Court in respect of persons who were supposed to be the protectors of the citizens and committed violence under the shield of uniform and authority in the four walls of a police station or lock-up, the victims being totally helpless. It will be useful to note what was said in para 18 which reads :

> *"However, in spite of the constitutional and statutory provisions aimed at safeguarding the personal liberty and life of a citizen, growing incidence of torture and deaths in police custody has been a disturbing factor. Experience shows that worst violations of human rights take place during the course of investigation, when the police with a view to secure evidence or confession often resorts to third-degree methods including torture and adopts techniques of screening arrest by either not recording the arrest or describing the deprivation of liberty merely as a prolonged interrogation. A reading of the morning newspapers almost everyday carrying reports of dehumanising torture, assault, rape and death in custody of police or other governmental agencies is indeed depressing. The increasing incidence of torture and death in custody has assumed such alarming proportions that it is affecting the credibility of the rule of law and the administration of criminal justice system. The community rightly feels perturbed. Society's cry for justice becomes louder."*

31. The Court also took a note of various other security forces and other agencies, where too there were instances of tortures and deaths in the custody. *N.C. Dhoundial v. Union of India* [(2004) 2 SCC 579], was a case where the Commission enquired the violation of human rights by the officials of CBI.

32. Respondent No. 2 has been a Police officer throughout his service career. We assume that he was a very efficient officer and investigated many cases including complicated and sensitive cases but what is relevant for the present purpose is the 'sanskar, to borrow words from *P.N. Duda case* [(1988) 3 SCC 167], i.e., conscious or sub-conscious bias in favour of investigating agencies.

33. Once again, we wish to make it clear that neither are we condemning any force nor upright officers of which there is no dearth, but are examining the confidence that is likely to be generated in the community at large on officers of such services being appointed as member of the Commission, particularly, when the language of Section 3(2)(d) does not admit of only one interpretation. When two interpretations are possible, the interpretation which promotes the object of the Act and public confidence deserves to be adopted.

34. The question can also be examined from another angle. The knowledge or experience of a police officer of human rights violation, represents only one facet of human rights violation and its protection, namely, arising out of crime. Human rights violations are of various forms which besides Police brutality are gender injustice, pollution, environmental degradation, mal-nutrition, social ostracism of Dalits etc. A Police officer can claim to have experience of only one facet. That is not the requirement of the section.

35. Let us also note some of the decisions, in which drawing aid from international covenants, law enacted by the Indian Parliament was construed and relief of protection of human rights was given.

36. In *Mackinnon Mackenzie and Co. Ltd. v. Audrey D'Costa* [(1987) 2 SCC 469], this Court considered the case of a "confidential lady stenographer" who complained that she and other women stenographers who were in the service of a company were being paid lower emoluments than their male counterparts. Taking note of the fact that India is a party to the international convention concerning equal remuneration for men and women, for work of equal value (the Equal Remuneration Convention, 1951), the Court adopted a principle embodied in the Convention to construe a law enacted by Parliament, the Equal Remuneration Act, 1976, to grant relief to the petitioner therein by holding the action of the employer to be an unconstitutional violation of the principles of equal pay for equal work.

37. In *Sheela Barse v. Secretary, Children's Aid Society* [(1987) 3 SCC 50 at 54], the petitioner complained about the state of affairs in an observation home for children. While issuing directions to the State of Maharashtra, it was held by this Court that the international instruments which had been ratified by India and which elucidated norms for the protection of children cast an obligation on the State to implement their principles. The Court said :

> *"Children are the citizens of the future era. On the proper bringing up of children and giving them the proper training to turn out to be good citizens depends the future of the country. In recent years, this position has been well realised. In 1959 the Declaration of All the Rights of the Child was adopted by the General Assembly of the United Nations and in Article 24 of the International Covenant on Civil and Political Rights, 1966, the importance of the child has been appropriately recognised. India as a party to these international charters having ratified the Declarations, it is an obligation of the Government of India as also the State machinery to implement the same in the proper way."*

38. In the aforesaid case, this Court travelled one step further than in *Mackinnon Mackenzie* [(1987) 2 SCC 469] and made not merely a reference to an international convention but a stronger expression of the binding nature of its obligations.

39. The endeavour of this Court to ensure a virtual judicial incorporation of treaty law into the *corpus juris* is demonstrated by its opinion in *Vishaka v. State of Rajasthan* [AIR 1997 SC 3011 at 3015], in the following words :

"The meaning and content of the fundamental rights guaranteed in the Constitution of India are of sufficient amplitude to encompass all the facets of gender equality including prevention of sexual harassment or abuse. Independence of judiciary forms a part of our constitutional scheme. The international conventions and norms are to be read into them in the absence of enacted domestic law occupying the field when there is no inconsistency between them. It is now an accepted rule of judicial construction that regard must be had to international conventions and norms for construing domestic law when there is no inconsistency between them and there is a void in the domestic law."

40. Again in *People's Union for Civil Liberties v. Union of India* [(1997) 3 SCC 433], dealing with the criticism against reading of conventions and covenants into the national laws, it was opined :

"For the present, it would suffice to state that the provisions of the covenant, which elucidate and go to effectuate the fundamental rights guaranteed by our Constitution, can certainly be relied upon by courts as facets of those funda-mental rights and hence, enforceable as such. So far as multilateral treaties are concerned, the law is, of course, different — and definite."

41. Thus, international treaties have influenced interpretation of Indian law in several ways. This Court has relied upon them for statutory interpretation, where the terms of any legislation are not clear or are reasonably capable of more than one meaning. In such cases, the courts have relied upon the meaning which is in consonance with the treaties, for there is a prima facie presumption that Parliament did not intend to act in breach of international law, including State treaty obligations. It is also well accepted that in construing any provision in domestic legislation which is ambiguous, in the sense that it is capable of more than one meaning, the meaning which conforms most closely to the provisions of any international instrument is to be preferred, in the absence of any domestic law to the contrary. In this view, Section 3(2)(d) is to be read keeping in view the Paris principles. Further, the proposal to appoint police officers on two earlier occasions was dropped when the Chairperson of NHRC expressed his opinion against appointments of such persons.

42. Thus, construing Section 3(2)(d) of the Act, a police officer would be ineligible to be appointed as a member of NHRC.

43. The challenge to the appointment of Respondent No. 2 was also made on two other grounds, namely, (1) Absence of effective consultation with the Committee members and, therefore, the recommendation was not in accord with Section 4 of the Act; and (2) breach of established norm of consultation with the Chairperson of NHRC.

44. Facts relevant for considering the aforesaid grounds have already been noticed. Under Section 4, every appointment has to be made after obtaining the recommendations of a Committee. The requirement of the section is not of 'consultation' but of recommendation of the Committee. It is true that the recommendations are required to be made after taking into consideration all relevant factors eschewing irrelevant factors. Since notice of the meeting had been given to the Leader of Opposition in the Council of States, it cannot be said that the recommendations of the Committee would stand vitiated as a result of his non-participation. There is nothing to even suggest that any request for deferring the meeting was made. Undoubtedly, for meaningful and purposeful recommendation, there ought to be complete disclosure of relevant factors considering that the appointment is being recommended for a highly expert body in relation to protection of human rights. The members of the Committee were not informed that on earlier two occasions, the views of the Chairperson of NHRC were sought and since the Chairperson was opposed to the appointment of a member of the force, the proposal was dropped. It is, however, unnecessary to examine its effect in view of the answer to the main question.

45. Regarding the second ground, namely, the requirement of consultation with the Chairperson of NHRC for appointment of members under Section 3(2)(d), the fact that the opinion of the Chairperson was sought on two earlier occasions would not tantamount to setting up of a convention requiring the Chairperson to be mandatorily consulted. Section 4 also does not postulate consultation with the Chairperson. However, having regard to the position of the Chairperson and the laudable objects the Commission is serving, its functions being of far-reaching public impact, we hope that till the amendment of the Act, the Central Government would consider developing a healthy convention of consulting the Chairperson regarding the appointment of the members and placing the opinion of the Chairperson before the Committee. We may also note that long time back the Commission had written to the Government suggesting amendments in the Act and incorporating a provision for mandatory consultation with the Chairperson regarding appointment of the members, but the matter still seems to be pending consideration of the Government. It deserves to be expedited.

46. Before parting, we reiterate that this Court should not be understood to have condemned, in any manner, the Police officers or members of Security Forces. They are, indeed, doing great service to the nation. Many of the officers in these services have dealt with the most difficult and intricate situations and problems and have contributed a lot in their solution. The question considered by us is only in the context of their expertise in the matters relating to human rights within the meaning of Section 3(2)(d) read with the Paris principles. We also wish to place on record our appreciation for the assistance rendered by Mr. Gulan E. Vahanvati, learned Solicitor General on request made by this Court.

47. In view of the aforesaid discussion, the appointment of Respondent No. 2 as member of the National Human Rights Commission is declared null and void but it shall not affect the validity of the decisions taken while he was a member of the Commission.

48. The petition is allowed accordingly and the rule made absolute.

D.M. Dharmadhikari, J.

49. With utmost respect, I am unable to endorse all the views and the conclusion recorded in his opinion by learned brother Sabharwal, J.

50. The statutory provisions under Section 3(2)(d), from its plain language, in my considered opinion, does not disqualify Respondent No. 2 from holding the position of member of the National Human Rights Commission.The composition of the Commission as provided in Section 3(2) of the Act with Judges on its membership in majority, is not as pluralistic as indicated in the "Paris principles".

51. Judges, by the very nature of their office and duties, with the life of seclusion expected of them, not only for independence but also for appearance of independence, renders them almost "cut off" from society. They lose touch with ground realities existing in the society. Their knowledge in matters relating to human rights is hearsay i.e. through the cases that happen to come before them in the law courts and which they get a chance to deal with and decide as Judges on the seat of the court. Their lack of practical experience in the field of human rights is required to be supplemented by such members of the Commission who are either actively in public life or directly dealing with the incidents and occurrences of violations of human rights. Such persons, as envisaged by use of a wide language in clause (d) of sub-section (2) Section 3, may include reputed human rights activists or high-ranking police officers who have acquired experience in investigation and prevention of human rights violations.

52. The expression "from amongst persons having knowledge of, or practical experience in, matters relating to human rights" as used in clause (d) of sub-section (2) of Section 3 is wide enough to allow the Selection Committee constituted under Section 4 to select any suitable person, who in the opinion of the Selection Committee, possesses knowledge and practical experience in matters of human rights. The expression and the language used in clause (d), neither expressly nor by implication, exclude suitable police officers with high record of experience and integrity.

53. Human rights violations, to a great extent, are crimes punishable under different kinds of criminal laws. Police officers dealing with such crimes as investigators, as protectors of law or as preventers of such crimes cannot be held to be disqualified or considered unsuitable for membership of the Commission.

54. In accordance with Section 11(1)(b) of the Act, the Commission has to be aided and assisted by a team of police and investigative staff "under an officer not below the rank of a Director General of Police". The Central Government is obliged by Section 11 to provide suitable police officers and staff for efficient performance of the functions of the Commission. In their capacity as members of the staff for aiding and assisting the Commission in discharge of its functions, there are several police officers of that category attached to the Commission who are directly dealing with human rights violations and thereby get a chance to acquire necessary knowledge and practical experience in the field of human rights. Such police officers who have aided and assisted the Commission in discharge of its functions, gain knowledge and experience in the same field for being chosen to act as members under clause (d) of sub-section (2) of Section 3.

55. Public perception, to which learned Brother has given great importance, of the police as a force, can change only if high-ranking police officers with exemplary record of service and of integrity are given chance to act as members of the Commission.

56. Learned Brother has referred to the "Paris principles" which were accepted by the countries which were parties to International Covenants on Civil, Social and Political Rights. International law and guidelines have been taken aid of by this Court in interpreting the domestic law only if it has found some gap to be filled in the latter or the provisions of domestic law are not clear and do not wholly carry the meaning and effect of international law which it intends to implement. "Paris principles" are at best merely in the nature of guidelines to be followed by covenanting countries who are parties to the resolutions taken in the international conferences on human rights. There is no obligation on acceptance of "Paris principles", to incorporate them word by word in statutory law. In the "Paris principles", a pluralistic composition of the Commission has been advised. Contrary to the Paris principles of a pluralistic composition of the Commission, under the Act, in respect of membership, Judges have a majority. A real pluralistic composition ought to include in its membership judges, human rights activists, scientists, academicians and even experienced police officers and social researchers.Merely because there are instances of human rights violations by some members of the police is no ground to exclude all police officers as a class from the membership of the Commission. The "Paris principles" can at best be taken aid of to understand and interpret the provisions of the Act but not to substitute or supplement it.

57. In my view, selection of a high-ranking police officer known for high integrity and character with record of commendable service cannot be held to be beyond the purview of Section 3(2)(d) of the Act. Section 3(2)(d) empowers the Selection Committee to induct 2 members other than Judges, having knowledge and practical experience in matters relating to human rights. Judges, by the very nature of their office and conduct, no doubt, as members not only make the Commission an independent body but also impart it an appearance of independence. Yet, as the membership of the Commission has to be of a pluralistic complexion, induction by selection of members, either from the police force or public would in no manner adversely affect the independence, efficacy or functioning of the Commission. A police officer, on his appointment to the Commission, would enjoy same rights and independence of action as other members do.

58. With utmost respect, I fail to agree with the observations and conclusions of learned brother Sabharwal, J. that, under the provisions of sub-section (2) of Section 3, police officers are not intended to be included in the membership of the National Human Rights Commission.

59. There are and would be police officers who have gained and are likely to gain knowledge and practical experience in matters relating to human rights by virtue of their duties. They are seen working courageously on occurrences and events relating to human rights. Apart from the knowledge of investigative techniques, from the very nature of their job and functions, they acquire knowledge as to how and where human rights are violated. They also know what preventive action is required to be taken and what course has to be adopted for protection of human rights. A police officer qua purely a police officer, with no knowledge or practical experience in handling matters of human rights, may be found unfit to be chosen as member but a police officer with necessary knowledge and experience in matters of human rights cannot be held to be disqualified merely because he is a police officer.

60. There are instances in India itself where police officers working in terrorist areas or for jail reforms have received national and international recognition and awards. Construing Section 3(2)(d) narrowly by excluding from its purview police officers altogether would deprive the chance of serving as members of the Commission to even police officers with record of exemplary service in the field of human rights. To disqualify them completely would have a demoralising effect on the police force as such.

61. The Selection Committee, provided in Section 4(1) of the Act, which has to recommend appointment to the membership of the Commission, is a pluralistic body comprising elected representatives of the people and political parties in power and in opposition. The perception of the Selection Committee regarding fitness of a particular person chosen for membership, by considering him to be possessing required knowledge and practical experience in the matters relating to human rights, cannot be faulted by the Court by substituting its own opinion for the opinion of the Selection Committee. Such a course of action is not legally permissible to the Court. The Court cannot sit over the selection of the Selection Committee unless there is found to be any infraction of law under which the selection was made.

62. The credentials and biodata of respondent No. 2 who has been chosen for membership of the Commission have been highlighted by the Union of India in its counter-affidavit. The relevant portion reads thus :

> *"Respondent No. 2 is a distinguished officer of the Indian Police Service, having retired as Director of the Central Bureau of Investigation (CBI). In the course of his career from 1966 to 2003, he has had occasion to supervise the conduct of investigation and prosecution of several offences, including serious offences against human rights. Among the cases investigated by CBI during the tenure of Respondent No. 2 as Director were the Punjab mass cremation cases and the Gujarat riot cases both of which involved serious violations of human rights. The investigation of the Punjab mass cremation case by CBI was on the directions of this Hon'ble Court and the case has now been transferred to the Commission for deciding the issue of compensation. The Gujarat riot cases are also pending before this Hon'ble Court, in which the CBI investigation reports are being placed before this Hon'ble Court. Other human rights cases handled by CBI during this period include inter alia cases of police encounters such as the death of Vashisht Narayan Singh in Azamgarh, U.P. and Varghese in Kerala. Cases of police torture in West Bengal (torture of minor boys named Manjeet Gowala and Pinter Jadav in Darjeeling) and cases of picking up of a citizen Shri Kuldip Singh in Amritsar and treating him as untraced, have also been investigated by CBI. In many of these cases CBI has commenced prosecution against police officers. Further Respondent No. 2 is also the Vice-President (Asia) of Interpol, an international police organisation. In this capacity also, he has been involved in developing mechanisms for police cooperation in investigation and prosecution of crimes across borders, including terrorism, human safety and human trafficking, which are all offences against human rights. The functions of the Commission under the Act include enquiry and investigation functions. For this purpose, the Commission has been given the power of investigation under Section 14, including the power to utilise the services of any officer or investigation agency of the Government and consider the report of such investigation. The staff of the Commission, since its inception include a senior officer of the Indian Police Service as*

Director General (Investigation) of the Commission and the functions of the Investigation Division of the Commission are carried on under the supervision and direction of the Commission itself. It is submitted that there is no illegality in an officer of the Indian Police Service being considered for appointment as a member of the Commission. During the course of their careers, police officers garner in vast practical experience in police methodology, investigative techniques and other practical matters relating to human rights. It is submitted that such experience would inter alia aid the Commission in identifying cases of police malpractice and the Commission would be able to look behind cases of cover-up and attempts to shield guilty police officers. It is, therefore, submitted that Respondent 2 has adequate knowledge and practical experience in matters relating to human rights, qualifying him for appointment to the Commission under Section 3(2)(d) of the Act."

63. I do not think that the abovementioned record of service of Respondent No. 2, in any manner, makes him disqualified for appointment as member of the Commission. His record of service shows his knowledge and practical experience in matters relating to human rights. It is another thing to make a general statement that for membership under Section 3(2)(d), well-known human rights activists or members of reputed NGOs who are actively involved in the field of human rights would have been better choices but the court is concerned only with the legality of the appointment and not the wisdom of the selection body. Merely because a more suitable person ought to have been chosen is no ground to invalidate the appointment of Respondent 2, who cannot be held to be disqualified under Section 3(2)(d). He has, in fact, served on the Commission for a period of almost one year.

64. So far as the observations made by learned brother Sabharwal, J. suggesting the need of developing a healthy convention of consulting the Chairperson for appointment of members of the Commission are concerned, I am in respectful agreement with him.

65. In view of my dissent on the main issue of validity of appointment of Respondent No. 2, I do not consider it necessary to elaborate my views in any greater detail particularly on the interpretation of Section 3(2)(d) of the Act, because in any event, on disagreement between us, the case will have to be decided by a larger Bench of this Court.

Order Of The Court

66. In view of difference of opinion between us, the matter is referred to a larger Bench. We are of the view that the matter deserves to be heard expeditiously.

In the Supreme Court of India

Writ Petition (Civil) No. 105 of 2004
People's Union for Civil Liberties (PUCL) v. Union of India & Anr.[10]

Date of Judgement : 29.04.2005

Bench : N. Santosh Hegde, B.P. Singh and S.B. Sinha, JJ.

[In continuation of the earlier proceedings, a 3 Judge Bench heard the issue. The 3 Judge Bench did not agree with the view of Justice Y.K. Sabharwal that the Paris Principles or any subsequent UN General Assembly Resolution could be read into Municipal Law and therefore, dismissed the Writ Petition while agreeing with the view expressed by Justice D.M. Dharmadhikari.]

Judgment

N. Santosh Hegde, J.

1. In this writ petition filed under Article 32 of the Constitution, the petitioner is challenging a decision of the first respondent Union of India appointing Respondent 2 as a member of the National Human Rights Commission (the Commission). The primary basis of the challenge to his appointment is on the ground that prior to the impugned appointment the Respondent No. 2 was holding the post of Director, Central Bureau of Investigation and was also holding the post of Vice-President (Asia), Interpol. According to the petitioner, the appointment of a person who served in the police force as a member of NHRC is contrary to the provisions of the Protection of Human Rights Act, 1993 (the Act), apart from being opposed to the very aims and objects for which the said Commission was constituted. The petitioner urges that such appointment would undermine the status and international recognition of the Commission as an institution for protection of human rights. It is also urged that the appointment of the Respondent No. 2 is also opposed to the Constitution on the grounds that it is arbitrary and violative of Article 14. It is submitted that it is also violative of international covenants. For this purpose, the petitioner has heavily relied on the principles laid down in the meeting of representatives of the national institutions in Paris wherein certain principles were evolved with regard to protection of human rights which principles came to be known as "Paris Principles". According to the petitioner, these principles were subsequently endorsed by the UN

10. (2005) 5 SCC 363

Commission of Human Rights and the UN General Assembly. The petitioner further contends that the UN Resolution dated 19.12.1993 concerning national institutions for protection of human rights, the compliance with the Paris Principles has become mandatory and since the Paris Principles prohibited the appointment of a civil servant like a police officer to such a Commission, such appointment of the Respondent No. 2 would send wrong signals to the international community as well as to the United Nations. The petitioner also urges that the appointment of the Respondent No. 2 has been made without consulting the Chairperson of the Commission which was the practice since the inception of the Commission. It is also urged that such appointment would have a direct impact on the effective implementation of human rights and fundamental rights enshrined in the Constitution including the right to life under Article 21. According to the petitioner, under Section 3(2)(d) of the Act, two members of the Commission should have knowledge of, and practical experience in matters relating to human rights; which definition has been defined under Section 2(1)(d) of the Act to mean :

> *"Human Rights means the rights relating to life, liberty, equality and dignity of the individual guaranteed by the Constitution or embodied in the International Covenants and enforceable by courts in India."*

2. According to the petitioner, a person who headed a prosecution agency cannot be taken as a person who has knowledge of, or practical experience in matters relating to human rights. The petitioner also urges that the appointment of the Respondent No. 2 as a member of the Commission could lead to potential conflict of interest between CBI and the Commission, as the Commission is often called upon to decide on complaints of violation of fundamental rights by CBI and also the police. According to the petitioner, the appointment of Respondent No. 2 destroys the independence of the Commission.

3. The first respondent, Union of India, in its counter opposed the writ petition contending that the appointment of the Respondent No. 2 as a member of the Commission is in accordance with the Act and the Respondent No. 2 is qualified to be a member of the Commission under the Act. The first respondent contends that the composition of the Commission is provided under Section 3(2)(d) of the Act which provides that a person having knowledge of and practical experience in matters relating to human rights is eligible for such appointment. It is further submitted that respondent No. 2 is a distinguished officer of the Indian Police Service, having retired as the Director of CBI. It is submitted that in the course of his career between 1966 and 2003, he has had occasions to supervise the investigation and prosecution of several offences including the serious offences against human rights. As an example, the first respondent has stated that as the Director of CBI, the Respondent No. 2 was responsible for investigating the Punjab mass cremation cases and the Gujarat riot cases; both of which involved serious violation of human rights. It was also submitted that as an institution, CBI is often entrusted by this Court to conduct inquiries into sensitive matters where violation of human rights is involved and the Respondent No. 2 has been a part of such investigations. It is also pointed out by the learned Solicitor General appearing for the Union of India that the petition does not make any personal allegation against the Respondent No. 2 as to any act of violation of human rights either by him personally or as being party to such violation. It is also submitted that the second respondent as the Vice-President (Asia), Interpol has been involved in developing mechanism in police cooperation and prosecution of crimes across borders including terrorism, human safety and human trafficking which are all offences against human rights. The first respondent has submitted that there is no illegality in appointing an officer of the Indian Police Service as a member of the Commission. It is further stated that on the contrary, very often during the course of their careers police officers garner vast practical experience in police methodology, investigative techniques and other practical matters relating to human rights enforcement. It is submitted that such experience would, inter alia, aid the Commission in identifying the areas of police malpractices and the Commission will be able to look behind the causes of cover-up and attempts to shield the guilty Police Officers.

4. It is denied that the appointment of the Respondent No. 2 would send wrong signals to the international community or to the United Nations. The first respondent states that though on a prior occasion the Chairperson of the Commission was consulted with regards to the appointment of a former police officer of the Indian Police Service and the said Chairperson had expressed his disagreement on such appointment, such consultation is not mandatory in all the cases; more so in the background of the fact that statute does not require any such consultation. Therefore, non-consultation with the Chairperson of the Commission would not in any manner vitiate the appointment of the 2nd respondent. The first respondent also denied the argument advanced by the petitioner that there has been a violation of Article 14 of the Constitution in the appointment of the Respondent No. 2. Relying on the judgment of this Court in *R.K. Jain v. Union of India* [(1993) 4 SCC 119], it is submitted that the judicial review in the matter of appointments is confined to the area of examining whether the appointee possesses the statutory qualifications or not and such power of judicial review does not extend to reassessing the merit of the particular appointee. It is also contended that the provisions of the Act are in conformity with the Paris Principles and neither the Paris Principles nor the UN Resolution prohibit a former civil servant or a police officer from becoming a member of the Human Rights Commission. More importantly, it is submitted that once the Indian legislature enacts a law pursuant to an international convention then the legislative area in that field being covered it is the municipal law alone that prevails hence, the validity of the appointment of the Respondent No. 2 can only be examined with reference to the provisions of the Act.

5. This petition came up for consideration before a Bench of two learned Judges of this Court. Since the said two learned Judges had a difference of opinion in regard to the question involved, by their reasoned order, they referred the matter to a larger Bench because of which the matter is now before this Bench of three Judges.

6. Having heard learned counsel for the parties and on the basis of their pleadings and arguments recorded hereinabove, at the outset we must notice that neither the Paris Principles nor the U.N. Resolution and much less does the Act either expressly or impliedly exclude the inclusion of a police officer in the Commission. The argument of the petitioner is that taking into consideration the object of the Act and the public perception of the police as violators of human rights, Section 3(2)(d) should be so interpreted to exclude police officers from becoming members of the Commission. We do not think such an interpretation is permissible when the statute is express in its language. We should note herein that there is no challenge to

the validity of the Act, therefore, we will have to proceed on the basis that the Act is intra vires. From the argument of the learned counsel for the petitioners, the question for consideration is whether Section 3(2)(d) of the Act requires any interpretation or a construction which would exclude police officers from becoming member of the Commission. Section 3(2)(d) which refers to two members to be appointed to the Commission reads thus :

> *"two members to be appointed from amongst persons having knowledge of, or practical experience in, matters relating to human rights."*

7. A plain reading of this Section does not give any room for interpretation because the language is quite clear. In our view, it only means that any two persons having knowledge of, or practical experience in, matters relating to human rights are eligible to be members of the Commission. This clear language of the section cannot be distorted by any inference based on any public perception or prejudice. It is relevant to note herein that this section does not exclude any class of persons so long as they have the knowledge of, or practical experience in, matters relating to human rights which is a requirement to be satisfied by the Selection Committee. In the absence of any clear and specific exclusionary provision in the statute, the court should plainly treat it as a general provision instead of delving in search of any possible hidden or implied exclusion. It was so said in *A.R. Antulay v. Ramdas Sriniwas Nayak* [(1984) 2 SCC 500].While so saying this Court in para 18 of the said judgment held that :

> *"It is a well-established canon of construction that the court should read the section as it is and cannot rewrite it to suit its convenience; nor does any canon of construction permit the court to read the section in such manner as to render it to some extent otiose.... The legislature provided for both the positive and the negative. It positively conferred power on Special Judge to take cognizance of offences and it negatively removed any concept of commitment. It is not possible therefore, to read Section 8(1) as canvassed on behalf of the appellant that cognizance can only be taken upon a police report and any other view will render the safeguard under Section 5-A illusory."*

8. If we apply the said principle of law to the facts of the case, there being no exclusion in Section 3(2)(d) of the Act and the language being clear, we cannot by looking back into the Paris Principles or the U.N. Resolution interpret an exclusionary clause to keep police officers from being members of the Commission in spite of the Act not providing for the same.

9. Having dealt with the provisions of the Act in regard to the qualification of two members to be appointed under Section 3(2)(d) of the Act, we will now refer to the argument of public perception about the police, about which, lengthy arguments supported by various judgments of the Court have been addressed by the learned counsel for the petitioner. Learned counsel for the petitioner submitted that it is a well-known fact that police force all over the world, especially in India, are the biggest violators of human rights hence it would be doing violence to the object of the Act if a police officer is selected as a member of the Commission. Having very carefully gone through the entire Statement of Objects and Reasons of the Act, we do not find that the objects as reflected in the Act indicate a perception of the police force of the country as a violator of human rights. Further, the objects of the Act do not envisage an exclusion of the members of any force from being considered for membership of the Commission. Learned counsel for the petitioner did place reliance on a number of reported cases of this Court, in support of his contention that the judicial and public perception of the police force in India is such that the police force is considered as the biggest violator of human rights. He relied on the judgment of this Court in *Paramjit Kaur v. State of Punjab* [(1999) 2 SCC 131], *D.K. Basu v. State of W.B.* [(1997) 1 SCC 416], *Munshi Singh Gautam v. State of M.P.* [JT (2004) 10 SC 547], *N.C. Dhoundial v. Union of India* [(2004) 2 SCC 579]. He also placed reliance on the report of the National Human Rights Commission (Annual Report 2001-02 at page 362). Learned Solicitor General, opposing this contention of the petitioner submitted that the criticism of the police in the aforementioned judgments of the Court is based on the facts of each one of those cases and none of the judgments cited hereinabove has in terms said that the police force in India as an institution, is a violator of human rights. He submitted that the police force has more than 2.2 million personnel working under various conditions prevailing in different parts of the country. It is possible that some of them commit violation of human rights but that would not ipso facto make each and every police personnel by presumption, a violator of human rights. Such an inference, according to learned Solicitor General, would amount to expressing an institutional bias in regard to an institution which many a times has rendered meritorious service to the nation, both in maintaining law and order, investigation of crimes and facing various other internal and external threats. He submitted that such a general condemnation of an institution like the police force would only demoralise the said force, consequence of which could be disastrous. In our opinion the learned Solicitor General has rightly relied on certain passages from the judgment of this Court in *State of Uttar Pradesh v. Mohammad Naim* [AIR 1964 SC 703], wherein this Court had deprecated the practice of courts making sweeping and general observations against the entire police force of a State though the case related to only one police officer. In such a situation, this Court held that such general remarks were neither justified on the facts of the case nor were they necessary for disposal of the said case, hence, expunged such general remarks.

10. While we cannot take exception in regard to the remarks made against the police in each one of the above cases relied on by the learned counsel for the petitioner, we certainly feel that these remarks cannot be so generalised as to make every personnel of the force, consisting of nearly 2.2 million people, violators of human rights solely on the ground that out of thousands of cases investigated and handled by them, in some cases the personnel involved have indulged in violation of human rights. Learned counsel for the petitioner, however, contended that the judgments apart, the public perception of the Indian police force as a whole is so poor that it considers the police as an organisation to be a violator of human rights. Therefore, selecting a retired police officer as a member of the Commission would lead to erosion of confidence of the people in the Commission. We are sincerely unable to gauge this public perception or its magnitude so as to import this concept of institutional bias. There are no statistics placed before this Court to show that there has been any census or poll conducted which would indicate that a substantial majority of the population in the country considers the police force as an institution which violates human rights nor do we think that by such generalisations we could disqualify a person who is otherwise eligible from becoming a member of the commission.

11. Public displeasure as presently perceived is not confined to the police force only. The views expressed in the media very often show that this displeasure is reflected against many a department of the Government including constitutional bodies and if public displeasure or perception were to be the yardstick to exclude people from holding constitutional or statutory offices then many such posts in the country may have to be kept vacant.

12. Then again what is the yardstick to measure public perception. Admittedly, there is no barometer to gauge the perception of the people. In a democracy there are many people who get elected by a thumping majority to high legislative offices. Many a times public perception of a class of society in regard to such people may be that they are not desirable to hold such post but can such a public opinion deprive such people from occupying constitutional or statutory offices without there being a law to the contrary? There is vast qualitative difference between public prejudice and judicial condemnation of an institution based on public perception. At any rate, as stated above, public perception or public opinion has no role to play in selection of an otherwise eligible person from becoming a member of the Commission under the Act.

13. A perusal of Section 4 of the Act shows that the appointment of Chairperson and other members shall be made after obtaining the recommendations of the Committee consisting of :

- The Prime Minister;
- The Speaker of the House of People;
- The Minister Incharge of the Ministry of Home Affairs in the Government of India;
- Leader of Opposition in the House of the People;
- Leader of Opposition in the Council of States;
- Deputy Chairman of the Council of States.

14. Proviso to the above section further stipulates that no sitting Judge of the Supreme Court or sitting Chief Justice of the High Court shall be appointed except after consultation with the Chief Justice of India. There is absolutely no requirement under the Act that this Committee consisting of such high office-holders of this country should further consult the Chairman of the Commission before appointing a member. The entire argument of the petitioner in this regard rests on the fact that on some previous occasion the Committee did consult the Chairperson of the Commission and in the present case this was not done. We are in agreement with the learned Solicitor General on this point that when a statute vests a function in a committee comprising such high dignitaries holding high constitutional positions, it would be impermissible to read into the statute the requirement of consultation with the Chairman of the Commission. The provision for appointment of Chairperson and other members of the Commission contemplates a self-contained procedure and no other mandatory provision can be imported into the Act where none actually exists. The allegation made by the petitioner in regard to non-consultation with the Chairman in the appointment of the Respondent No. 2 is vague and the same cannot be accepted from the counter-affidavit filed.It is further argued by the learned counsel for the petitioner that there was no proper consultation amongst the members of the Selection Committee. This is based on the fact that one of the members, who was then the Leader of Opposition in the Council of States, did not respond to the intimation sent to him in regard to the selection of the members since he was in hospital at that point of time. A perusal of the Act does not show that there is any quorum fixed for the selection nor does it provide for any meeting nor has any particular procedure been provided for. Under the Act, consultation by circulation is not impermissible. In such a situation, if one out of six did not respond, it would not vitiate the opinion of the other five members. On the contrary section 4(2) specifically says that no appointment of a Chairperson or a member shall be invalid merely by reason of any vacancy in the Committee. In the instant case the Prime Minister, the Speaker of the House of the People, Minister in charge of the Ministry of Home Affairs in the Government of India, Leader of Opposition in the House of the People and Deputy Chairman of the Council of States having agreed on the appointment of the Respondent No. 2, we find no statutory error in the appointment of the second Respondent No. 2.

15. In the ordinary course, the above analysis itself would have been sufficient to dispose of this petition. However, since this matter has been referred to this Bench due to the divergence of views between Hon'ble Sabharwal and Dharmadhikari, JJ. it is in the fitness of things that we note their judgments also and particularly the judgment of Hon'ble Sabharwal, J. as our conclusions are different from his conclusions.

16. In arriving at his decision Hon'ble Sabharwal, J. has treated the Paris Principles and the U.N. General Assembly Resolution as covenants. Thereafter, he has applied the law applicable to international covenants and imported the obligations under the Paris Principles and the U.N. General Assembly Resolution as if they are binding as legal obligations on India even in the municipal context. While doing so he has relied upon the judgments of this Hon'ble Court in *Mackinon Mackenzie v. Audrey D'Costa* [AIR 1987 SC 1281]; *Sheela Barse v. Secretary, Children's Aid Society* [(1987) 3 SCC 50]; *People's Union for Civil Liberties v. Union of India* [(1997) 3 SCC 433]; and *Vishaka v. State of Rajasthan* [(1997) 6 SCC 241].

17. Having noted the above we would with respect like to point out that neither the Paris Principles nor the subsequent U.N. General Assembly Resolution can be exalted to the status of a covenant in international law. Therefore merely because India is a party to these documents does not cast any binding legal obligation on it. Further, all the above cases which Hon'ble Sabharwal, J. has relied upon deal with the obligations of the Indian State pursuant to its being a party to a covenant/treaty or a convention and not merely a declaration in the international fora or a U.N. General Assembly Resolution.

18. Apart from the above, the fact that the field in relation to the constitution of NHRC is covered by an Act of the Indian Parliament, it follows that neither the Paris Principles nor the U.N. General Assembly Resolution can override the express provisions of the Act. Therefore, we are not in agreement with the decision of Hon'ble Sabharwal, J. After considering the views expressed by Hon'ble Dharmadhikari, J. on this aspect of the case, we are in agreement with the same.

19. For the reasons stated above this petition fails and is dismissed.

In the Supreme Court of India

Writ Petition (Civil) No. 389 of 2002 with Writ Petition (Criminal) Nos. 89 and 129 of 2002, 28 and 48 of 2003

People's Union for Civil Liberties (PUCL) & Anr. v. Union of India.[11]

Date of Judgement : 16.12.2003

Bench: S. Rajendra Babu and G.P. Mathur, JJ.

[PUCL had challenged various provisions of the Prevention of Terrorism Act, 2002 on several legal and Constitutional grounds. In the judgment, the Supreme Court has given various important observations pertaining to human rights and civil liberties, though holding that POTA was constitutionally valid.]

Judgment

S. Rajendra Babu, J.

W.P. (C) No. 389/2002 and W.P. (Crl.) No. 89/2002 :

1. In this batch of Writ Petitions before us the constitutional validity of various provisions of the Prevention of Terrorism Act, 2002 (hereinafter POTA) is in challenge.

2. The Petitioners' contended before us that since the provisions of POTA, in pith and substance, fall under Entry 1 (Public order) of List II Parliament lacks legislative competence. To authenticate this contention, the decision in *Rehman Shagoo v. State of Jammu Kashmir* [(1960) 1 SCR 680] is relied upon. According to them, the menace of terrorism is covered by the entry "Public order" and to explain the meaning thereof, our attention is invited to decisions in *Romesh Thappar v. State of Madras* [1950 SCR 594], *Dr.Ram Manohar Lohia v. State of Bihar* [(1966) 1 SCR 709] and *Madhu Limaye v. SDM, Monghyr* [(1970) 3 SCC 746]. The Petitioners thus submitted that terrorist activity is confined only to State(s) and therefore State(s) only have the competence to enact a legislation.

3. The learned Attorney General refuting this contention submitted that the acts of terrorism, which are aimed at weakening the sovereignty and integrity of the country cannot be equated with mere breaches of law and order and disturbances of public order or public safety. He argued that the concept of "sovereignty and integrity of India" is distinct and separate from the concepts of "public order" or "security of State" which fall under List II enabling

11. (2004) 9 SCC 580

States to enact legislation relating to public order or safety affecting or relating to a particular State. Therefore, the legislative competence of a State to enact laws for its security cannot denude Parliament of its competence under List I to enact laws to safeguard national security and sovereignty of India by preventing and punishing acts of terrorism. Learned Attorney General distinguished the decision in *Rehman Shagoo*[(1960) 1 SCR 680] and submitted that the legislation dealt with therein is fundamentally and qualitatively different from POTA. He also argued before us that *Rehman Shagoo* [(1960) 1 SCR 680] cannot mitigate the binding ratio and unanimous conclusion reached by this Court on the point of legislative competence in *Kartar Singh v. State of Punjab* [1994 (3) SCC 569], that Parliament can enact such law.

4. In deciding the point of legislative competence, it is necessary to understand the contextual backdrop that led to the enactment of POTA, which aims to combat terrorism. Terrorism has become the most worrying feature of contemporary life. Though violent behaviour is not new, the present-day 'terrorism' in its full incarnation has obtained a different character and poses extraordinary challenges to the civilised world. The basic edifices of a modern State, like democracy, State security, rule of law, sovereignty and integrity, basic human rights etc. are under the attack of terrorism. Though the phenomenon of terrorism is complex, a 'terrorist act' is easily identifiable when it does occur. The core meaning of the term is clear even if its exact frontiers are not. That is why the anti-terrorist statutes — the earlier Terrorism and Disruptive Activities (Prevention) Act, 1987 (TADA) and now POTA, do not define 'terrorism' but only 'terrorist acts'. (See *Hitendra Vishnu Thakur v. State of Maharashtra* [(1994) 4 SCC 602]).

5. Paul Wilkinson, an authority on terrorism related works, culled out five major characteristics of terrorism. They are :

1. It is premeditated and aims to create a climate of extreme fear or terror.
2. It is directed at a wider audience or target than the immediate victims of violence.
3. It inherently involves attacks on random and symbolic targets, including civilians.
4. The acts of violence committed are seen by the society in which they occur as extra-normal, in literal sense, that they breach the social norms, thus causing a sense of outrage.
5. Terrorism is used to influence political behaviour in some way — for example to force opponents into conceding some or all of the perpetrators' demands, to provoke an overreaction, to serve as a catalyst for more general conflict, or to publicise a political cause.

6. In all acts of terrorism, it is mainly the psychological element that distinguishes it from other political offences, which are invariably accompanied with violence and disorder. Fear is induced not merely by making civilians the direct targets of violence but also by exposing them to a sense of insecurity. It is in this context that this Court held in *Mohd. Iqbal M. Shaikh v. State of Maharashtra* [(1998) 4 SCC 494], that :

> "*. . . it is not possible to give a precise definition of terrorism or to lay down what constitutes terrorism. But . . . it may be possible to describe it as use*

of violence when its most important result is not merely the physical and mental damage of the victim but the prolonged psychological effect it produces or has the potential of producing on the society as a whole. ... if the object of the activity is to disturb harmony of the society or to terrorize people and the society with a view to disturb the even tempo, tranquillity of the society, and a sense of fear and insecurity is created in the minds of a section of the society at large, then it will, undoubtedly, be held to be a terrorist act..."

7. Our country has been the victim of an undeclared war by the epicentres of terrorism with the aid of well-knit and resourceful terrorist organisations engaged in terrorist activities in different States such as Jammu & Kashmir, North-East States, Delhi, West Bengal, Maharashtra, Gujarat, Tamil Nadu and Andhra Pradesh. The learned Attorney General placed material to point out that the year 2002 witnessed 4038 terrorist-related violent incidents in J&K in which, 1008 civilians and 453 security personnel were killed. The number of terrorists killed in 2002 was 1707 out of which 508 were foreigners. In the year 2001, there were as many as 28 suicide attacks while there were over 10 suicide attacks in 2002 in which innocent persons and a large number of women and children were killed. The major terrorist incidents in the recent past includes attack on the Indian Parliament on 13.12.2001, attack on Jammu & Kashmir Assembly on 01.10.2001, attack on Akshardham Temple on 24.09.2002, attack on US Information Center at Kolkata on 22.01.2002, Srinagar CRPF Camp attack on 22.11.2002, IED blast near Jawahar Tunnel on 23.11.2002, attack on Raghunath Mandir on 24.11.2002, bus bomb blast at Ghatkopar in Mumbai on 02.12.2002, attack on villagers in Nadimarg in Pulwama district in Jammu & Kashmir on the night of 23.03.2003/24.03.2003 etc. There were attacks on Red Fort and on several government installations, security forces' camps and in public places. Gujarat witnessed gruesome carnage of innocent people by unleashing unprecedented bout of terror. People in Bihar, Andhra Pradesh and Maharashtra etc. have also experienced the terror trauma. The latest addition to this long list of terror are the recent twin blasts at Mumbai that claimed about 50 lives. It is not necessary to swell this opinion by narrating all the sad episodes of terrorist activities that the country has witnessed.

8. All these terrorist strikes have certain common features. They could be very broadly grouped into three :

1. Attack on the institution of democracy, which is the very basis of our country(By attacking Parliament, Legislative Assembly etc). And the attack on economic system by targeting economic nerve centres.
2. Attack on symbols of national pride and on the security/strategic installations (eg. Red Fort, Military installations and camps, Radio stations etc.).
3. Attack on the civilians to generate terror and fear psychosis among the general populace. The attack at worshipping places to injure sentiments and to whip communal passions. These are designed to position the people against the Government by creating a feeling of insecurity.

9. Terrorist acts are meant to destabilise the nation by challenging its sovereignty and integrity, to raze the constitutional principles that we hold dear, to create a psyche of fear and anarchism among common people, to tear apart the secular fabric, to overthrow democratically elected government, to promote prejudice and bigotry, to demoralise the security forces, to thwart the economic progress and development and so on. This cannot be equated with a usual law and order problem within a State. On the other hand, it is inter-State, inter-national or cross-border in character. Fight against the overt and covert acts of terrorism is not a regular criminal justice endeavour. Rather, it is defence of our nation and its citizens. It is a challenge to the whole nation and invisible force of Indian-ness that binds this great nation together. Therefore, terrorism is a new challenge for law enforcement. By indulging in terrorist activities organised groups or individuals, trained, inspired and supported by fundamentalists and anti-Indian elements are trying to destabilise the country. This new breed of menace was hitherto unheard of. Terrorism is definitely a criminal act, but it is much more than mere criminality. Today the Government is charged with the duty of protecting the unity, integrity, secularism and sovereignty of India from terrorists, both from outside and within the borders. To face terrorism we need new approaches, techniques, weapons, expertise and of course new laws. In the above said circumstances Parliament felt that a new anti-terrorism law is necessary for a better future. This parliamentary resolve is epitomised in POTA.

10. The terrorist threat that we are facing is now on an unprecedented global scale. Terrorism has become a global threat with global effects. It has become a challenge to the whole community of civilised nations. Terrorist activities in one country may take on a trans-national character, carrying out attacks across one border, receiving funding from private parties or a Government across another and procuring arms from multiple sources. Terrorism in a single country can readily become a threat to regional peace and security owing to its spillover effects. It is, therefore, difficult in the present context to draw sharp distinctions between domestic and international terrorism. Many happenings in the recent past caused the international community to focus on the issue of terrorism with renewed intensity. The Security Council unanimously passed Resolutions 1368 (2001) and 1373 (2001); the General Assembly adopted Resolution 56/1 by consensus, and convened a special session. All these resolutions and declarations inter alia call upon member States to take necessary steps to 'prevent and suppress terrorist acts' and also to 'prevent and suppress the financing of terrorist acts'. India is a party to all these resolves. Anti-terrorism activities on the global level are mainly carried out through bilateral and multilateral cooperation among nations. It has, thus, become our international obligation also to pass necessary laws to fight terrorism.

11. The attempts by the State to prevent terrorism should be based on well-established legal principles. The 'Report of the Policy Working Group of the United Nations on Terrorism' urged the global community to concentrate on a triple strategy to fight against terrorism. They are :

(a) Dissuade disaffected groups from embracing terrorism;

(b) Deny groups or individuals the means to carry out acts of terrorism; and

(c) Sustain broad-based international cooperation in the struggle against terrorism.

12. Therefore, the anti-terrorism laws should be capable of dissuading individuals or groups from resorting to terrorism, denying the opportunities for the commission of acts of terrorism by creating inhospitable environments for terrorism and also leading the struggle against terrorism. Anti-terrorism law is not only a penal statute but also focuses on pre-emptive rather than defensive State action. At the same time, in the light of global terrorist threats, collective global action is necessary. Lord Woolf, C.J. in *A, X and Y v. Secretary of the State for the Home Department* [2002 EWCA Civ. 1502] has pointed out that :

> "... *Where international terrorists are operating globally and committing acts designed to terrorize the population in one country, that can have implications which threaten the life of another. This is why a collective approach to terrorism is important.*"

13. Parliament has passed POTA by taking all these aspects into account. The terrorism is not confined to the borders of the country. Cross-border terrorism is also threatening the country. To meet such a situation, a law can be enacted only by Parliament and not by a State Legislature. Piloting the Prevention of Terrorism Bill in the joint session of Parliament on 26.03.2002 the Hon'ble Home Minister said :

> "... *The Government of India has been convinced for the last four years that we have been here and I am sure even the earlier Governments held that terrorism and more particularly, State-sponsored cross-border terrorism is a kind of war. It is not just a law and order problem. This is the first factor, which has been responsible for Government thinking in terms of an extraordinary law like POTO.*
>
> ... *So, first of all, the question that I would like to pose to all of you and which we have posed to the nation is: 'Is it just in Jammu and Kashmir that we are facing an aggravated law and order situation or is it really when we say it is a proxy war, do we really believe that it is a proxy war?'... But when you have terrorist organisations being trained, financed by a State and it becomes State-sponsored terrorism and all of them are enabled to infiltrate into our country, it becomes a challenge of a qualitatively different nature...*"

(emphasis supplied)

14. From this it could be gathered that the Parliament has explored the possibility of employing the existing laws to tackle terrorism and arrived at the conclusion that the existing laws are not capable. It is also clear to the Parliament that terrorism is not a usual law and order problem.

15. The protection and promotion of human rights under the rule of law is essential for the prevention of terrorism. Here comes the role of law and Court's responsibility. If human rights are violated in the process of combating terrorism, it will be self-defeating. Terrorism often thrives where human rights are violated, which adds to the need to strengthen action to combat violations of human rights. The lack of hope for justice provides breeding grounds for terrorism. Terrorism itself should also be understood as an assault on basic rights. In all cases, the fight against terrorism must be respectful to the human rights. Our Constitution laid down clear limitations on State actions within the context of the fight against terrorism. To maintain this delicate balance by protecting 'core' human rights is the responsibility of court in a matter like this. Constitutional soundness of POTA needs to be judged by keeping these aspects in mind.

16. Now, we will revert to the issue of legislative competence. Relying on *Rehman Shagoo* [(1960) 1 SCR 680], Petitioners argued that Parliament lacks competence since 'terrorism' in pith and substance is covered under Entry 1 (Public Order) of List II. Conclusion of this contention depends upon the true meaning of the Entry 'Public Order'.

17. A Constitution Bench of this Court in *Rehman Shagoo* [(1960) 1 SCR 680], examined the constitutionality of the Enemy Agents (Ordinance) No. VIII of S. 2005) promulgated by His Highness the Maharaja under Section 5 of the Jammu & Kashmir Constitution Act, S. 1996. For a proper understanding of the ratio in *Rehman Shagoo* [(1960) 1 SCR 680], it is necessary to understand the background in which the impugned Ordinance was promulgated(See: *Prem Nath Kaul v. State of Jammu & Kashmir* [1959 Supp (2) SCR 270], to understand the background that prevailed in the then Kashmir). Because any interpretation divorced from the context and purpose will lead to bad conclusions. It is a well-established canon of interpretation that the meaning of a word should be understood and applied in accordance with the context of time, social and conditional needs. *Rehman Shagoo* [(1960) 1 SCR 680] was concerned with the interpretation of Instrument of Accession and the power of the Maharaja to issue the impugned Ordinance therein. The same was promulgated to protect the State of Kashmir from external raiders and to punish them and those who assist them. The situation that prevailed during the latter half of the 1940s is fundamentally different from today. The circumstances of independence, partition, State reorganisation, and the peculiar situation prevailing in the then Kashmir etc. need to be taken into account. It is only in that context this Court said in *Rehman Shagoo*[(1960) 1 SCR 680] that the impugned Ordinance :

> *"...In pith and substance deals with public order and criminal law and procedure; the mere fact that there is an indirect impact on armed forces in s. 3 of the Ordinance will not make it in pith and substance a law covered by Item (1) under the head 'Defence' in the Schedule."*

18. Therefore, *Rehman Shagoo* [(1960) 1 SCR 680], is distinguishable and cannot be used as an authority to challenge the competence of Parliament to pass POTA. The problems that prevailed in India immediately after independence cannot be compared with the menace of terrorism that we are facing in the twenty first century. As we have already discussed above, the present-day problem of terrorism is affecting the security and sovereignty of the nation. It is not State specific but trans-national. Only Parliament can make a legislation to meet its challenge. Moreover, the entry 'Public Order' in the State List only empowers the States to enact a legislation relating to public order or security in so far as it affects or relates to a particular State. Howsoever wide a meaning is assigned to the Entry 'Public order', the present day problem of terrorism cannot be brought under the same by any stretch of imagination. Thus, *Romesh Thappar* [1950 SCR 594], *Dr. Ram Manohar Lohia* [(1966) 1 SCR 709] and *Madhu Limaye* [(1970) 3 SCC 746] (all cited earlier) cannot be resorted to read 'terrorism' into 'Public

Order'. Since the Entry Public Order or any other entries in List II do not cover the situation dealt with in POTA, the legislative competence of Parliament cannot be challenged. Earlier a Constitution Bench of this Court, while dealing with the very same argument, held in *Kartar Singh case* [1994 (3) SCC 569] as follows :

> *"Having regard to the limitation placed by Article 245(1) on the legislative power of the legislature of the State in the matter of enactment of laws having application within the territorial limits of the State only, the ambit of the field of legislation with respect to 'public order' under Entry 1 in the State List has to be confined to disorders of lesser gravity having an impact within the boundaries of the State. Activities of a more serious nature which threaten the security and integrity of the country as a whole would not be within the legislative field assigned to the States under Entry 1 of the State List but would fall within the ambit of Entry 1 of the Union List relating to defence of India and in any event under the residuary power conferred on Parliament under Article 248 read with Entry 97 of the Union List.*
>
> ***
>
> *The terrorism, the Act (TADA) contemplates, cannot be classified as mere disturbances of 'public order' disturbing the 'even tempo of the life of community of any specified locality' — in the words of Hidayathulla, C.J. in Arun Ghosh v. State of West Bengal [(1970) 1 SCC 98] but it is much more, rather a grave emergent situation created either by external forces particularly at the frontiers of this country or by anti-nationals throwing a challenge to the very existence and sovereignty of the country in its democratic polity.*
>
> ***
>
> *In our view, the impugned legislation does not fall under Entry 1 of List II, namely, Public Order. No other entry of List II has been invoked. The impugned Act, therefore, falls within the legislative competence of Parliament in view of Article 248 read with Entry 97 of List I and it is not necessary to consider whether it falls under any of the entries in List I or List III. We are, however, of the opinion that the impugned Act could fall within the ambit of Entry 1 of List I, namely, 'Defence of India'." [pp.633, 634, 635]"*

19. While this is the view of the majority of Judges in *Kartar Singh case* [1994 (3) SCC 569], K. Ramaswamy, J. held that Parliament does possess power under Article 248 and Entry 97 of List I of the Seventh Schedule and could also come within the ambit of Entry 1 of List III. Sahai, J. held that the legislation could be upheld under Entry 1 of List III. Thus, all the Judges are of the unanimous opinion that Parliament had legislative competence though for different reasons.

20. Considering all the above said aspects, the challenge advanced by the Petitioners, for the want of legislative competence of Parliament to enact POTA is not tenable.

21. Another issue that the Petitioners has raised at the threshold is the alleged misuse of TADA and the large number of acquittals of the accused charged under TADA. Here we would like to point out that this Court cannot go into and examine the 'need' of POTA. It is a matter of policy. Once legislation is passed the Government has an obligation to exercise all available options to prevent terrorism within the bounds of the Constitution. Moreover, we would like to point out that this Court has repeatedly held that mere possibility of abuse cannot be counted as a ground for denying the vesting of powers or for declaring a statute unconstitutional (See *State of Rajasthan v. Union of India* [(1978) 1 SCR 1], *Collector of Customs v. Nathella Sampathu Chetty* [AIR 1962 SC 316], *Kesavananda Bharati v. State of Kerala* [1973 (4) SCC 225] and *Mafatlal Industries Ltd. v. Union of India* [(1997) 5 SCC 536] etc).

Meaning of the word 'abets' in the context of POTA

22. Pertaining to the validity of individual sections, the petitioners primarily contended that Section 3(3) of POTA provides that whoever 'abets' a terrorist act or any preparatory act to a terrorist act shall be punishable and this provision, fails to address the requirement of 'mens rea' element. They added that this provision has been incorporated in POTA in spite of the contrary observation of this Court in *Kartar Singh* [1994 (3) SCC 569], wherein it was held that the word 'abets' needs to have the requisites of intention or knowledge. Consequently, they want us to strike down Section 3(3) as the same is prone to misuse.

23. In *Kartar Singh* [1994 (3) SCC 569], this Court was concerned with the expression "abet" as defined under Section 2(1)(a) of TADA and hence considered the effect of different provisions of the TADA to ascertain true meaning thereof. As the meaning of the word "abet" as defined therein is vague and imprecise, actual knowledge or reason to believe on the part of the person to be brought within the definition should be brought into that provision instead of reading down that provision. That kind of exercise is not necessary in POTA.

24. Under POTA the word "abets" is not defined at all. Section 2(1)(i) of POTA says "words and expressions used but not defined in this Act and defined in the Code shall have the meanings respectively assigned to them in the Code". According to Section 2(1)(a) of POTA "Code" means 'Code of Criminal Procedure, 1973 (2 of 1974)'. Whereas, Section 2(y) Cr.P.C. refers to Indian Penal Code for meaning of the word 'abets'. Therefore, the definition of 'abets', as appears in the IPC, will apply in a case under POTA. In order to bring a person abetting the commission of an offence, under the provisions of IPC it is necessary to prove that such person has been connected with those steps of the transactions that are criminal. 'mens rea' element is sine qua non for offences under IPC. Learned Attorney General does not dispute this position. Therefore, the argument advanced pertaining to the validity of Section 3(3) citing the reason of the absence of 'mens rea' element stands rejected.

Section 4

25. Section 4 provides for punishing a person who is in 'unauthorised possession' of arms or other weapons. The petitioners argued that, since the knowledge element is absent the provision is bad in law. A similar issue was raised before a Constitution Bench of this Court in *Sanjay Dutt v. State (II)* [(1994) 5 SCC 410]. Here this Court in Para 19 observed that :

> "...*Even though the word 'possession' is not preceded by any adjective like 'knowingly', yet it is common ground that in the context the word 'possession' must mean possession with the requisite mental element, that is, conscious possession and not mere custody without the awareness of the nature of such possession. There is a mental element in the concept of possession. Accordingly, the ingredient of 'possession' in Section 5 of the TADA Act means conscious possession. This is how the ingredient of possession in similar context of a statutory offence importing strict liability on account of mere possession of an unauthorised substance has been understood.*"

26. The finding of this Court, squarely to the effect that there exists a mental element in the word possession itself, answers the Petitioners argument. The learned Attorney General also maintains the stand that Section 4 pre-supposes conscious possession. Another aspect pointed out by the petitioners is about the 'unauthorised' possession of arms and argued that the unauthorised possession could even happen, for example, by non-renewal of license etc. In the light of *Sanjay Dutt case* [(1994) 5 SCC 410], this section pre-supposes knowledge of terrorist act for possession. There is no question of innocent persons getting punished. Therefore, we hold that there is no infirmity in Section 4.

Sections 6, 7, 8, 10, 11, 15, 16 and 17

27. Contentions have been raised in regard to provisions relating to seizure, attachment and forfeiture of proceeds of terrorism.

28. Provisions relating to seizure, attachment and forfeiture have to be read together. Section 2(1)(c) of POTA sets out the meaning of 'proceeds of terrorism' and reads as follows :

> " *'proceeds of terrorism' shall mean all kinds of properties which have been derived or obtained from commission of any terrorist act or have been acquired through funds traceable to a terrorist act, and shall include cash, irrespective of person in whose name such proceeds are standing or in whose possession they are found.*"

29. Explanation to Section 3 gives the meaning of 'a terrorist act' in the context of sub-section (1) of Section 3, so as to include the act of raising funds intended for the purpose of terrorism. Section 6 debars a person from holding or possessing any proceeds of terrorism and also makes it clear that it is liable to be forfeited. Section 7 authorises an investigating officer, not below the rank of Superintendent of Police with the prior approval in writing of the Director General of Police of the State, to seize such property or attach the same and serve a copy of such an order on the person concerned, if he has reason to believe that any property in relation to which an investigation is being conducted represents proceeds of terrorism. Section 8 provides for forfeiture of the proceeds of terrorism by a court irrespective of the fact whether or not the person from whose possession it is seized or attached is prosecuted in a Special Court for an offence under POTA. Section 9 provides for issue of a show-cause notice before forfeiture of proceeds of terrorism and an order for forfeiture cannot be made if such person establishes that he is a bona fide transferee of such proceeds for value without knowing that they represent proceeds of terrorism. Under Section 10, an appeal lies against an order made under Section 8 of POTA. Sub-section (2) thereof states that, where an order made under Section 8 is modified or annulled by the High Court, the person against whom an order of forfeiture has been made under Section 8 is acquitted, such property shall be returned to him and in either case if it is not possible for any reason to return the forfeited property, adequate compensation should be paid to him, which will be equivalent to the price and interest from the date of seizure of the property. Although the petitioners have challenged the various provisions of POTA relating to seizure, forfeiture and attachment of the property, ultimately, they did not pursue with that argument and submitted that the various facets of challenge to the aforesaid provisions can only be examined in the context of an actual fact situation and for the present they wanted an interpretation of the expressions used in Section 10(2) to apply even to a case of forfeiture of the proceeds of terrorism against a person who is prosecuted under POTA. Even that aspect can only be considered when an actual situation arises and not in the abstract. Therefore, we need not examine in detail these provisions except to notice the background in which these provisions have been enacted.

30. The order of forfeiture, by reason of Section 11, has been made independent of imposition of other punishments to which a person may be liable. Under Section 12, Designated Authority has been permitted to investigate the claims made by a third party. These provisions have to be seen as against Section 16, which provides for forfeiture of property of any person prosecuted and ultimately convicted. Here only on conviction, forfeiture of property can take place. In this connection, it is relevant to take note of the provisions of Sections 15, 16 and 17. Section 15 renders certain transfers to be null and void in cases where after the issue of an order under Section 7 or notice under Section 9 any property is transferred by any mode whatsoever, such transfer shall for the purpose of the Act be ignored and if such property is subsequently forfeited, the transfer of such property shall be deemed to be null and void. Section 16 enables a special court trying a person for an offence under the Act to pass an order that all or any of the properties, movable or immovable or both belonging to him, during the period of such trial, be attached, if not already attached under the Act. On conviction of such person, the special court may, by an order, declare that any property, movable or immovable or both belonging to the accused and specified in the order, shall stand forfeited to the Central Government or the State Government, as the case may be. Section 17 provides that in cases where any share of a company shall stand forfeited, then, the company shall, on receipt of the order of the special court, notwithstanding anything contained in the Companies Act, 1956 or the articles of association of the company, forthwith register the Central Government or the State Government, as the case may be, as the transferee of such shares.

31. Funding and financing play a vital role in fostering and promoting terrorism and it is only with such funds terrorists are able to recruit persons for their activities and make payments to them and their family to obtain arms and ammunition for furthering terrorist activities and to sustain the campaign of terrorism. Therefore, seizure, forfeiture and attachment of properties are essential in order to contain terrorism and is not unrelated to the same. Indeed, it is relevant to notice a resolution passed by the United Nations Security Council(Resolution No. 1373 dated 28.09.2001), which emphasised the need to curb terrorist activities by freezing and forfeiture of funds and financial assets employed to further terrorist activities. It will also be interesting to notice the United Nations International Convention for the Suppression of the Financing of Terrorism but at the same time it is not necessary to go into those details in the present context. The scheme of the provisions indicate that the principles of natural justice are duly observed and they do not confer any arbitrary power and forfeiture can only be made by an order of the court against which an appeal is also provided to the High Court and the rights of bona fide transferee are not affected. Therefore, for the present, it is not necessary to pronounce the constitutional validity of these provisions and we proceed on the basis that they are valid.

32. Number of changes have been made in the provisions which existed in TADA and which exist in POTA. The relevant discussion in the challenge to Section 8 of TADA by majority in *Kartar Singh* [1994 (3) SCC 569], is contained in paras 149-57 and para 452 by Sahai J. who has concurred with the majority. The validity of Section 8 of TADA was upheld, only if it was applied in the manner indicated in para 156 of the judgment which is as under :

> *"The discretionary power given to the Designated Court under Sections 8(1) and (2) is to be exercised under strict contingencies, namely, that (1) there must be an order of forfeiture and that order must be in writing; (2) the property either movable or immovable or both must belong to the accused convicted of any offence of TADA Act or rule thereunder; (3) the property should be specified in the order; (4) even though attachment can be made under Section 8(2) during the trial of the case, the forfeiture can be ordered only in case of conviction and not otherwise."*

33. However, ultimately, they do not press these contentions to be considered in these proceedings by stating that the various facets as set above can really be seen in actual fact situation and for the present, they call upon the court to clarify that the expression "modified" or "annulled" used in Section 10(2) shall apply even in a case of forfeiture of the proceeds of terrorism against a person who is not prosecuted under POTA.

34. It is not necessary to interpret these expressions and as and when an appropriate case arises, appropriate interpretation can be given on the said expressions. There is a scheme for forfeiture of the proceeds of terrorism followed by a show cause notice to be issued and thereafter on a decision being made, an appeal lies thereto and the order of forfeiture, by itself, will not prevent the court from inflicting any other punishment for which the person may be liable under the Act. The effect of modification and annulment of an order made by court under Section 8 of the Act is set out in sub-section (2) of Section 10. Therefore, as rightly submitted on behalf of the petitioners, these aspects can appropriately be dealt with, depending upon the fact situation arising in a given case. Therefore, it is not necessary to express any opinion on these aspects of the matter.

Section 14

35. The constitutional validity of Section 14 is challenged by advancing the argument that, it gives unbridled powers to the investigating officer to compel any person to furnish information if the investigating officer has reason to believe that such information will be useful or relevant to the purpose of the Act. It is pointed out that the provision is without any checks and is amenable to misuse by the investigating officers. It is also argued that it does not exclude lawyers or journalists who are bound by their professional ethics to keep the information rendered by their clients as privileged communication. Therefore, the Petitioners submitted that Section 14 is violative of Articles 14, 19, 20(3) and 21 of the Constitution. Learned Attorney General maintained that the Act does not confer any arbitrary or unguided powers; that such power is restricted to furnish information in one's possession in relation to terrorist offence 'on points or matters where the investigating officer has reason to believe (not suspect) that such information would be useful for or relevant to the purposes of the Act'; that this provision is essential for the detection and prosecution of terrorist offences; and that the underlying rationale of the obligation to furnish information is the salutary duty of every citizen.

36. Section 39 of the Code of Criminal Procedure, 1973, casts a duty upon every person to furnish information regarding offences. Criminal justice system cannot function without the cooperation of people. Rather it is the duty of everybody to assist the State in detection of the crime and bringing criminals to justice. Withholding such information cannot be traced to right to privacy, which itself is not an absolute right (See: *Sharda v. Dharmpal* [2003 (4) SCC 493]). Right to privacy is subservient to that of security of State. Highlighting the necessity of people's assistance in detection of crime this Court observed in *State of Gujarat v. Anirudhsing* [1997 (6) SCC 514] that :

> "*...It is the salutary duty of every witness who has the knowledge of the commission of crime, to assist the State in giving evidence...*"

37. Section 14 confers power to the investigating officer to ask for furnishing information that will be useful for or relevant to the purpose of the Act. Furthermore, such information could be asked only after obtaining a written approval from an officer not below the rank of a Superintendent of Police. Such power to the investigating officers is quite necessary in the detection of terrorist activities or terrorist.

38. It is a settled position of law, that a journalist or lawyer does not have a sacrosanct right to withhold information regarding crime under the guise of professional ethics. A lawyer cannot claim a right over professional communication beyond what is permitted under Section 126 of the Evidence Act. There is also no law that permits a newspaper or a journalist to withhold relevant information from courts though they have been given such power by virtue of Section 15(2) of the Press Council Act, 1978 as against Press Council(See also: *M.S.M. Sharma v. ShriSri Krishan Sinha* [1959 Supp (1) SCR 806] and *Sewakram Sobhani v. R.K. Karanjia* [1981 (3) SCC 208], which quoted *Arnold v. King Emperor* [1913-14 (41) IA 149], with approval and also *British Steel Corporation v. Granada Television* [1981 (1) All ER 417 (HL)] and *Branzburg v. Hayes* [1972 (408) US 665]). Of course the investigating officers will be circumspect and cautious in requiring them to disclose information. In the process of obtaining information, if any right of a citizen is violated, nothing prevents him from resorting to other legal remedies.

39. Inasmuch as the main purpose of Section 14 of POTA is only to allow the investigating officers to procure certain information that is necessary to proceed with the further investigation we find there is no merit in the argument of the petitioners and we uphold the validity of Section 14.

Sections 18 and 19

40. Sections 18 and 19 deal with the notification and de-notification of terrorist organisations. Petitioners submitted that under Section 18(1) of POTA, a schedule has been provided giving the names of terrorist organisations without any legislative declaration; that there is nothing provided in the Act for declaring organisations as terrorist organisation; that this provision is therefore, unconstitutional as it takes away the fundamental rights of an organization under Articles 14, 19(1)(a) and 19(1)(c) of the Constitution; that under Section 18(2) of the Act, the Central Government has been given unchecked and arbitrary powers to 'add' or 'remove' or 'amend' the Schedule pertaining to terrorist organisations; that under the Unlawful Activities (Prevention) Act, 1967, an organization could have been declared unlawful only after the Central Government has sufficient material to form an opinion and such declaration has to be made by a Notification wherein grounds have to be specified for making such declaration; that therefore such arbitrary power is violative of Articles 14, 19 and 21 of the Constitution. Pertaining to Section 19, the main allegation is that it excessively delegates power to Central Government in the appointment of members to the Review Committee and they also pointed out that the inadequate representation of judicial members will affect the decision-making and consequently it may affect the fair judicial scrutiny; that, therefore, Section 19 is not constitutionally valid.

41. The learned Attorney General contended, that there is no requirement of natural justice which mandates that before a statutory declaration is made in respect of an organization which is listed in the schedule a prior opportunity of hearing or representation should be given to the affected organization or its members; that the rule of *audi alteram partem* is not absolute and is subject to modification; that in light of the post-decisional hearing remedy provided under Section 19 and since the aggrieved persons could approach the Review Committee there is nothing illegal in the Section; that furthermore, the constitutional remedy under Articles 226 and 227 is also available; that therefore, having regard to the nature of the legislation and the magnitude and prevalence of the evil of terrorism it cannot be said to impose unreasonable restrictions on the Fundamental Rights under Article 19(1)(c) of the Constitution.

42. The right of citizens to form associations or unions that is guaranteed by Article 19(1)(c) of the Constitution is subject to the restriction provided under Article 19(4) of the Constitution. Under Article 19(4) of the Constitution the State can impose reasonable restrictions, inter alia, in the interest of sovereignty and integrity of the country. POTA is enacted to protect sovereignty and integrity of India from the menace of terrorism. Imposing restriction under Article 19(4) of the Constitution also includes declaring an organization as a terrorist organization as provided under POTA. Hence Section 18 is not unconstitutional.

43. It is contended that before making the notification whereby an organization is declared as a terrorist organization there is no provision for pre-decisional hearing. But this cannot be considered as a violation of *audi alteram partem* principle, which itself is not absolute. Because in the peculiar background of terrorism it may be necessary for the Central Government to declare an organization as terrorist organization even without hearing that organization. At the same time under Section 19 of POTA the aggrieved persons can approach the Central Government itself for reviewing its decision. If they are not satisfied by the decision of the Central Government they can subsequently approach the Review Committee and they are also free to exercise their Constitutional remedies. The post-decisional remedy provided under POTA satisfies the *audi alteram partem* requirement in the matter of declaring an organization as a terrorist organization(See: *Mohinder Singh Gill v. Chief Election Commissioner* [1978 (1) SCC 405]; *Swadeshi Cotton Mills v. Union of India* [1981 (1) SCC 664]; *Olga Tellis v. Bombay Municipal Corporation* [1985 (3) SCC 545]; *Union of India v. Tulsiram Patel* [1985 (3) SCC 398]). Therefore, the absence of pre-decisional hearing cannot be treated as a ground for declaring Section 18 as invalid.

44. It is urged that, Section 18 or 19 is invalid based on the inadequacy of judicial members in the Review Committee. As per Section 60, Chairperson of the Review Committee will be the person who is or has been a Judge of a High Court. The mere presence of non-judicial members by itself cannot be treated as a ground to invalidate Section 19. (See: *Kartar Singh case* [1994 (3) SCC 569] at page 683, para 265 of SCC.)

45. As regards the reasonableness of the restriction provided under Section 18, it has to be noted that the factum of declaration of an organization as a terrorist organization depends upon the 'belief' of the Central Government. The reasonableness of the Central Government's action has to be justified based on material facts upon which it formed the opinion. Moreover the Central Government is bound by the order of the Review Committee. Considering the nature of legislation and magnitude or presence of terrorism, it cannot be said that Section 18 of POTA imposes unreasonable restrictions on fundamental right guaranteed under Article 19(1)(c) of the Constitution. We uphold the validity of Sections 18 and 19.

Sections 20, 21 and 22

46. The petitioners assailed Sections 20, 21 and 22 mainly on the ground that no requirement of *mens rea* for offences is provided in these sections and the same is liable to misuse, therefore, it has to be declared unconstitutional. The learned Attorney General argued that Section 21 and its various sub-sections are penal provisions and should be strictly construed both in their interpretation and application; that on a true interpretation of the Act having regard to the well-settled principles of interpretation, Section 21 would not cover any expression or activity which does not have the element or consequence of furthering or encouraging terrorist activity or facilitating its commission; that support *per se* or mere expression of sympathy or arrangement of a meeting which is not intended or designed and which does not have the effect to further the activities of any terrorist organization or the commission of terrorist acts are not within the mischief of Section 21 and hence is valid.

47. Here the only point to be considered is, whether these Sections exclude *mens rea* element for constituting offences or not. At the outset it has to be noted that Sections 20, 21 and 22 of POTA is similar to that of Sections 11, 12 and 15 of the Terrorism Act, 2000 of the United Kingdom. Such provisions are found to be quite necessary all over the world in anti-terrorism efforts. Sections 20, 21 and 22 are penal in nature that demand strict construction. These provisions are a departure from the ordinary law since the said law was found to be inadequate and not sufficiently effective to deal with the threat of terrorism. Moreover, the crime referred to herein under POTA is aggravated in nature. Hence special provisions are contemplated to combat the new threat of terrorism. Support, either verbal or monetary, with a view to nurture terrorism and terrorist activities is causing new challenges. Therefore Parliament finds that such support to terrorist organisations or terrorist activities needs to be made punishable. Viewing the legislation in its totality, it cannot be said that these provisions are obnoxious.

48. But the Petitioners' apprehension regarding the absence of *mens rea* in these Sections and the possibility of consequent misuse needs our elucidation. It is the cardinal principle of criminal jurisprudence that *mens rea* element is necessary to constitute a crime. It is the general rule, that a penal statute presupposes *mens rea* element. It will be excluded only if the legislature expressly postulates otherwise. It is in this context that this Court said in *Kartar Singh case* [1994 (3) SCC 569] (at page 645 para 115 of SCC) that :

> *"Unless a statute either expressly or by necessary implication rules out 'mens rea' in case of this kind, the element of mens rea must be read into the provision of the statute."*

49. *Mens rea,* by necessary implication, could be excluded from a statute only where it is absolutely clear that the implementation of the object of the Statute would otherwise be defeated. Here we need to find out whether there are sufficient grounds for inferring that Parliament intended to exclude the general rule regarding *mens rea* element. (See: *State of Maharashtra v. Mayer Hans George* [AIR 1965 SC 722], *Nathulal v. State of M.P.* [AIR 1966 SC 43], *Inder Sain v. State of Punjab* [(1973) 2 SCC 372], for the general principles concerning the exclusion or inclusion of *mens rea* element vis-à-vis a given statute.) The prominent method of understanding the legislative intention, in a matter of this nature, is to see whether the substantive provisions of the Act require *mens rea* element as a constituent ingredient for an offence. Offence under Section 3(1) of POTA will be constituted only if it is done with an 'intent'. If Parliament stipulates that the 'terrorist act' itself has to be committed with a criminal intention, can it be said that a person who 'professes' (as under Section 20) or 'invites support' or 'arranges, manages or assists in arranging or managing a meeting' or 'addresses a meeting' (as under Section 21) has committed the offence if he does not have an intention or design to further the activities of any terrorist organization or the commission of terrorist acts? We are clear that it is not. Therefore, it is obvious that the offence under Section 20 or 21 or 22 needs positive inference that a person has acted with intent of furthering or encouraging terrorist activity or facilitating its commission. In other words, these sections are limited only to those activities that have the intent of encouraging or furthering or promoting or facilitating the commission of terrorist activities. If these sections are understood in this way, there cannot be any misuse. With this clarification we uphold the constitutional validity of Sections 20, 21 and 22.

Section 27

50. Under Section 27, a police officer investigating a case can seek a direction through the Court of Chief Judicial Magistrate or the Court of a Chief Metropolitan Magistrate for obtaining samples of handwriting, fingerprints, footprints, photographs, blood, saliva, semen, hair, voice of any accused person reasonably suspected to be involved in the commission of an offence under the Act. The court can also draw adverse inference if an accused refuses to do so.

51. The Petitioners argued that this Section falls foul of Articles 14, 20(3) and 21 of the Constitution for the reason: that no power has been left with the Court to decide whether the request for samples from a suspect person sought for by the investigating officer is reasonable or not; that no power has been given to the Court to refuse the request of the investigating officer; that it is not obligatory for the Court to record any reason while allowing the request; and that the Section is a gross violation of Article 20(3), because it amounts to compel a person to give evidence against himself. Relying mainly on *State of Bombay v. Kathi Kalu Oghad* [1962 (3) SCR 10], learned Attorney General submitted that the argument pertaining to the violation of Article 20(3) is not sustainable.

52. We do not think, as feared by the Petitioner, that this section fixes a blanket responsibility upon the Court to grant permission immediately upon the receipt of a request. Upon a close reading of the Section, it will become clear that upon a 'request' by an investigating police officer it shall only 'be lawful' for the court to grant permission. Nowhere is it stated that the Court will have to positively grant permission upon a request. It is very well within the ambit of Court's discretion. If the request is based on a wrong premise, the Court is free to refuse the request. This discretionary power granted to the Court presupposes that the Court will have to record its reasoning for allowing or refusing a request. Pertaining to the argument that the Section *per se* violates Article 20(3), it has to be noted that a Bench consisting of 11 Judges in *Kathi Kalu Oghad case* [1962 (3) SCR 10], had looked into a similar situation and it is ruled therein (at pages 30-32) that :

> *"...The giving of finger impression or of specimen signature or of handwriting, strictly speaking, is not 'to be a witness'.... When an accused person is called upon by the court or any other authority holding an investigation to give his finger impression or signature or a specimen of his handwriting, he is not giving any testimony to the nature of a personal testimony. The giving of a personal testimony'must depend upon his volition. He can make any kind of statement or may refuse to make any statement. But his finger impressions or his handwriting, in spite of efforts at concealing the true nature of it by dissimulation cannot change their intrinsic character. Thus, the giving of finger impressions or of specimen writing or of signatures by an accused person, though it may amount to furnishing evidence in the larger sense, is not included within the expression 'to be a witness'.*
>
> *...They are only materials for comparison in order to lend assurance to the Court that its inference based on other pieces of evidence is reliable..."*
>
> (emphasis Supplied)

53. This being the position in law, the argument of the Petitioners pertaining to the violation of Article 20(3) is not sustainable. It is meaningful to look into Section 91 Cr.P.C. that empowers a criminal court as also a police officer to order any person to produce a document or other thing in his possession for the purpose of any inquiry or trial(See: *State of Gujarat v. Shyamlal Mohanlal Choksi* [AIR 1965 SC 1251] in this regard.). Moreover, this Section is only a step in aid for further investigation and the samples so obtained can never be considered as conclusive proof for conviction. Consequently, we uphold the constitutional validity of Section 27.

Section 30

54. Section 30 contains provision for the protection of witness. It gives powers to the Special Court to hold proceedings in-camera and to taking measures for keeping the identity of the witness secret.

55. Petitioners challenged the constitutional validity of this Section by levelling the argument that the right to cross-examine is an important part of fair trial and principles of natural justice which are guaranteed under Article 21; that even during emergency fundamental rights under Articles 20 and 21 cannot be taken away; that Section 30 is in violation of the dictum in *Kartar Singh case* [1994 (3) SCC 569], because it does not contain the provision of disclosure of names and identities of the witness before the commencement of trial; that fair trial includes the right for the defence to ascertain the true identity of an accuser; that, therefore, the same has to be declared unconstitutional. Learned Attorney General submitted that such provisions or exercise of such powers are enacted to protect the life and liberty of a person who is able and willing to give evidence in prosecution of grave criminal offences; that the Section is not only in the interest of witness whose life is in danger but also in the interest of the community which lies in ensuring that heinous offences like terrorist acts are effectively prosecuted and punished; that if the witnesses are not given immunity they would not come forward to give evidence and there would be no effective prosecution of terrorist offences and the entire object of the Act would be frustrated; that cross-examination is not a universal or indispensable requirement of natural justice and fair trial; that under compelling circumstances it can be dispensed with natural justice and fair trial can be evolved; that the Section requires the Court to be satisfied that the life of the witness is in danger and the reasons for keeping the identity of the witness secret are required to be recorded in writing; that, therefore, it is reasonable to hold that the Section is necessary for the operation of the Act.

56. Section 30 of POTA is similar to Section 16 of TADA, the constitutional validity of which was upheld by this Court in *Kartar Singh case* [1994 (3) SCC 569] (see pages 683-689 of SCC). In order to decide the constitutional validity of Section 30 we don't think it is necessary to go into the larger debate, which learned Counsel for both sides have argued, that whether right to cross-examine is central to fair trial or not because right to cross-examination *per se* is not taken away by Section 30. This section only confers discretion to the court concerned to keep the identity of witness secret if the life of such witness is in danger. We cannot shy away from the unpleasant reality that often witnesses do not come forward to depose before court even in serious cases. This precarious situation creates challenges to our criminal justice administration in general and terrorism-related cases in particular. Witnesses do not volunteer to give evidence mainly due to fear for their lives. Ultimately, the non-conviction affects the larger interest of the community, which lies in ensuring that the executors of heinous offences like terrorist acts are effectively prosecuted and punished. The legislature drafted Section 30 by taking all these factors into account. In our view, a fair balance between the rights and interest of witness, rights of accused and larger public interest has been maintained under Section 30. It is also aimed to assist the State in justice administration and encourage others to do the same under the given circumstances. Anonymity of witness is not the general rule under Section 30. Identity will be withheld only in exceptional circumstance when the Special Court is satisfied that the life of the witness is in jeopardy. Earlier this Court has endorsed a similar procedure. (See: *Gurbachan Singh v. State of Bombay* [1952 SCR 737], *Hira Nath Mishra v. Principal, Rajendra Medical College* [1973 (1) SCC 805] and *A.K. Roy v. Union of India* [1982 (1) SCC 271] .) While deciding the validity of Section 16 of TADA, this Court quoted all these cases with approval. (See also the subsequent decision in *Jamaat-e-Islami Hind v. Union of India* [1995 (1) SCC 428]).

57. The need for the existence and exercise of power to grant protection to a witness and preserve his or her anonymity in a criminal trial has been universally recognised. Provisions of such nature have been enacted to protect the life and liberty of the person who is able and willing to give evidence in support of the prosecution in grave criminal cases. A provision of this nature should not be looked at merely from the angle of protection of the witness whose life may be in danger, if his or her identity is disclosed but also in the interest of the community to ensure that heinous offences like terrorist acts are effectively prosecuted and punished. It is a notorious fact that a witness who gives evidence which is unfavourable to an accused in a trial for terrorist offence would expose himself to severe reprisals which could result in death or severe bodily injury or that of his family members. If such witnesses are not given appropriate protection, they would not come forward to give evidence and there would be no effective prosecution of terrorist offences and the entire object of the enactment may possibly be frustrated. Under compelling circumstances, this can be dispensed with by evolving such other mechanism, which complies with natural justice and thus ensures a fair trial.

58. The observations made in this regard by this Court in the decisions to which we have adverted to earlier have been noticed by this Court in *Kartar Singh case* [1994 (3) SCC 569], which has upheld the validity of a similar provision subject, of course, to certain conditions which now forms part of Section 30. The present position is that Section 30(2) requires the court to be satisfied that the life of a witness is in danger to invoke a provision of this nature. Furthermore, reasons for keeping the identity and address of a witness secret are required to be recorded in writing and such reasons should be weighty. In order to safeguard the right of an accused to a fair trial and basic requirements of the due process, a mechanism can be evolved whereby the special court is obligated to satisfy itself about the truthfulness and reliability of the statement or disposition of the witness whose identity is sought to be protected.

59. Our attention has been drawn to the legal position in USA, Canada, New Zealand, Australia and UK as well as the view expressed in the European Court of Human Rights in various decisions. However, it is not necessary to refer any of them because the legal position has been fully set out and explained in *Kartar Singh* [1994 (3) SCC 569] and provision of POTA in Section 30 clause (2) has been modelled on the guidelines set out therein. We may further notice that the effort of the court has been to balance the right of the witness as to his life and liberty and the right of the community in effective prosecution of heinous criminal offences with the right of the accused to a fair trial. This is done by devising a mechanism or arrangement to preserve anonymity of the witness when there is an identifiable threat to the life or physical safety of the witness or others whereby the court satisfies itself about the weight to be attached to the evidence of the witness. In some jurisdictions an independent counsel has been appointed for the purpose to act as *amicus curiae* and after going through the deposition evidence assist the court in forming an opinion about the weight of the evidence in a given case or in appropriate cases to be cross-examined on the basis of the questions formulated and given to him by either of the parties. Useful reference may be made in this context to the recommendations of the Law Commission of New Zealand.

60. The necessity to protect the identity of the witness is not a factor that can be determined by a general principle. It is dependent on several factors and circumstances arising in a case and, therefore, the Act has left the determination of such question to an appropriate case.

61. Keeping secret the identity of witness, though in the larger interest of the public, is a deviation from the usual mode of trial. In extraordinary circumstances we are bound to take this path, which is less travelled. Here, the Special Courts will have to exercise utmost care and caution to ensure fair trial. The reason for keeping identity of the witness has to be well substantiated. It is not feasible for us to suggest the procedure that has to be adopted by the Special Courts for keeping the identity of witness a secret. It shall be appropriate for the concerned Courts to take into account all the factual circumstances of individual cases and to forge appropriate methods to ensure the safety of individual witness. With these observations we uphold the validity of Section 30.

Section 32

62. This section made it lawful of certain confessions made to police officers to be taken into consideration.

63. Concerning the validity and procedural difficulties that could arise during the process of recording confessions, the petitioners submitted that there is no need to empower the police to record confession since the accused has to be produced before the Magistrate within forty-eight hours, in that case the Magistrate himself could record the confession; that there is no justification for extending the time-limit of forty-eight hours for producing the person before the Magistrate; that it is not clear in the section whether the confession recorded by the police officer will have validity after the Magistrate has recorded the fact of torture and has sent the accused for medical examination; that it is not clear as to whether both the confession before the police officer as well as confessional statement before the Magistrate shall be used in evidence; that the Magistrates cannot be used for mechanically putting seal of approval on the confessional statements by the police; that, therefore, the section has to be nullified. Validity of this section was defended by the learned Attorney General by forwarding the arguments that the provisions relating to the admissibility of confessional statements, which are similar to that of Section 32 in POTA was upheld in *Kartar Singh case* [1994 (3) SCC 569]; that the provisions of POTA are an improvement over TADA by virtue of enactment of Sections 32(3) to 32(5); that the general principles of law regarding the admissibility of a confessional statement is applicable under POTA; that the provision which entails the Magistrate to test and examine the voluntariness of a confession and complaint of torture is an additional safeguard and does not in any manner inject any constitutional infirmity; that there cannot be perennial distrust of the police; that Parliament has taken into account all the relevant factors in their totality and same is not unjust or unreasonable.

64. At the outset it has to be noted that Section 15 of TADA, that was similar to this section, was upheld in *Kartar Singh case* [1994 (3) SCC 569] (pages 664-683 of SCC). While enacting this section Parliament has taken into account all the guidelines, which were suggested by this Court in *Kartar Singh case* [1994 (3) SCC 569]. Main allegation of the Petitioners is that there is no need to empower the police to record confession since the accused has to be produced before the Magistrate within forty-eight hours in which case the Magistrate himself could record the statement or confession. In the context of terrorism the need for making such a provision so as to enable police officers to record the confession was explained and upheld by this Court in *Kartar Singh case* [1994 (3) SCC 569] (page 680 para 253 of SCC). We need not go into that question at this stage. If the recording of confession by the police is found to be necessary by the Parliament and if it is in tune with the scheme of law, then an additional safeguard under Sections 32(4) and (5) is afortiori legal. In our considered opinion the provision that requires producing such a person before the Magistrate is an additional safeguard. It gives that person an opportunity to rethink over his confession. Moreover, the Magistrate's responsibility to record the statement and the enquiry about the torture and provision for subsequent medical treatment makes the provision safer. It will deter the police officers from obtaining a confession from an accused by subjecting him to torture. It is also worthwhile to note that an officer who is below the rank of a Superintendent of Police cannot record the confessional statement. It is a settled position that if a confession was forcibly extracted, it is a nullity in law. Non-inclusion of this obvious and settled principle does not make the section invalid (See: *Kartar Singh case* [1994 (3) SCC 569] page 678, para 248-49 of SCC). Ultimately, it is for the court concerned to decide the admissibility of the confessional statement (See: *Kartar Singh case* [1994 (3) SCC 569], page 683, para 264 of SCC). Judicial wisdom will surely prevail over irregularity, if any, in the process of recording confessional statement. Therefore we are satisfied that the safeguards provided by the Act and under the law are adequate in the given circumstances and we don't think it is necessary to look more into this matter. Consequently, we uphold the validity of Section 32.

Section 49

65. Section 49 mainly deals with the procedure for obtaining bail for an accused under POTA.

66. Petitioners' main grievance about this section is that under Section 49(7), a court could grant bail only if it is satisfied that there are grounds for believing that an accused 'is not guilty of committing such offence', since such a satisfaction could be attained only after recording of evidence there is every chance that the accused will be granted bail only after minimum one year of detention; that the proviso to Section 49(7), which is not there under TADA, makes it clear that for one year from the date of detention no bail could be granted; that this section has not incorporated the principles laid down by this Court in *Sanjay Dutt case* [(1994) 5 SCC] (at page 439 para 43-48 of SCC), wherein it is held that if a challan is not filed after expiry of 180 days or extended period, the indefeasible right of an accused to be released on bail is ensured, provided that the same is exercised before filing of challan; that the prosecution is curtailing even this right under POTA. Therefore, the petitioners want us to make the section less stringent according to the settled principles of law. Learned Attorney General submitted that the provisions regarding bail are not onerous nor do they impose any excessive burden or restriction on the right of the accused; that similar provisions are found in Section 37 of the NDPS Act, 1985 and in Section 10 of the U.P. Dacoity Affected Areas Act; that on a true construction of Sections 49(6) and (7), it is not correct to conclude that the accused cannot apply for bail at all for a period of one year; that the right of the accused to apply for bail during the period of one year is not completely taken away; that the stringent provision of bail under Section 49(7) would apply only for the first one year of detention and after its expiry the normal bail provisions under Cr.P.C. would apply; that there is no dispute that the principle laid down by this Court in *D.K. Basu v. State of West Bengal* [1997 (1) SCC 416] will apply; that in the light of effective safeguards provided in the Act and effective remedies against adverse orders there is no frailty in Section 49.

67. Section 49 of the Act is similar to Section 20 of TADA, constitutional validity of which has been upheld by this Court in *Kartar Singh case* [1994 (3) SCC 569] (pages 691-710 of SCC). Challenge before us is limited to the interpretation of Sections 49(6) and (7). By virtue of Section 49(8), the powers under Sections 49(6) and (7) pertaining to bail are in addition to and not in derogation to the powers under the Code or any other law for the time being in force on granting of bail. The offences under POTA are more complex than that of ordinary offences. Usually, the overt and covert acts of terrorism are executed in a chillingly efficient manner as a result of high conspiracy, which is invariably linked with anti-national elements both inside and outside the country. So an expanded period of detention is required to complete the investigation. Such a comparatively long period for solving the case is quite justifiable. Therefore, the investigating agencies may need the custody of the accused for a longer period. Consequently, Sections 49(6) and (7) are not unreasonable. In spite of this, bail could be obtained for an accused booked under POTA if the 'court is satisfied that there are grounds for believing that he is not guilty of committing such offence' after hearing the Public Prosecutor. It is the general law that before granting the bail the conduct of the accused seeking bail has to be taken into account and evaluated in the background of the nature of crime said to have been committed by him. That evaluation shall be based on the possibility of the likelihood of his either tampering with the evidence or committing the offence again or creating threat to the society. Since, the satisfaction of the court under Section 49(7) has to be arrived at based on the particular facts and after considering the abovementioned aspects, we do not think the unreasonableness attributed to Section 49(7) is fair(See *Kartar Singh case* [1994 (3) SCC 569], page 707 para 349-352 of SCC).

68. Proviso to Section 49(7) reads as under :

> *"Provided that after the expiry of a period of one year from the date of detention of the accused for an offence under this Act, the provisions of sub-section (6) of this section shall apply."*

69. It is contended that this proviso to Section 49(7) of POTA is read by some of the courts as a restriction on exercise of power for grant of bail under Section 49(6) of POTA and such power could be exercised only after the expiry of the period of one year from the date of detention of the accused for offences under POTA. If the intention of the legislature is that an application for bail cannot be made prior to expiry of one year after detention for offences under POTA, it would have been clearly spelt out in that manner in Section 49(6) itself. Sections 49(6) and 49(7) of POTA have to be read together and the combined reading of these two sections is to the effect that Public Prosecutor has to be given an opportunity of being heard before releasing the accused on bail and if he opposes the application, the court will have to be satisfied that there are grounds for believing that he is not guilty of having committed such offence. It is by way of exception to Section 49(7) that the proviso is added which means that after the expiry of one year after the detention of the accused for offences under POTA, the accused can be released on bail after hearing the Public Prosecutor under ordinary law without applying the rigour of Section 49(7) of POTA. It also means that the accused can approach the court for bail subject to conditions of Section 49(7) of POTA within a period of one year after the detention for offences under POTA.

70. Proviso to Section 49(7) provides, that the condition enumerated in sub-section (6) will apply after the expiry of one year. There appears to be an accidental omission or mistake of not including the word 'not' after the word 'shall' and before the word 'apply'. Unless such a word is included, the provision will lead to an absurdity or become meaningless. Even otherwise, read appropriately, the meaning of the proviso to Section 49(7) is, that an accused can resort to ordinary bail procedure under the Code after that period of one year. At the same time, the proviso does not prevent such an accused to approach the court for bail in accordance with the provisions of POTA under Sections 49(6) and (7) thereof. This interpretation is not disputed by the learned Attorney General. Taking into account the complexities of the terrorism related offences and intention of the Parliament in enacting a special law for its prevention, we do not think that the additional conditions regarding bail under POTA are unreasonable. We uphold the validity of Section 49.

71. There is no challenge to any other provisions of the Act.

72. In the result, these petitions stand dismissed, subject, however, to the clarifications that we have set out above on the interpretation of the provisions of the enactment while dealing with the constitutionality thereof.

W.P. (Crl.) 129/2002

73. A case was registered against the petitioner under Section 13(1)(*a*) of the Unlawful Activities (Prevention) Act, 1967, Sections 21(2) and (3) of the Prevention of Terrorism Act, 2002 (POTA) read with Sections 109 and 120B of the Indian Penal Code on 04.07.2002. When the petitioner returned to Chennai from Chicago on 11.07.2002, he was arrested at Chennai Airport and was produced before a Judicial Magistrate, Madurai on 12.07.2002. He had been remanded. He has been detained in jail since then pursuant to the remand order of the Judicial Magistrate, Madurai. A notification was issued constituting the Special Court, Chennai at Poonamallee for trial of the offences under POTA. The petitioner was produced before the Special Court on 07.08.2002 and he has been continued to be remanded to jail from time to time. On 09.10.2002, his remand had been extended beyond the period of 90 days.

74. In this case, though several questions have been raised, two questions have been specifically urged, namely :

> (1) Whether Sections 21(1) and (3) of the Prevention of Terrorism Act, 2002 are offending Articles 19(1)(a) and 19(1)(c) of the Constitution of India and therefore unconstitutional?
>
> (2) Does the mere expression of sympathy for Tamils in Sri Lanka for whom the Liberation of Tigers of Tamil Eelam has become the sole-representative recognised by the International Community amount to support to a terrorist organisation under the Prevention of Terrorism Act, 2002 thereby empowering the State to curtail personal liberty?

75. We have upheld the constitutional validity of Section 21 of POTA in the decision pronounced by us in Writ Petition (C) No. 389 of 2002 above and, therefore, the first question does not survive for consideration.

76. So far as the second question is concerned, we have heard Shri F.S. Nariman and Shri Anil B. Divan, learned senior counsel appearing for the petitioner, apart from Shri Rajinder Sachhar and Shri B.S. Malik, the learned senior counsel appearing for the petitioner in connected matters, on the interpretation of Section 21 of POTA. Shri P.P. Rao, appearing for the State of Tamil Nadu, has made elaborate submissions and adverted to various affidavits filed by the Union of India. However, it is not necessary for us to examine any of these aspects in these proceedings. We have carefully considered the arguments advanced by the learned counsel and that of the learned Attorney General for India on this aspect of the matter. We think, the proper course that has to be adopted in a case of this nature where a criminal case has already been lodged and the same is pending consideration before the Special Court, it would not be appropriate for us to express our views on the question of facts arising in this case. We are sure that the Special Court will decide the matter in the light of decision pronounced by us in Writ Petition (C) No. 389 of 2002 above.

77. The writ petition is disposed of with the aforesaid observations.

W.P. (Crl.) 28/2003

78. The petitioner in this writ petition seeks for declaration that Section 21(2) and the proviso to Sections 49(6) and 49(7) of POTA are illegal and ultra vires the Constitution of India.

79. In as much as we have upheld the constitutional validity of Section 21(2) and the proviso to Sections 49(6) and 49(7) of POTA in the judgment pronounced by us in Writ Petition (C) No. 389 of 2002 above, this writ petition is dismissed.

WP (Crl.) 48/2003

80. In this writ petition, apart from challenging the constitutional validity of Sections 1(4), 3 to 9, 14, 18 to 24, 26, 27, 29 to 33, 36 to 53, which has been upheld by us in the judgment pronounced by us in Writ Petition (C) No. 389 of 2002 above, the constitutional validity of Entry 21 of the Schedule to POTA is also challenged.

81. On that aspect, no specific arguments have been addressed by any of the parties. This matter will have to be heard separately and hence, this writ petition is de-linked from other matters.

In the Supreme Court of India

Writ Petition (Civil) No. 196 of 2001

People's Union for Civil Liberties (PUCL) v. Union of India & Ors.[12]

Date of Order : 28.11.2001

Bench : B.N. Kirpal and K.G. Balakrishnan, JJ.

[This Petition was filed by PUCL asserting the Right to Food. The Supreme Court has given several directions and has monitored developments for more than a decade. Only important orders have been included in the compilation.]

Order

1. After hearing learned counsel for the parties, we issue, as an interim measure, the following directions :

1. TARGETED PUBLIC DISTRIBUTION SCHEME (TPDS)

(i) It is the case of the Union of India that there has been full compliance with regard to the allotment of foodgrain in relation to TPDS. However, if any of the States gives a specific instance of non-compliance, the Union of India will do the needful within the framework of the Scheme.

(ii) The States are directed to complete the identification of BPL families, issuing of cards and commencement of distribution of 25 kg grain per family per month latest by 01.01.2002.

(iii) The Delhi Government will ensure that TPDS application forms are freely available and are given and received free of charge and there is an effective mechanism in place to ensure speedy and effective redressal of grievances.

2. ANTYODAYA ANNA YOJANA

(i) It is the case of the Union of India, there has been full compliance with regard to the allotment of foodgrains in relation

12. (2007) 1 SCC 728

to Antyodaya Anna Yojana. However, if any of the States gives a specific instance of non-compliance, the Union of India will do the needful within the framework of the Scheme.

(ii) We direct the States and the Union Territories to complete identification of beneficiaries, issuing of cards and distribution of grain under this Scheme latest by 01.01.2002.

(iii) It appears that some Antyodaya beneficiaries may be unable to lift grain because of penury. In such cases, the Centre, the States and the Union Territories are requested to consider giving the quota free after satisfying itself in this behalf.

3. MID DAY MEAL SCHEME (MDMS)

(i) It is the case of Union of India, that there has been full compliance with regard to the Mid-Day Meal Scheme (MDMS). However, if any of the States gives a specific instance of non-compliance, the Union of India will do the needful within the framework of the Scheme.

(ii) We direct the State Governments/Union Territories to implement the Mid-Day Meal Scheme by providing every child in every government and government-assisted primary schools with a prepared mid-day meal with a minimum content of 300 calories and 8-12 grams of protein each day of school for a minimum of 200 days. Those Governments providing dry rations instead of cooked meals must, within three months start providing cooked meals in all government and government-aided primary schools in all half the districts of the State (in order of poverty) and must within a further period of three months extend the provision of cooked meals to the remaining parts of the State.

(iii) We direct the Union of India and FCI to ensure provision of fair average quality grain for the Scheme on time. The States/ Union Territories and FCI are directed to do joint inspection of food grains. If the food grain is found, on joint inspection, not to be of fair average quality, it will be replaced by FCI prior to lifting.

4. NATIONAL OLD AGE PENSION SCHEME (NOAPS)

(i) It is the case of the Union of India that there has been full compliance with regard to the National Old Age Pension Scheme. However, if any of the States gives a specific instance of non-compliance, the Union of India will do the needful within the framework of the Scheme.

(ii) The States are directed to identify the beneficiaries and to start making payments latest by 01.01.2002.

(iii) We direct the State Governments/Union Territories to make payments promptly by the 7th of each month.

5. ANNAPURNA SCHEME

The States/Union Territories are directed to identify the beneficiaries and distribute the grain latest by 01.01.2002.

6. INTEGRATED CHILD DEVELOPMENT SCHEME (ICDS)

(i) We direct the State Governments/Union Territories to implement the Integrated Child Development Scheme (ICDS) in full and to ensure that every ICDS disbursing centre in the country shall provide as under:

(a) Each child up to 6 years of age to get 300 calories and 8-10 grams of protein;

(b) Each adolescent girl to get 500 calories and 20-25 grams of protein;

(c) Each pregnant woman and each nursing mother to get 500 calories and 20-25 grams of protein;

(d) Each malnourished child to get 600 calories and 16-20 grams of protein;

(e) Have a disbursement centre in every settlement.

(ii) It is the case of the Union of India that there has been full compliance of its obligations, if any, under the Scheme. However, if any of the States gives a specific instance of non-compliance, the Union of India will do the needful within the framework of the Scheme.

7. NATIONAL MATERNITY BENEFIT SCHEME (NMBS)

(i) We direct the State Governments/Union Territories to implement the National Maternity Benefit Scheme (NMBS) by paying all BPL pregnant women Rs. 500/- through the Sarpanch 8-12 weeks prior to delivery for each of the first two births.

(ii) It is the case of the Union of India that there has been full compliance with its obligations under the Scheme. However, if any of the States gives a specific instance of non-compliance, the Union of India will do the needful within the framework of the Scheme.

8. NATIONAL FAMILY BENEFIT SCHEME

(i) We direct the State Governments/Union Territories to implement the National Family Benefit Scheme and pay a BPL family Rs 10,000 within four weeks through a local Sarpanch, whenever the primary breadwinner of the family dies.

9. We direct that a copy of this order be translated in regional languages and in English by the respective States/Union Territories and prominently displayed in all gram panchayats, government school buildings and fair price shops.

10. In order to ensure transparency in selection of the beneficiaries and their access to these Schemes, the gram panchayats will also display the list of all the beneficiaries under the various Schemes. Copies of the Schemes and the list of the beneficiaries shall be made available by the gram panchayats to members of public for inspection.

11. We direct Doordarshan and AIR to adequately publicise various Schemes and this order.

2. We direct the Chief Secretaries of each of the States and Union Territories to ensure compliance with this order. They will report compliance by filing affidavits in this Court within 8 weeks from today with copies to the Attorney-General and the counsel for the petitioner.

3. We grant liberty to the Union of India to file affidavit pursuant to the order of this Court dated 21.11.2001.

4. List the matter for further orders on 11.02.2002. In the meanwhile, liberty is granted to the parties to apply for further directions, if any.

In the Supreme Court of India

Writ Petition (Civil) No. 196 of 2001

People's Union for Civil Liberties (PUCL) v. Union of India & Ors.[13]

Date of Order : 29.04.2004

Bench : Y.K. Sabharwal and B.N. Agarwal, JJ.

Order

1. With the assistance of learned counsel, we have perused various documents including Report No. 1 of 2000 prepared by CAG and a working paper on Health, Nutrition and Family Welfare Programme Review of Progress during the Ninth Plan period by the Planning Commission, Government of India (February 2001). It is evident that the Integrated Child Development Scheme (ICDS) is perhaps the largest of all the food supplementation programmes in the world, was initiated in the year 1975 with the following objectives as per the aforesaid document prepared by the Planning Commission :

> (i) To improve the health and nutrition status of children of 0-6 years by providing supplementary food and by coordinating with State Health Departments to ensure delivery of required health inputs;
>
> (ii) To provide conditions necessary for pre-school children's psychological and social development through early stimulation and education;
>
> (iii) To provide pregnant and lactating women with food supplements;
>
> (iv) To enhance the mother's ability to provide proper child care through health and nutrition education;
>
> (v) To achieve effective coordination of policy and implementation among the various departments to promote child development.

2. From the facts and figures given in the documents it appears that despite the fact that for the development of children, in particular, mal-nourished and under-nourished children, the Scheme is elaborate and intends to cover all the children under the age group of 0-6 years, but it appears that a lot more deserves to be done in this field to ensure that nutritious food reaches

13. (2004) 12 SCC 108

to those who are under nourished or mal-nourished or others covered under the scheme.

3. The food is supplied to children through Anganwadi Centres (AWCS). In all, there are 6 lakh centers. The norms of the Government of India provide for one centre for the population of 1000 (700 in case of tribal area). According to the petitioner, going by the said norms there should be 14 lac AWCS. It appears that according to the calculation of the Government of India, AWCS would be 12 lakhs. We direct the Government of India to file within 3 months an affidavit stating the period within which it proposes to increase the number of AWCS so as to cover the 14 lakh habitations. We notice that the norm for supply of nutritious food worth rupee one for every child was fixed in the year 1991. The Government of India should consider the revision of the norm of rupee one and incorporate their suggestion in the affidavit.

4. In respect of sanctioned AWCS, we direct that the same shall be made fully operational by 30.06.2004. We further direct that the sanctioned AWCS shall supply nutritious food/ supplement to the children, adolescent girls and to pregnant and lactating women under the Scheme for 300 days in a year.

5. We direct the Chief Secretaries to file reports showing that, for the period from 01.04.2003 till 31.03.2004 from the sanctioned AWCS how many children, adolescent girls and pregnant and lactating women were supplied nutritious food/supplement and for how many days during the said period. The report shall be filed by 31.07.2004. List the matter in the month of August, 2004.

6. The question regarding Below Poverty Line Scheme will also be taken up on that day instead of July, 2004.

7. Not to be treated as part heard.

In the Supreme Court of India

Writ Petition (Civil) No. 196 of 2001 with I.A. Nos. 40-41 of 2004
People's Union for Civil Liberties (PUCL) v. Union of India & Ors.[14]

Date of Order : 07.10.2004

Bench : Y.K. Sabharwal and Tarun Chatterjee. JJ.

Order

1. We have gone through the 5th (August, 2004) Report of the Commissioners S/Shri Dr. N.C. Saxena and N.R. Sankaran. First of all, we wish to place on record our compliments and appreciation for the enormous work done by the learned Commissioners and presenting the Report under consideration.

2. The Report is in three parts. First part is divided into 14 sections covering different schemes. Under Section 1, Integrated Child Development Scheme (ICDS) has been considered. Part II sets out summary of findings and Part III sets out recommendations. We would first consider the aspect of ICDS. In order to fully appreciate the problem, it would be useful to notice the background briefly.

3. ICDS, as noticed in the Order dated 29.04.2004 is perhaps the largest of all the food and supplementation programmes in the world that was initiated in the year 1975 with the following objectives as per the document prepared by Planning Commission :

> 1. To improve the health and nutrition status of children 0-6 years by providing supplementary food and by coordinating with State health departments to ensure delivery of required health inputs;
>
> 2. To provide conditions necessary for pre-school children's psychological and social development through early stimulation and education;
>
> 3. To provide pregnant and lactating women with food supplements;
>
> 4. To enhance the mother's ability to provide proper child care through health and nutrition education;
>
> 5. To achieve effective coordination of policy and implementation among the various departments to promote child development.

14. (2004) 12 SCC 104

4. The Scheme intends to cover all the children under age group of 0-6 years. The food is supplied to the children through Anganwadi Centres (For short, 'AWCS'). The norms of the Government of India provide for one Centre for a population of one thousand (700 in case of tribal area). It is not in serious dispute, as contended by Mr. Mohan Parasaran, learned Additional Solicitor General that according to norms, there should be approximately 14 lakh AWCS. Admittedly, nearly 6 lakh Centres have been sanctioned. Many of the sanctioned Centres are also not operational as is evident from the report under consideration. The problem seems to be more acute in States like Bihar, Uttar Pradesh and Jharkhand. It deserves to be noticed that the directions in respect of ICDS were issued as far back in 28.11.2001. The order dated 29.04.2004 notices that most of those covered by the Order dated 28.11.2001 are not getting the benefit under ICDS. That observation was made on the basis of figures which were provided under the National Family Benefit Health Scheme on conducting survey. The result was that a large number of children between the age group of 0-6 years were malnourished. That Order also noticed that the position was alarming in the aforesaid three States as well as the State of Uttaranchal. By Order dated 29.04.2004, the Government of India was directed to file within three months an affidavit stating the period within which it proposed to sanction the remaining number of AWCS. The Government of India was also directed to consider the revision of norms of supply of nutritious food worth rupee one to every child in the Centres as norm of rupee one was fixed way back in the year 1991 and incorporate its suggestion in the affidavit.

5. It is most unfortunate that instead of three months, nearly six months have expired, the Government of India has still not filed the affidavit and instead an oral application has been made by learned Additional Solicitor General for grant of further time to file an affidavit in terms of the Order dated 29.04.2004. We are shocked at the attitude of the Central Government which is in respect of giving nutritious food to all children though in practice it concerns those unfortunate sections of the society who can ill-afford to provide nutritious food to the children of the aforesaid age group. In absence of the affidavit, we could have straight away issued directions for the sanction of the remaining AWCS and for increase of norm of rupee one to rupees two but having regard to the totality of the circumstances, we grant one final opportunity to the Central Government to file affidavit within a period of two weeks whereafter we would consider these two aspects, namely, (i) sanction of 14 lakh AWCS; (ii) increase of norm of rupee one to rupees two.

6. We make it clear that if the affidavit is not filed, this Court will be left with no option but to issue directions for implementation of the two aspects.

7. Now, we would deal with the aspect of sanctioned AWCS and their working. In the Order dated 29.04.2004, it was directed that the sanctioned AWCS shall be made fully operational by 30.06.2004. Further, direction issued was that the sanctioned AWCS shall supply nutritious food/supplement to children, adolescent girls and to pregnant and lactating women under the Scheme for 300 days in a year. The report presents a gloomy picture both in regard to the operation of the sanctioned AWCS in some of the States like Uttar Pradesh, Bihar and Jharkhand and the position in those in which they are operational. Instances have been given in the Report where for months the supplies were not made to the children. For example, in the State of Jharkhand, the sanctioned AWCS were not working from May to December, 2003.

No satisfactory reply is forthcoming from that State. Further, there are material discrepancies in two affidavits filed by the said State, one in September and the one handed over in the Court today. In the September affidavit, it was deposed on oath that 16,689 AWCS were operational. In the affidavit filed today, the figure of operational AWCS is stated to be 7429. According to the Report, on an average, 42 paisa as against the norm of rupee one was being allocated per beneficiary per day by the State of Jharkhand. The position in Bihar and Uttar Pradesh is also no better. Out of 394 sanctioned ICDS projects, only 249 were operational in the State of Bihar. As per the affidavit dated 30.09.2004, all the projects were being made operational from 04.10.2004. Whether that has happened or not, Mr. B.B. Singh, learned counsel appearing for the State is unable to state for want of instructions. Be that as it may, if all have not been made operational, since 04.10.2004 has already passed and gone we direct that the same shall be made operational in period not later than one week from today.

8. In the State of Uttar Pradesh, though percentage of non-functional/non-operational AWCS is more as per the Report but according to the State, admittedly 24 per cent are not operational. In the affidavit, it has been claimed that the remaining will be made operational by 30.11.2004. We direct the State Government to make operational all sanctioned AWCS by 30.11.2004. After that, we would not entertain any application for extension of time.

9. The Report also mentions that some of AWCS are operating from private houses including those of grain dealers which it is suggested is not a healthy way of working as it is likely to increase the chances of pilferage of the grain etc. We are happy to note that as stated in the affidavit of the State of Uttar Pradesh, it has made efforts to shift AWCS to primary schools. It is a good example for other States to follow. The report also mentions about the attempt to centralise the procurements in some of the States which has many fallouts. It has been explained in one of the affidavits that the procurements is at district level and not at the State level. Further, the problem of using contractors for procurement has also been mentioned in the report suggesting that it should be done by agencies and officers at the Government level. These are only by way of illustrations as to facts and figures given in Section 1 of the report relating to Integrated Child Development Services.

10. Having heard Mr. Colin Gonsalves, learned Senior Counsel appearing for the petitioner and learned Additional Solicitor General appearing for the Central Government and learned counsel appearing for the State Governments in particular, the States of Bihar, Jharkhand and Uttar Pradesh, for present, we issue the following directions :

1. The aspect of sanctioning 14 lakh AWCS and increase of norm of rupee one to rupees 2 per child per day would be considered by this Court after two weeks.

2. The efforts shall be made that all SC/ST hamlets/habitations in the country have Anganwadi Centres as early as possible.

3. The contractors shall not be used for supply of nutrition in Anganwadis and preferably ICDS funds shall be spent by making use of village communities, self-help groups and Mahila Mandals for buying of grains and preparation of meals.

4. All State Governments/Union Territories shall put on their website full data for the ICDS Schemes including where AWCS are operational, the number of beneficiaries category-wise, the funds allocated and used and other related matters.

5. All State Governments/Union Territories shall use the Pradhanmantri Gramodaya Yojna fund (PMGY) in addition to the state allocation and not as a substitute for state funding.

6. As far as possible, the children under PMGY shall be provided with good food at the Centre itself.

7. All the State Governments/Union Territories shall allocate funds for ICDS on the basis of norm of one rupee per child per day, 100 beneficiaries per AWC and 300 days feeding in a year, i.e., on the same basis on which the Centre makes the allocation.

8. BPL shall not be used as an eligibility criteria for ICDS.

9. All sanctioned projects shall be operationalised and provided food as per these norms and wherever utensils have not been provided, the same shall be provided (Instance of Jharkhand State has been noticed in the Report where utensils have not been provided). The vacancies for the operational ICDS shall be filled forthwith. (Instance of Uttar Pradesh where vacancies have not been filled up is quite alarming though in the affidavit it has been stated that a drive has been initiated to fill up the vacancies.)

10. All the State Governments/Union Territories shall utilise the entire State and Central allocation under ICDS/PMGY and under no circumstances, the same shall be diverted and preferably also not returned to the Centre and, if returned, a detailed explanation for non-utilisation shall be filed in this Court.

11. All States/Union Territories shall make earnest effort to cover the slums under ICDS.

12. The Central Government and the States/Union Territories shall ensure that all amounts allocated are sanctioned in time so that there is no disruption whatsoever in the feeding of children.

11. Our attention has been drawn to what is stated at page 20 in box 2 regarding failure of authorities to take appropriate action despite the Commissioner's intervention in the case of Madhya Pradesh pertaining to the area mentioned therein and the non-payment to the workforce. We direct the State Government to either make payment of wages to the labourers or file an affidavit giving detailed explanation within two weeks.

12. List the matter after two weeks.

In the Supreme Court of India

I.A. Nos. 34, 35, 40, 49, 58, 59, 60, 61 and 62 in Writ Petition (Civil) No. 196 of 2001
People's Union for Civil Liberties (PUCL) v. Union of India & Ors.[15]

Date of Judgement : 13.12.2006

Bench : Dr. Arijit Pasayat and S.H. Kapadia, JJ.

Judgment

Dr. Arijit Pasayat, J.

1. Grievance is made by the petitioner about the non-implementation of the directions given by this Court to the Central Government and the State Governments relating to Integrating Child Development Scheme (in short "ICDS"). The Scheme is meant for children of the age group of 0-6, pregnant women, lactating mothers and adolescent girls. Undisputedly, funds are released by the Central Government to the State Governments who are required to implement the Scheme. The State Governments, it is alleged, have failed to match the grants given by the Central Government.

2. We shall deal with this aspect a little later in detail.

3. Dr. N.C. Saxena, Commissioner, and Sh. Harsh Mander, the Special Commissioner were appointed pursuant to the orders passed by this Court for giving their reports on the question whether the Scheme has been implemented in the manner desired by this Court by various orders.

4. A bare reading of the reports shows the grim realities and apparent lethargy of some of the States in implementing the Scheme.

5. By report dated 19.07.2006 the following recommendations are made by the Committee :

(1) Reassert the figure of 14 lakhs AWCs as a benchmark estimate of the minimum number of AWCs required for universalisation of ICDS, based on existing norms.

(2) Direct the Government of India to raise the number of AWCs to 14 lakhs within three years.

(3) Direct the Government of India to formulate improved norms for the creation and placement of AWCs, in the light of this report, and in

15. (2007) 1 SCC 719

consultation with the Commissioners. The improved norms should be consistent with universalisation in the sense that implementation of these norms would ensure convenient access to an Anganwadi (or mini-Anganwadi, as the case may be) to all children and eligible women.

(4) Clarify that universalisation of ICDS involves extending all ICDS services (not just supplementary nutrition) to all children below the age of six, all pregnant or lactating women and all adolescent girls.

(5) Direct Chief Secretaries of all the State Governments/UTs to submit affidavits to the Honourable Supreme Court with details of all habitations with a majority of SC/ST households, the availability of AWCs in these habitations, and the plan of action for ensuring that all these habitations have functioning AWCs within two years.

(6) Direct Chief Secretaries of all the State Governments/UTs to submit affidavits to the Honourable Supreme Court on the steps that have been taken with regard to the interim order of this Court of 07.10.2004 directing that "contractors shall not be used for supply of nutrition in anganwadis and preferably ICDS funds shall be spent by making use of village communities, self-help groups and mahila mandals for buying of grains and preparation of meals". Chief Secretaries of all the State Governments/UTs must also commit to a time-frame within which the decentralisation of the supply of SNP through local community efforts will be made.

6. Under Chapter 1.4 "Will India meet the Nutrition MDG?" the Report indicates as follows :

"The Millennium Development Goals (MDGs) are a set of internationally agreed goals that countries and institutions have committed to reach by 2015. The second MDG target, which we refer to as the nutrition MDG, is to halve between 1990 and 2015 :

(i) the prevalence of underweight children (under five years of age)

(ii) the proportion of population below a minimum level of dietary energy consumption.

A few studies, using different assumptions, have considered the likelihood that India will attain the second nutrition MDG. Although their projections differ, in sum it seems unlikely that the prevalence of malnutrition in India will fall from its level of 54% in 1990 to 27% by 2015. NFHS data shows that, in 1998/99, even the wealthiest quintile had a prevalence of malnutrition (33%) that far exceeded the MDG goal. Our projections indicate that economic growth alone is unlikely to be sufficient to lower the prevalence of malnutrition. When combined with policy interventions, the projections are rosier, but a rapid scaling up of health, nutrition, education and infrastructure interventions is needed if MDG is to be met."

7. In the earlier report i.e. 6th report, dated 21.11.2005 the following observations of the Commissioner are relevant :

"Compliance with the 28.11.2001 order and coverage of ICDS beneficiaries.— Significant orders of this Court were passed regarding the implementation of ICDS on 28.11.2001 stating that the services of ICDS must be made available to every child up to 6 years of age, every adolescent girl, every pregnant woman and nursing mother, that every malnourished child must get an enhanced ration and that there must be an ICDS disbursement centre in every settlement. The order was the first amongst many regarding the implementation of the ICDS..

The Statewise coverage of beneficiaries under ICDS as it currently stands as per the Department of Women and Child Development, is given in Table 1.1. The number of children in the 0-6 year age group being provided supplementary nutrition services under ICDS stands at 403 lakhs. In comparison, as per the 2001 census of India, the 0-6 year population in India stands at 1578 lakhs. Thus, as many as 1201 lakhs or 74% of children entitled to ICDS are currently left out of its net.

The coverage of adolescent girls in the 11-18 year age group is worse than that of children in the 0-6 year age group. The Kishori Shakti Yojana (KSY), under which adolescent girls are covered remains limited to 2000 TCDS projects. The total coverage of adolescent girls stands at a mere 2.4 lakhs. In comparison, as per the census of 2001, the total female population in the 11-18 year age group stands at approximately 844 lakhs. The coverage of adolescent girls has therefore virtually not taken off with a mere 0.3% of adolescent girls being covered under the Scheme. It is important to note that of the 35 States and UTs only Chhattisgarh, Gujarat, Haryana, Meghalaya, Rajasthan, Uttar Pradesh and Andaman and Nicobar Islands have reported to the Commissioner that adolescent girls are being covered under ICDS. Other States such as Bihar, Goa, Jharkhand and Orissa have pointedly stated that adolescent girls are not being covered under ICDS, although blocks were identified for the implementation of the project as far back as in 1991-92. Thus an entire section of beneficiaries remains completely ignored in the implementation of the scheme.

The number of pregnant women and nursing mothers is estimated to be 4% of the total population at any point in time as per ICDS Scheme guidelines. The current coverage of 81.05 lakh beneficiaries in this category, therefore, is less than 20% of the estimated number of persons who should be covered by the scheme."

8. The essence of the previous orders dated 28.11.2001, 29.04.2004 and 07.10.2004 of this Court can be summed up as follows :

(1) Almost five years ago (on 28.11.2001), the Hon'ble Supreme Court issued an interim order calling for the universalisation of ICDS, in the sense that (1) every habitation should have a functional ICDS centre (Anganwadi), and (2) ICDS services should be extended to all children up to the age of six years, all pregnant or nursing mothers and all adolescent girls. This order was reiterated and extended on 29.04.2004 and 07.10.2004, along with further directions on ICDS.

(2) We are concerned that very little progress has been made towards the implementation of these orders. In the 2004-05 financial year, the Government of India sanctioned the opening of 1.88 lakh new Anganwadi centres towards implementation of the above quoted orders. It is a matter of concern, that these Anganwadi Centres have not so far been operationalised. The Hon'ble Court may seek an explanation from the Ministry of Women and Child Development, Government of India, in this regard.

(3) In fact, the Government of India has not only failed to implement aforementioned orders of the Hon'ble Court, but challenged the basic principles of universalisation outlined in these orders. The aim of this note is to clarify some key issues and present recommendations for further orders.

9. Anganwadi centres are hereinafter referred to as AWCs.

10. As noted above, the reports of the Commissioner present a grim picture. Though directions were given by this Court in relation to universalisation of coverage under ICDS, immediate operationalisation of all sanctioned projects/centres without delay, utilisation of all funds allocated, the implementation by the Central Government and the State Governments is more in breach than observance. In the earlier orders dated 29.04.2004, 07.10.2004 the submissions made by the petitioner regarding universalisation were accepted to the effect that about 14 lakh AWCs should be made functional. The data available indicates that till now only 9,52,764 centres have been sanctioned (including 1.8 lakh new AWCs) under the first phase of expansion that was sanctioned in 2005. It appears that the Central Government has announced sanction of 1.07 lakh in the last week of August 2006, which means the total number of sanctioned centres would be around 10.5 lakhs leaving a deficit of 3.5 lakh centres. It appears that even the earlier expansion of 1.88 lakh centres which were sanctioned have not yet become operational.

11. In its letter dated 23.01.2006, the Central Government in its letter addressed to the Commissioners rejected the figure of 14 lakhs suggested by the petitioner on the ground that it was based on a survey of drinking water facilities, whereby any population cluster of at least 250 persons counts as a separate "habitation". According to norms suggested by the petitioner, one AWC was intended "for every 1000 population". This was suggested on a practical basis because one AWC cannot serve more than 1000 persons i.e. about 200 households. Since many of the AWCs have a single worker even 1000 persons appear to be a high cut-off.

12. The suggestions presently given are that a full-fledged AWC should be made operational for a population of 300 persons or above. This is stated to be on the basis of 7th All-India Educational Survey (in short "AIES"). Though the Central Government has accepted the need for revision of the norms for creation or placement of AWCs, very little appears to have been done. An Inter-Ministerial Task Force (in short "IMTF") was constituted for this purpose. It has submitted its report sometime earlier this year.

13. Whatever be the norms suggested, immediate steps should be taken to make all the sanctioned centres functional and operational without further delay. The petitioner has placed on record various materials to contend that the benchmark needs to be substantially reduced to provide a rational base. The data available shows that about 79% of the sanctioned centres have been made operational and the data placed by the petitioner shows that only about 69.4% of the sanctioned centres are providing supplementary nutrition.

14. According to the data provided regarding the funds allocation and utilisation, following is the position :

> *"Till 2004-05 financial year, norms for per beneficiary per day allocation of funds to be made by the State/UT Governments were those set in 1991. In the last financial year (in December 2004), the DoWCD took the long overdue step of revising the financial norms for money to be spent per beneficiary per day for the provision of supplementary nutrition. The cost norms have been changed to the following :*

Table 1.3. : Norms for per beneficiary per day allocation of funds under State/UT Plans

Beneficiary	*Old Rates**	*New Rates***
Children (6-72 months)	*Re 0.95 per child per day*	*Rs 2 per child per day*
Severely malnourished children (6-72 months)	*Rs 1.35 per child per day*	*Rs 2.70 per child per day*
Pregnant women and nursing mothers/adolescent girls (KSY)	*Rs 1.15 per beneficiary per day*	*Rs 2.30 per beneficiary per day*

** Rates set by DoWCD, GOI in 1991.*

*** Rates set by DoWCD, GOI in December 2004.*

This is based on DoWCD Letter No. F. No. 19-5/2003-CD-I (pt) dated 19.10.2004.

15. As mentioned in the Sixth Report of the Commissioners to this Court, over the years the funds allocated by the State Governments for Supplementary Nutrition Programme (in short "SNP") has been low and the utilisation of allocated funds has also been poor. According to data from DoWCD, the following is the position of allocation and expenditure by States and GOI for SNP in 2005-06 :

Statement indicating budget allocation by States, releases made by GOI and expenditure reported during 2005-06 for Supplementary Nutrition Programme (SNP) under Integrated Child Development Services (ICDS) Scheme.

Rs (in lakhs)

Budget allocation for SNP by the States in the year 2005-06		Releases made by GOI	Total Allocation	Expenditure including State share	% Utilisation
Plan	Non-plan	During 2005-06*		Reported by the States during 2005-06*	
1	2	3	4	5	6
1,97,512.0	884,351.13	97,458.55	3,79,321.76	2,18,801.73	57.7

*expenditure up to 15.02.2006.

This is based on DoWCD, GOI's letter to Commissioners [Letter No. 19-5/2003-CD-I (Vol. 111) dated 28.08.2006].

16. It is thus seen that the extent of utilisation of funds allocated for SNP is on an average only 57.7% for the country as a whole. Despite allocations made by the States and a corresponding grant given by the Centre, huge amounts of money is being left unspent and rightful beneficiaries are being denied critically needed supplementary nutrition.

17. Further, shortfall in allocation required to cover all the children under the age of 6 in the country under the SNP programme is about 60%.

Total allocation	Total no. of children under 6 (according to Census 2001)	Required allocation*	Shortfall	% shortfall
3,79,321.76	1578.6	9,47,178.87	5,67,857.11	59.95%

*The figures are in lakhs.

18. The calculation is at the rate of Rs. 2 per child per day for 300 days. The calculations above have been made only taking into account children under 6 years of age in the country. However, the allocations are for the entire SNP programme of ICDS which is to also cover pregnant women, lactating mothers and adolescent girls; taking this into account the shortfall in allocation would be even larger.

19. Certain States have been performing particularly badly in respect to most of the indicators seen above. The following is the data in relation to these States.

State	No. of AWCs sanctioned	No. of AWCs providing SNP	% providing service
Punjab	17,421	14,730	84.6
Haryana	16,359	13,546	82.8
Uttar Pradesh	1,37,557	1,02,881	74.8
Jharkhand	30,854	19,571	63.4
Bihar	80,415	50,503	62.8
West Bengal	74,640	45,285	60.7
Madhya Pradesh	59,324	35,549	59.9
Assam	32,075	4330	13.5
Manipur	4501	0	0.0

20. Further, even though the other States have a higher number of centres that are providing SNP, in terms of the utilisation and allocation of funds they are performing badly.

State	Total allocation (Centre + State)	Expenditure (up to 15-2-2006)	% utilisation
Manipur	1334.24	1329.16	99.6
Jharkhand	16,473.84	12,711.01	77.2
Uttar Pradesh	67,569.73	45,916.19	68.0
Assam	9666.67	5337.64	55.2
Madhya Pradesh	20,877.53	9457.82	45.3
Bihar	43,040.62	18,989.12	44.1
Haryana	13,628.80	4046.03	29.7
West Bengal	45,345.67	11,845.38	26.1
Punjab	14,814.55	3599.65	24.3

The basis for working out the above details is DoWCD, GOI's letter to Commissioners [Letter No. 19-5/2003-CD-I (Vol. III), 28.08.2006]

21. While, none of the States are utilising the funds allocated to them for the purpose of SNP, per cent of utilisation is less than even 30% in the States of Haryana, West Bengal and Punjab. In the case of Manipur it is suspicious as to where the funds have been spent as according to the data given by the Department of Women and Child Development, number of beneficiaries under SNP in Manipur is nil.

22. In the following table the funds required for SNP to cover all the children under the age of 6 (based on the norm of Rs. 2 per child per day for 300 days) has been calculated. As can be seen in the table below, in States like Assam, Uttar Pradesh, Madhya Pradesh, Punjab, West

Bengal and Haryana, there is a shortfall of more than 60% of funds that are actually required to cover all children under 6. This combined with the fact that these States do not fully utilise even what is currently being allocated to them shows that many deserving beneficiaries are being left out of the supplementary nutrition programme of ICDS.

State	Total allocation (Centre + States)	0-6 population as per 2001 census	Amount required to be allocated for the 0-6 population (in Rs crores)	% shortfall
Manipur	1334.24	3.1	1876.146	28.88
Jharkhand	16,473.84	48.0	28,777.128	42.75
Bihar	43,040.62	162.3	97,407.234	55.81
Assam	9666.67	43.5	26,101.488	62.97
Uttar Pradesh	67,569.73	304.7	1,82,832.252	63.04
Madhya Pradesh	20,877.53	106.2	63,709.938	67.23
Punjab	14,814.55	30.6	18,332.952	67.53
West Bengal	45,345.67	111.3	66,796.944	70.69
Haryana	13,628.80	32.6	19,554.48	75.11

The above details are culled out from DoWCD, GOI's letter to Commissioners Letter No. 19-5/2003-CD-1(Vol. III) 28.08.2006 which has been referred to in detail above.

23. Keeping in view the submissions made and considering the materials placed on record we direct as follows :

(1) The Government of India shall sanction and operationalise a minimum of 14 lakh AWCs in a phased and even manner starting forthwith and ending December 2008. In doing so, the Central Government shall identify SC and ST hamlets/habitations for AWCs on a priority basis.

(2) The Government of India shall ensure that population norms for opening of AWCs must not be revised upward under any circumstances. While maintaining the upper limit of one AWC per 1000 population, the minimum limit for opening of a new AWC is a population of 300 may be kept in view. Further, rural communities and slum-dwellers should be entitled to an "Anganwadi on demand" (not later than three months) from the date of demand in cases where a settlement has at least 40 children under 6 but no anganwadi.

(3) The universalisation of ICDS involves extending all ICDS services (supplementary nutrition, growth monitoring, nutrition and health education, immunisation, referral and pre-school education) to every child under the age of 6, all pregnant women and lactating mothers and all adolescent girls.

(4) All the State Governments and Union Territories shall fully implement ICDS by, inter alia,

(i) allocating and spending at least Rs. 2 per child per day for supplementary nutrition out of which the Central Government shall contribute Re 1 per child per day;

(ii) allocating and spending at least Rs. 2.70 for every severely malnourished child per day for supplementary nutrition out of which the Central Government shall contribute Rs. 1.35 per child per day;

(iii) allocating and spending at least Rs. 2.30 for every pregnant woman, nursing mother/adolescent girl per day for supplementary nutrition out of which the Central Government shall contribute Rs. 1.15.

(5) The Chief Secretaries of the States of Bihar, Jharkhand, Madhya Pradesh, Manipur, Punjab, West Bengal, Assam, Haryana and Uttar Pradesh, shall appear personally to explain why the orders of this Court requiring the full implementation of ICDS were not obeyed.

(6) Chief Secretaries of all the State Governments/UTs are directed to submit affidavits with details of all habitations with a majority of SC/ST households, the availability of AWCs in these habitations, and the plan of action for ensuring that all these habitations have functioning AWCs within two years.

(7) Chief Secretaries of all the State Governments/UTs are directed to submit affidavits giving details of the steps that have been taken with regard to the order of this Court of 07.10.2004 directing that "contractors shall not be used for supply of nutrition in Anganwadis and preferably ICDS funds shall be spent by making use of village communities, self-help groups and mahila mandals for buying of grains and preparation of meals". Chief Secretaries of all the State Governments/UTs must indicate a time-frame within which the decentralisation of the supply of SNP through local community shall be done.

(8) It is a matter of concern that 15 States and Union Territories have not submitted any affidavit in compliance with the order dated 07.10.2004. They are the States of Orissa, Uttar Pradesh, Sikkim, Arunachal Pradesh, Nagaland, Goa, Punjab, Manipur, Tamil Nadu, Andhra Pradesh, Mizoram, Haryana, Bihar and the National Capital of Delhi and the Union Territory of Lakshadweep. Within four weeks reply shall be filed through the Chief Secretary concerned as to why action for contempt shall not be initiated for the lapse.

24. The matters shall be listed after three months. Upto date statistic report shall be filed by the different States, Union Territories and the Central Government.

In the Supreme Court of India

Shreya Singhal v. Union of India
with
PUCL v. Union of India & Ors
WP. (Crl.) 199/2013

Date of Judgement : 24.03.2015

Bench : Justice Jasti Chalameswar and Justice Rohinton Fali Nariman

Summary of the findings

PUCL had challenged the constitutional validity of section 66A of the IT Act by filing an independent Writ Petition. This Writ Petition has been decided along with other Writ Petitions carrying the title of the lead case, Shreya Singhal v. Union of India. These Writ Petitions were filed after it was found that many citizens across the country were getting arrested under the said provision in its wanton abuse. Vide judgment dated 24.03.2015, Section 66-A was struck down in its entirety as being violative of Article 19(1)(a) of the Constitution of India. It was a landmark and celebrated judgment in Indian free speech jurisprudence as it set out several rigorous tests for constitutionally permissible restrictions on speech. The Supreme Court held that it would breach the fundamental right of every citizen to have the freedom of speech of expression of his/her views on the internet.

The impugned provision, Section 66A made it a criminal offence to send electronically any information that is 'grossly offensive', 'menacing', causes 'annoyance', 'obstruction', 'insult', 'hatred' amongst other things. It was argued by PUCL that this provision was constitutionally invalid as it infringed upon the fundamental right to "freedom of speech and expression" as recognised by Article 19(1)(a) of the Constitution of India. The Court agreed with this contention and held that the only restrictions which may be imposed on the rights of an individual under Article 19(1)(a) are those which have been set out under Clause (2) of Article 19. It was held that if the restriction has no proximate relationship with the achievement of one of the designated subject matters under Article 19(2), it cannot be said that the restriction is a "reasonable restriction" under Article 19(2). It specifically held that 'public interest' cannot be used as a ground to curb free speech. The Court also came to the conclusion that the wording of Section 66A was completely open-ended, undefined, and vague and that as the contours of the offence were not clearly demarcated, it was open to abuse by the authorities. In this regard, the Supreme Court, used the 'chilling effect' doctrine to strike down the impugned provision as unconstitutional.

The other findings given in the judgment was that it upheld the constitutionality of section 69A of the Information Technology Act, which provides a system for the blocking of information online by way of an order from a member of Central Government. It was upheld as appropriate safeguards were built into the specific provision by the legislature. The Supreme Court also read down Section 79 of the IT Act which deals with the liability of intermediaries. The provision will now be read as providing for intermediary liability only where an intermediary has received actual knowledge from a court order or on being notified by Government that unlawful acts related to Article 19(2) are going to be committed, and that intermediary had failed to expeditiously remove or disable access to such information.

In the Supreme Court of India

PUCL v. UNION OF INDIA & ORS
WP. (Crl.) 199/2013

WRITTEN SUBMISSIONS OF MR. SANJAY PARIKH, ADVOCATE FOR THE PETITIONER ON SECTION 66A OF THE INFORMATION TECHNOLOGY ACT, 2000

1. The phrase "freedom of Speech and expression" contained in Article 19(1)(a) has been given a very vide interpretation by this Hon'ble Court in several judgments. The freedom of speech and expression includes "Freedom of propagation of ideas", "right to circulate one's ideas, opinion and views", "right of citizens to speak, publish and express their views as well as right of people to read" as well as the right to know about the affairs of the government. Case law for the above proposition is given below :

   Vide PUCL Vs UOI 2003 (4) SCC 399 in Para 16, 24-27, 38-45.

   In para 44 (page 440) this Hon'ble Court has given a list of decisions in which the meaning and dimensions of the phrase, "freedom of speech and expression", have been given.

2. Freedom of speech can be restricted only in the interest of the security of the State, friendly relations with foreign state, public order, decency or morality or in relation to contempt of court, defamation or incitement to an offence. *The only restriction which may be imposed on the rights of an individual under Article 19(1)(a) are those which Clause (2) of the Article 19 permits and no other*. Case law for the above proposition is given below :

(I) Vide Sakal Papers (P) Ltd Vs UOI 1962 (3) SCR 842 at page 857, 862, 863 and 868

At page 863

"For, the scheme of Art. 19 is to enumerate different freedoms separately and then to specify the extent of restrictions to which they may be subjected and the objects for securing which this could be done. A citizen is entitled to enjoy each and every one of the freedoms together and cl. (1) does not prefer one freedom to another. That is the plain meaning of this clause. It follows from this that the State cannot make a law which directly restricts one freedom even for securing the better enjoyment of another freedom.

All the greater reason, therefore for holding that the State cannot directly restrict one freedom by placing an otherwise permissible restriction on another freedom".

At page 868

"To repeat, the only restrictions which may be imposed on the rights of an individual under Art. 19(1)(a) are those which cl. (2) of Art. 19 permits and no other"

(II) PUCL v. UOI 2003 (4) SCC 399 at 438

Para 39

"So legislative competence to interfere with a fundamental right guaranteed under Article 19(1)(a) is limited as provided under Article 19 (2)."

3. To bring a challenge within the exceptions contained under Article 19(2) it must be established :

(I) Impugned legal provision has proximate and reasonable nexus and not far-fetched, hypothetical, problematic or too remote;
(II) The connection is immediate, real and rational;
(III) Impugned legal provision is clear, unambiguous and not vague;

a. Vide Kameshwar Prasad v. State of Bihar 1962 Suppl (3) SCR 369 at 371, 373, 374, 378, 380 till 385.

The question considered by this Hon'ble court was whether Rule 4A, as far it lays an embargo on any form of demonstration could be sustained as falling within the scope of Article 19(2) and (3). Reliance was placed on the judgement in Superintendent, Central Prison v. Ram Manohar Lohia (1960 (2) SCR 821) and after acknowledging that the connection has to be intimate, real and rational it was observed:

At page 383-384

"The threat to public order should therefore arise from the nature of the demonstration prohibited. No doubt, if the rule were so framed as to single out those types of demonstration which were likely to lead to a disturbance of public tranquillity or which would fall under the other limiting criteria specified in Art. 19(2) the validity of the rule could have been sustained. The vice of the rule, in our opinion, consists in this that it lays a ban on every type of demonstration — be the same however innocent and however incapable of causing a breach of public tranquillity and does not confine itself to those forms of demonstrations which might lead to that result".

The Court struck down the entire Rule as it was not possible to separate the legal from the unconstitutional portion. (P 384).

b. Vide <u>Superintendent, Central Prison</u> v. <u>Ram Manohar Lohia</u> (1960 (2) SCR 821, at page 826, 827, 830, 832, 833, 834, 835, and 836)

Section 3 of the UP Special Powers Act, 1932 was under challenge in this case. After referring to the judgement of federal court in <u>Rex</u> v. <u>Basudeva</u>AIR 1950 FC 67, this Hon'ble Court observed that :

"The decision in our view lays down the correct test. The limitation imposed in the interests of public order to be a reasonable restriction, should be one which has a proximate connection or nexus with public order, but not one far-fetched, hypothetical or problematic or too remote in the chain of its relation to public order."

That is why it has been submitted that the phrase itself in an impugned provision should constitute the offence. For example, the expression, "annoyance", should result in the incitement of an offence or public disorder. The nexus cannot be established by giving hypothetical, imaginary or far-fetched meaning to the expression "annoyance" or "grossly offensive" etc.

Finally, while examining the impugned provision, this Hon'ble Court very clearly laid down the test to bring in an expression within Article 19(2). It stated:

<u>Page 836-837</u>

"We shall now test the impugned section, having regard to the aforesaid principles. Have the acts prohibited under s. 3 any proximate connection with public safety or tranquility ? We have already analysed the provisions of s. 3 of the Act. In an attempt to indicate its wide sweep, we pointed out that any instigation by word or visible representation not to pay or defer payment of any exaction or even contractual dues to Government, authority or a landowner is made an offence. Even innocuous speeches are prohibited by threat of punishment. There is no proximate or even foreseeable connection between such instigation and the public order sought to be protected under this section. We cannot accept the argument of the learned Advocate General that instigation of a single individual not to pay tax or dues is a spark which may in the long run ignite a revolutionary movement destroying public order. We can only say that fundamental rights cannot be controlled on such hypothetical and imaginary considerations. It is said that in a democratic set up there is no scope for agitational approach and that if a law is bad the only course is to get it modified by democratic process and that any instigation to break the law is in itself a disturbance of, the public order. If this argument without obvious limitations be accepted, it would destroy the right to freedom of speech which is the very foundation

of democratic way of life. Unless there is a proximate connection between the instigation and the public order, the restriction, in our view, is neither reasonable nor is it in the interest of public order. In this view, we must strike down s. 3 of the Act as infringing the fundamental right guaranteed under Art. 19(1)(a) of the Constitution.".

In support of the above finding, reliance was also placed another constitution bench judgement, Chintaman Rao v. State of Madhya Pradesh (1950 SCR 759 at 756). In this case, this Hon'ble Court also held that the entire section being void as infringing Article 19(1)(a) of the constitution must be struck down as the doctrine of severability is inapplicable — to enable the Court to affirm the validity of a part and reject the rest.

c. Vide S. Rangarajan Vs P. Jagjivan Ram 1989 (2) SCC 574 (at 586)(Para 21, 41, 45 & 53).

In para 45, this Hon'ble Court observed that the anticipated danger should not be remote, conjectural or farfetched and that it should be have a proximate and direct nexus with the expression. Thereafter, it was observed, "in other words, the expression should be inseparably locked up with the action, contemplated like the equivalent of a "spark in a power keg". In para 51, this Hon'ble Court emphasised that freedom of expression cannot be suppressed on account of threats of demonstration and violence and that is the obligatory duty of the state to protect the freedom of expression. While concluding, the Court further emphasised in Para 53, content of Article 19(1)(a) and 19(2) as follows :

"We end here as we began on this topic. Freedom of expression which is legitimate and constitutionally protected, cannot be held to ransom by an intolerant group of people. The fundamental freedom under Article 19(1)(a) can be reasonably restricted only for the purposes mentioned in Article 19(2) and the restriction must be justified on the anvil of necessity and not the quicksand of convenience or expediency. Open criticism of government policies and operations is not a ground for restricting expression. We must practice tolerance to the views of others. Intolerance is as much dangerous to democracy as to the person himself."

4. Merely because the internet has a wider reach and speed in publishing information and also its implications, the content of Article 19(1)(a) cannot be diluted. The restriction has to full fill the parameters under Article 19(2). The tests propounded in Kameshwar Prasad (Supra) and Ram Manohar Lohia (Supra) are required to be established to invoke Article 19(2).

a. Vide Secretary, Ministry of Information and Broadcasting v. Cricket Association of Bengal, 1995 (2) SCC 161 at 195, 208, 213, 226, 228.

In this case, this Hon'ble Court was considering what telecasting means and what are its legal dimensions and consequences. After referring to the judgements on Article 19, in para 37 the following question was posed:

"The next question which is required to be answered, is whether there is any distinction between the freedom of the print media and that of the electronic media such as radio and television and is so, whether it necessitates more restrictions on the latter media."

There is a detailed discussion on Eric Barendt's book titled, "Broadcasting Law" as well as the judgement of the US Supreme Court in the Red Lion Broadcasting Case, 395 US 367. In para 43 the law on freedom of speech and expression under Article 19(1)(a) as restricted by Article 19(2) was summarised. It is also held that (vide para 45), burden is on the authority to justify the restriction.

The question which was posed in para 37 has been answered in para 78, where the court stated that (at page 227) :

"But to contend that on that account the restrictions to be imposed on the right under Article 19 [1] (a) should be in addition to those permissible under Article 19 [2] and dictated by the use of public resources in the best interests of the society at large, is to misconceive both the content of the freedom of speech and expression and the problems posed by the element of public property in, and the alleged scarcity of, the frequencies as well as by the wider reach of the media. If the right to freedom of speech and expression includes the right to disseminate information to as wide a section of the population as is possible, the access which enables the right to be so exercised is also an integral part of the said right. The wider range of circulation of information or its greater impact cannot restrict the content of the right nor can it justify its denial. The virtues of the electronic media cannot become its enemies. It may warrant a greater regulation over licensing and control and vigilance on the content of the programme telecast. However, this control can only be exercised within the framework of Article 19 [2] and the dictates of public interests. To plead for other grounds is to plead for unconstitutional measures." [Emphasis supplied]

5. The expressions which have been used in 66A have not been defined. This can be compared with Section 66 where the term dishonestly and fraudulently have been defined and given them same meaning as provided in the IPC. In 66B, 66C, 66D, 66E, 66F, 67, 67A and 67B the offence for which punishment has been provided has been defined. However, in 66A, the expressions, grossly offensive, menacing character, annoyance, inconvenience, danger, obstruction, insult etc. have not been defined. These expressions are absolutely vague and are subjected to different interpretation. None of these expressions can be, if subjected to the tests of proximity and nexus, can either cause incitement of an offence or public disorder. It is only by imaginations hypothesis

and subjective inputs that these expressions can be brought within the sweep of Article 19(2). What can cause annoyance to a person may not cause annoyance to another; the subject matter which is alleged to cause annoyance can be totally innocuous; it can also be objectionable. But Article 19(1)(a) does not allow the distant, far-fetched and imaginative interpretations to bring an expression within Article 19(2). It is for this reason that Section 66A violates Article 19(1)(a). It is not permissible to bring in the definitions of these expressions, given in IPC offences for upholding Section 66A.

6. By a general or vague provision, the right of speech and expression cannot be curtailed. Section 66A is general and vague, therefore, arbitrary and unreasonable and violative of Articles 14 and 21 of the Constitution. The basic principle of legal jurisprudence is, that a law is void for vagueness if its prohibitions are not clearly defined. Such laws result in unfairness and are attendant with dangers of arbitrary and discriminatory applications. Case law in support of the above proposition is given below :

a. Vide Kartar Singh Vs State of Punjab 1994 (3) SCC 569 at 644 (Para 112) and page 648 (Para 130).

7. The intelligible differentia between the medium and of print/broadcast, real life speech and speech on the internet, is that speech on the internet travels faster. There is however, no rational nexus between creating new categories of criminal offences and any permissible aim sought to be achieved under Article 19(2). This is especially noticeable in the case of Section 66A, rather than other offences such as Cyber Terrorism or Hacking as covered under the Information Technology Act, 2000.

   Re: Secretary of Ministry of Information and Broadcasting v. Cricket Association of Bengal, 1995 (2) SCC 161 at 195.

8. Section 66A is also bad in law inasmuch as it mixes up minor and major offences and does not contain any differentiation between the penalties for them. It includes, "criminal intimidation" and, "annoyance" both as bundled together within it and violates the principles of proportionality. Similar offences already exist under the Indian Penal Code, 1860 which applies to online content equally. These offences have definitions and ingredients providing adequate notice. This is not so in the case of Section 66A which merely contains phrases. Hence, this also leads to a mixing up of major and minor offences, in a bundle of phrases under 66A leading to the same penal consequence. In support of the above proposition, case law is cited below.

Vide Om Kumar and Ors v. Union of India (2001 (2) SCC 386)

> *"On account of a Chapter on Fundamental Rights in Part III of our Constitution right from 1950, Indian courts did not suffer from the disability similar to the one experiences by English Courts for declaring as unconstitutional legislation on the principles of proportionality or reading them in a manner consistent with the charter of rights. Ever since 1950, the principle of, "proportionality" has indeed been applied vigorously to legislative (and administrative action) in India. While dealing with the*

validity of legislation infringing fundamental freedoms enumerated in Article 19(1) of the Constitution of India – such as freedom of speech and expression, freedom to assemble peacefully, freedom to form associations and unions...."

9. International Covenants to which India is a party such as the ICCPR (Article 19), have been interpreted with respect to the access on the Internet. Specific reference is made to the summary of recommendations of the Report of the Special Rapporteur on the Promotion and Protection of the Right to Freedom of Opinion and Expression, dated 6 May 2011. The Report recognises the importance of the right to freedom of expression protected both under the UDHR as well as under ICCPR, at the same time it is also considered the new and expanded horizons of internet which may pose serious concerns. Paragraphs 10 to 19 are important. Paragraph 16 is quoted below for ready reference.

   Para 16

   "The Special Rapporteur welcomes the recently adopted general comment No. 34 of the Human Rights Committee on Article 19 of the International Covenant, which underscores that when a State invokes a legitimate ground for restriction of the right to freedom of expression, it must demonstrate in specific and individualized fashion precise nature of the threat, the necessity and the proportionality of the specific action taken, in particular by establishing a direct and immediate connection between the expression and the threat."

   Further Para 29 and 37 are also important.

   Para 29

   "As highlighted in joint papers for a series of expert workshops on the prohibition of incitement of national, racial or religious hatred organized by the Office of the United Nations High Commissioner for Human Rights (OHCHR) in 2011, the Special Rapporteur remains concerned by the vague formulation of some domestic legal provisions that prohibit incitement. These include combating "incitement to religious unrest", "promoting division between religious believers and non-believers", "defamation of religion", "inciting to violation", instigating hatred and disrespect against the ruling regime", "inciting subversion of state power" and "offences that damage public tranquility". Such vague and broad terms clearly do not meet the criterion of legal clarity."

   Para 37

   "The four types of expression examined above (III.A) fall under the first category of the types of expression that constitute offences under

international criminal law and/or international human rights law and which States are required to prohibit at the domestic4 level. However, as they all constitute restrictions to the right to freedom of expression, they must also comply with the three-part test of prescription by: unambiguous law; pursuance of a legitimate purpose; and respect for the principles of necessity and proportionality."

The conclusions and recommendations are contained in Para 78 to 92 which were read out and not reproduced herein below.

In the Supreme Court of India

Civil Appellate Jurisdiction
Civil Appeal No. 4911 of 2008
(Special Leave Petition (Civil) No. 5145 of 2006)
People of Union for Civil Liberties
Versus
Govt. of NCT of Delhi & Ors.

Date of Judgement : 06.08.2008

Bench : K.G. Balakrishnan CJI & A.K. Mathur J

[Sh. YP Chibber, General Secretary, PUCL, had taken up the cause of sewage workers before the National Human Rights Commission in the year 1998. He had relentlessly pursued it before the NHRC which resulted in framing of detailed guidelines. As the guidelines were not implemented, resulting in deaths year after year of sewage workers, PUCL took up the cause before the Delhi High Court through a Writ Petition. It was prayed that the NHRC guidelines be implemented by the concerned authorities as well as payment of compensation to the injured/deceased. The High Court did not interfere on the ground that the issue being pending before the NHRC, parallel proceedings cannot continue. The said High court judgment was challenged before the Supreme Court which resulted in detailed directions by order dated 06.08.2008].

Order

1. Leave granted.

2. The appellant, a public charitable society, had filed a writ petition before the Delhi High Court alleging that there were large number of sewerage workers who met with accidents in the course of their employment; that these workers were engaged by the Municipal Corporation of Delhi/Delhi Jal Board; that the workers were not provided with safety equipments; and that the departments do not take precautionary measures to save the lives of these workers. The appellant alleges that under similar situation the Bombay High Court had entertained a writ petition and issued certain directions. The appellant wants that as regards Municipal Corporation of Delhi/Delhi Jal Board

also, similar directions should be issued. The appellant also prays that, the National Human Rights Commission (NHRC) has framed an elaborate scheme and the same shall be implemented by the Delhi Municipal Corporation. It also prays that the Delhi Jal Board, under whose jurisdiction the sewerage work is being done, shall also take care of all the lives of these workers. In view of the scheme formulated by the NHRC the High Court declined to interfere and the writ petition was dismissed. Challenging the same, the appellant is before this Court by way of this appeal.

3. Heard learned counsel for the appellant and also learned counsel for the respondents.

4. Counsel for the appellant pointed out that in spite of the scheme being approved by the NHRC, these organisations are not implementing the scheme effectively and sincerely, and the workers are met with serious accidents and they are not being taken care of well when they met with accidents.

5. Learned counsel for the Delhi Jal Board has stated that the scheme suggested/recommended by the NHRC has been fully implemented and the additional posts have also been created and a separate department, namely, Department of Safety and Disaster Management has been set up and a Special Consultant for Safety Measures appointed. It is also submitted that all the directions suggested by the NHRC are being fully implemented.

6. It is important to note that the NHRC has suggested very detailed guidelines and some of the guidelines deal primarily with measures to be taken when a sewerage worker is engaged to clean the sewerage. It is suggested by the NHRC that (i) emergency first aid treatment kits should be provided to take care of all minor injuries like cuts and burns; (ii) a physician's services should be available for emergencies; (iii)the workers should be educated about the hazards of waterborne diseases, such as typhoid and cholera through sewage and tetanus through cuts and wounds. Cuts and grazes should be covered with waterproof plasters. Effective immunization of workers against diseases such as typhoid, cholera, tetanus, etc. should be done by vaccination; (iv) the importance of personal hygiene should be emphasized and the workers should be instructed to keep finger-nails short and well trimmed, wash hands with soap and hot water before taking food or smoking and to keep fingers out of nose, mouth and eyes, because the hands carry most infections; (v) use of rubber glove should be insisted so that sewage or sludge does not come in direct contact with the hands. Before starting work, skin likely to be exposed to sewage should be covered with barrier cream or worker should be provided with wadder suit; (vi) the workers should be provided with a complete change of work clothes to be worn during working hours. Gum boots should also be provided for the workers; (vii) when the work is completed, all contaminated parts of the body should be thoroughly washed; (viii) in laboratory work only pipettes with rubber teats should be used to prevent contamination of the mouth, laboratory glassware should not be used for drinking purposes. In no event food should be prepared in the laboratory;

(ix) adequate facility of clean water and soap should be provided for the workers for cleaning their body after completion of the job; (x) the gangs/JE/site-in-charge must have telephone numbers for call of an ambulance, fire service, police and nearby hospital for any emergency; and (xi) those who are regularly engaged in sewerage work should be given proper training. These guidelines and the other guidelines issued by the NHRC may also be implemented by the Municipal Corporation/Delhi Jal Board whenever the occasion arises.

7. The appeal is disposed of accordingly. No costs.

Constitution of the PUCL

(Incorporating amendments up to September 4, 2010)

1. Name

The name of the organisation shall be the People's Union for Civil Liberties (PUCL).

2. Aims & Objects

The People's Union for Civil Liberties will try to bring together all those who are committed to the defence and promotion of civil liberties in India, irrespective of any differences which they may have in regard to political and economic institutions suitable for the country.

The aims and objects of the organisation will be :

(a) to uphold and promote by peaceful means civil liberties and the democratic way of life throughout India;

(b) to secure recognition to the principle of dignity of the individual;

(c) to undertake a constant review of penal laws and the criminal procedure with a view to bringing them in harmony with humane and liberal principles;

(d) to work for the withdrawal and repeal of all repressive laws including preventive detention;

(e) to encourage freedom of thought and defend the right of public dissent;

(f) to ensure the freedom of the press and independence of mass media like radio and television;

(g) to secure the rule of law and independence of the judiciary;

(h) to make legal aid available to the poor;

(i) to make legal assistance available for the defence of civil liberties;

(j) to work for the reform of the judicial system so as to remove inordinate delays, reduce heavy expenses, and eliminate inequities;

(k) to bring about prison reform;

(l) to oppose police excesses and use of third degree method;

(m) to oppose police discrimination on the ground of religion, race, caste, sex, or place of birth;

(n) to combat social evils which encroach on civil liberties, such as untouchability, casteism, and communalism;

(o) to defend in particular the civil liberties of the weaker sections of society and of women and children;

(p) to do all acts and things that may be necessary, helpful, or incidental to the above aims and objects.

3. Criteria of Membership

(a) Every adult person shall be eligible to be a member of the organisation if he/she believes that civil liberties must be maintained in India, now and in the future, irrespective of any economic and political changes that may take place in the country.

(b) Members of the political parties will be entitled to be members of the organisation in their individual capacity if they subscribe to its aims and objects. They will have all the rights of membership except that :

(i) the President, the Vice Presidents, the General Secretaries, other Secretaries, and the Treasurers of the organisation or any of its branches shall not be a member of any political party.

(ii) At least one-half of the members of the National Council and the National Executive Committee and of corresponding bodies at the State and local levels, shall be person who are not members of any political party.

(iii) Not more than 10% of the members of the National Council and the National Executive Committee, and of corresponding bodies at the State and local levels, shall be members of one political party.

(c) The membership fee will be Rs. 50/- per year, to be collected once a year. Student members and non-earning members who are below the age of 25 may pay Rs. 10/- per year as member's fee. The Executive Committees at every level will be entitled to admit persons from economically weaker sections of society, like workers and peasants, at a membership fee of Rs. 10/- per year.

(d) Those who pay Rs. 1000/- in a lump sum will be Life members. Those who pay Rs. 2000/- will be Patron members of the organisation.

(e) The National Council will have the right, by a two-third majority, to refuse membership to any person or to remove any person from membership. The Council of a State branch will have a similar right in the respective State.

3(A). Institutional Members

In addition to individual members there may be Institutional members also. All voluntary groups and institutions (but not political parties or groups affiliated to them) which agree with the objectives of the PUCL and desire to join it will be entitled to become Institutional Members in accordance with the Supplementary Rules laid down by the National Executive Committee (see at the end).

4. National Convention

(a) A National Convention of the organisation will be held once in two years.

(b) The National Convention will review the work of the organisation and lay down policies and programmes for future.

5. National Council

(a) The National Council will meet at least once a year.(amended in place of 'twice a year' by the National Council on 4th September 2010)

(b) The National Council will determine the policy and programme of the organisation, in conformity with the policies and programmes adopted by the National Convention.

(c) The National Council will elect the President, one or more Vice Presidents, one or more General Secretaries, one or more other Secretaries, and Treasurers for the ensuing term, as laid down in Clause 7(2).

6. The National Executive Committee

(a) The National Executive Committee will look after the growth and work of the organisation, in conformity with the policies and programmes adopted by the National Convention and the National Council.

(b) The National Executive Committee will promote the formation of branches of the organisation in every State in India.

(c) The National Executive Committee will promote the policies and programmes of the organisation during the interval between two National Convention and meetings of the National Council.

7. Elections and formation of National bodies, calling of National Convention

(1) At least six months before the next National Convention, the General Secretary would write to all the State branches that they should elect, preferably by consensus, representatives of their respective States for the National Council. The number of members to be elected by the States will be conveyed to them by the General Secretary in proportion to the total membership of the PUCL in the state according to the records with the National office at the time of the above mentioned letter from the General Secretary to the State branches. Besides these names, the General Secretary of the State branch will be an ex-officio member of the National Council. The names of the representatives of the State will be communicated to the General Secretary of the PUCL within two months of the receipt of his letter. (The national President and the General Secretary may nominate, if necessary, some members to the National Council/National Executive Committee).

(2) At least three months before the expiry of the term of the current President and other office bearers of the PUCL, a meeting of the National Council, constituting of the representatives of the States, including the State General Secretary, and

the nominees of the national President and the General Secretary, if any, will be held at a place fixed by the General Secretary of the PUCL in consultation with the President. This meeting of the National Council will decide, on the basis of consensus, and if necessary, by votes, the office bearers as mentioned in Clause 5(c) for the next term commencing from the date on which the next National Convention will be held.

(3) The aforesaid meeting of the National Council will also elect the National Executive Committee of the PUCL which will comprise of the President, the General Secretary, other office bearers, all the former presidents, and such other members as may be decided by consensus by the National Council or nominated by the national President and General Secretary.

(4) The outgoing President will be an ex-officio member of both the National Council and the National Executive Committee.

(5) The aforesaid meeting of the National Council will also decide the venue and the date of the National Convention. The National Executive Committee will act as the Subjects Committee and would meet on the date preceding the National Convention to decide upon the resolutions, etc., to be discussed by the Convention. Members of the PUCL who want to propose some resolution would send them to the General Secretary one month before the proposed date of the Convention.

8. State and District Branches

(a) With the sanction of the General Secretary, who in this matter will act in consultation with the President, members of any State may set up a state branch.

(b) As far as possible, in consultation with the General Secretary of the PUCL, the same pattern would be adapted at the State and district level for their functioning and elections.

(c) A State Council and State Executive Committee of the branch will be elected, as far as possible, according to the procedure laid down in Clause 7 above, in consultation with the General Secretary.

(d) The provisions analogous to clauses 4, 5, 6, and 7 above shall govern the State Convention, The State Council, the State Executive Committee, and the office-bearers of the State branch.

(e) Out of the membership fee collected in any State, one-third shall be sent to the National office and two-third shall remain with the State branch and shared equally with the district branch concerned.

(f) In case of Life members and Patrons members, 40% of the amount will be sent to the National office. The entire amount of such members enrolled directly with the Central office will be kept there.

9. Supplementary Rules

Supplementary Rules for the organisation shall be made by the National Executive Committee as and when necessary.

10. Amendments

The National Council will be entitled by the vote of a majority of its total membership to alter any part of this constitution except the aims and object of the organisation and the criteria of membership as specified in clause 3(a) above.

Former Presidents of PUCL :

V.M. Tarkunde (Justice) (1982 to 1984)
Rajni Kothari (Prof.) (1984 to 1986)
Rajindar Sachar (Justice) (1986 to 1995)
K G Kannabiran (1995 to 2009)
Prabhakar Sinha (Dr.) (2010- 2016)

Former General Secretaries :

Arun Shourie (1982 to 1986)
Rajni Kothari (1982 to 1984)
Dalip S. Swami (1986 to 1990)
Y.P. Chhibbar (1984 to 2008)
Pushkar Raj (2009-2012)

People's Union for Civil Liberties :

Founder : Jaya Prakash Narayan
President : Ravi Kiran Jain
General Secretary : V Suresh
Treasurer : Surendra Kumar

Vice Presidents :

Binayak Sen, G. Saraswathi (Ms.)
N.D. Pancholi, P.B. D'sa, Radhakant Saxena
Sanjay Parikh, Vinay Kantha

Secretaries :

Kavita Srivastava (Ms.), Nishant Akhilesh
Rohit Prajapati, Sudha Bharadwaj (Ms.)
Vandana Misra (Ms.), Y J Rajendra

Organising Secretaries :

Ajay T.G., Arjun Sheoran, Nishat Hussain (Ms.)
Ramashray Pd Singh

Regd. Office :

270-A Patparganj
Opp. Anandlok Apartments
Mayur Vihar-I, Delhi-110 091
Tel : 22750014
Fax (PP) 42151459
E-mail : puclnat@gmail.com
Pucl.natgensec@gmail.com
Website : www.pucl.org.